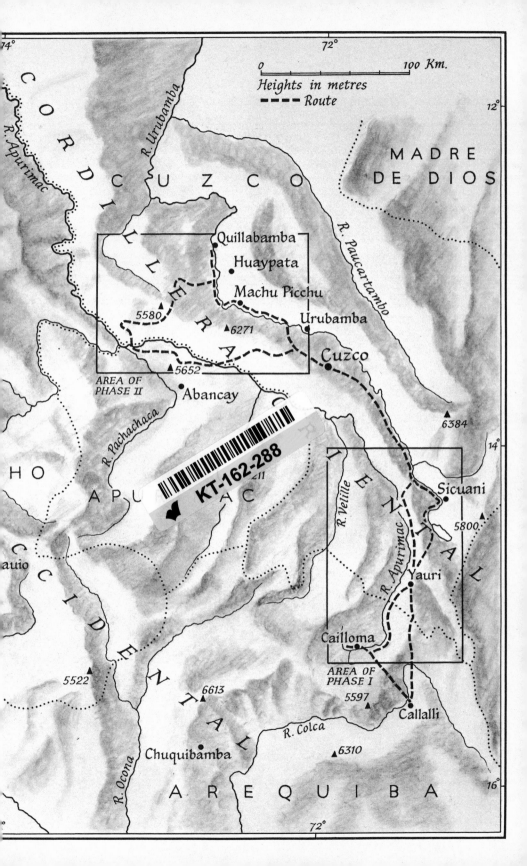

CORDILLERA

R. Apurimac

R. Urubamba

CUZCO

MADRE
DE DIOS

R. Paucartambo

Heights in metres
- - - Route

0   100 Km.

Quillabamba

Huaypata

Machu Picchu

Urubamba

▲5580

▲6271

Cuzco

AREA OF
PHASE II

▲5652

Abancay

R. Pachachaca

APU

211

AC

OCCIDENTAL

CHO

ORIENTAL

R. Velille

R. Apurimac

▲6384

Sicuani

▲5800

Yauri

Cailloma

AREA OF
PHASE I

▲5597

Callalli

▲5522

▲6613

Chuquibamba

▲6310

R. Ocona

R. Colca

AREQUIBA

ROAD TO ELIZABETH

ROAD TO ELIZABETH

A Quest in the Mountains of Peru

by

JOHN RIDGWAY

GUILD PUBLISHING LONDON

This edition published 1986
by Book Club Associates
by arrangement with
Victor Gollancz Ltd

Photoset in Great Britain by
Rowland Phototypesetting Ltd, Bury St Edmunds, Suffolk
and printed by St Edmundsbury Press Ltd
Bury St Edmunds, Suffolk
Colour plates originated and printed
by Acolortone Ltd, Ipswich

For Lizbet

Acknowledgements

I would like to thank the following persons:

My father, Reginald Ridgway, for his help and encouragement.
Clara de Guerola, for her support in Lima.
Nick Asheshov, for helping us find our feet in Lima and Cuzco.
Maria, in Cuzco, for her help with the documentation necessary
   to enter the Emergency Zone.
Our friends on the Altiplano.
The teachers of Peru.
Elizabeth Paullo.
The gallant men at the raft crossing of the Apurimac.
Theresa, Virginie, and Simeona of Accobamba.
Donia and Juan Huaman Chavez of Accobamba.
Cesar Ayala Bendita, for his friendship in Accobamba.
Len Young of Quillabamba.
Padre Santiago Echeverria of Quillabamba.
Captain George Hogg RN, and his secretary, Margaret, of the
   British Embassy in Lima.
Victoria Berg.
Nick Asheshov again, for bringing Lizbet from Accobamba to
   Lima, and much else besides.
Kay Allinson, Social Worker, Dornoch, Sutherland.
Ian Smith, Inverness, for keeping us on an even keel.

J.R.

List of Illustrations

Chapter One

Through the village we went and past the bread-lady's home on the right. Then, before we knew it, we were at the cemetery, a scattering of maybe fifteen abandoned graves beside a slight bend in the path. The child-graves were no more than a couple of feet long, their little wooden crosses drooping wearily, battered by the rain. People die young in Peru.

'Go quietly,' whispered Simeona, our Quechuan Indian guide. 'This family has suffered terribly. They are very nervous.'

The only sound was the squelch of our boots in the mud of the jungle path. We clambered over a broken-down wall covered by clinging, sodden undergrowth and found ourselves in a small, ill-kept meadow, looking downhill at the back of a single hut some thirty yards away. For a few seconds we hesitated, halted by a mixture of curiosity, excitement and apprehension about what we were going to find. Was it merely a chain of extraordinary coincidences that had brought us to this spot 9,000 feet up in the rain-forest in the eastern foothills of the Andes? Or had fate pulled us there? Now, at this critical moment, my mind yet again went back fifteen years to the first and only other time I had been in the area, and to the man who had captured my imagination so strongly. His name was Elvin Berg.

In 1970 I led an expedition to the head-waters of the Amazon. The journey was a tough one, and left me with many indelible memories; but no other incident created so powerful and lasting an impression as our discovery of a place called Osambre. One morning, five days and two 15,000-foot mountain passes from the end of the nearest dirt-road, our Indian guides told us that we were approaching some sort of small farm belonging to 'a German'. It seemed scarcely possible that any European could be living so far from civilisation, but we slogged on through the jungle, hoping that the rumour was true, for we were in an advanced stage of exhaustion from heat, hard walking, insect-bites and poor food, and we badly needed a rest.

Then, at the bottom of a natural defile, we came to a massive gate made of wooden poles piled horizontally between heavy timber posts—the outer defence of a jungle fortress. Ten minutes later we staggered up a small pasture and crawled over six more horizontal poles which barred the entrance to a farmyard-square formed by nine huts. We were met by a smiling, pale-faced, elderly man wearing a light-brown denim shirt and trousers, with a matching cloth cap placed squarely on a head of short brown hair. 'Welcome to Osambre,' he said in Spanish. 'I am Señor Abel Berg, and this is my son Elvin.'

Beside him stood a young man in his early twenties, clearly part-Indian, tall, powerful and conspicuously fit-looking, with a strong, handsome face. The father ushered us into a bare whitewashed room by the gate, and we watched in thirsty anticipation as Elvin unloaded a heap of pineapples, oranges and sweet lemons on to a rough wooden table. We were pretty well all-in, and just sat in silence, biting chunks from the thick, dripping pineapple slices which he cut for us. Outside, the farmyard was milling with life. A stream ran through the middle of it, with a soap-nut tree for washing clothes. A multitude of children, chickens, turkeys, ducks, geese, sheep, dogs and pigeons scuttled about inside a wall and high fence. Outside were pigs and cattle, but they were all brought in at nightfall for fear of the jaguars which came right up to the perimeter in the dark.

As we recovered, Abel told us something of the history of this Garden of Eden, which he himself had created. His father, a Norwegian also called Elvin Berg, had come out to Peru at the turn of the century and gone into the rubber business. He had married a Quechuan Indian girl, and Abel was their son.

2

Abel himself had been sent to the Naval Academy in Lima, the fees being paid by his uncle Olaf in Norway; but he was unhappy at school and ran away. After service in the Peruvian navy during the second world war, he married a Quechuan girl called Esther, and moved out to Osambre in 1945. At the time the place was just a patch of virgin jungle on the mountainside, but Abel combined Norwegian persistence with Peruvian good nature, and with his wife set about building a world of his own.

Together the pair created an enclave of almost total self-sufficiency. In due course the ample Esther gave birth to four sons and a daughter, far from any help. Hard work and careful planning produced food in over-abundance: oranges, sweet lemons, grapefruit and bananas were the commonest kinds of fruit, but there were also yucca, sugar-cane, soya, maize and all the animals. The jungle teemed with deer, pig and other game, and the Apurimac river, winding in its gorge some 1,500 feet below, provided a constant supply of fish which dried easily in the tropical sun. There was no waste-disposal problem, since the pigs ate everything, and there were no glass, tin, plastic or paper containers. The annual coffee and cocoa crops provided sufficient income for books, clothes and fertilizer, which were about the only imported goods the family seemed to need.

It all sounded idyllic—and so it proved. We spent three days at Osambre, and saw how the Bergs lived and worked in perfect harmony with a couple of families of nomadic Campa Indians —short, lithe and coal-black—from the deep jungle round about. Multi-coloured children, playing happily together in the yard, bore witness to 'integration'—a word they had never heard.

Many times during our stay Abel spoke of his belief that the Campas were the most 'tranquil' human beings he had ever known. With him I went to visit a Campa family who lived alone in what he called *Ceja de la Selva*—'the Eyebrow of the Jungle'. To him they were the very opposite of sophisticated people from the western world, who were the most 'un-tranquil'. His theory of *tranquilidad* appealed to me greatly, and on our last evening with him, as we sat out on a large cow-hide beneath a vast sky filled with stars, I concluded that, if he had anything to do with it, there would be Bergs living at Osambre for as long as there would be Ridgways at Ardmore, our home on the north-west coast of Scotland.

Yet if I admired Abel for his achievement, it was Elvin who most fired my imagination. At twenty-two he was supremely fit and strong, and had a tremendous zest for life. He favoured Army tropical-green lightweight trousers, belt and shirt, but softened the image by wearing an ancient pith helmet. A hunting-rifle was seldom out of his hands, and he was never happier than when he had at his side the much shorter Campa boy with whom he had been brought up.

When we left Osambre, Elvin insisted on coming with us. His energy and good nature seemed boundless, first as guide on our walk out through the jungle, and then as bow-man on an exciting 100-mile dash down the Apurimac river in a dug-out canoe. As we shot the rapids between great walls of white water, shaving shiny black reefs by inches, our lives were in his hands. If his judgment had once failed, we would have been no more than numbers on the river's death-list for the year.

Our debt to him could not be measured. When we met him, we had been weakened by problems of health at high altitude and long weeks of walking through the mountains—and to this had been added the sheer pressure of needing to hurry on down-river before the rainy season began. He had joined the expedition at a critical moment, and given us the impetus to get through the last leg before we reached the first point on the Amazon that was navigable by normal boats.

But my admiration for Elvin went beyond mere gratitude for practical assistance. Although I had known him for only a few days, he had become far more than a friend. To me he was an inspiration, an outstanding human being. When we parted, I gave him my wrist-watch as a small token of our affection—and I had never forgotten him. It was because of Elvin Berg, and my undying regard for him, that I had returned to the Eyebrow of the Jungle fifteen years later.

Chapter Two

In 1968 I founded my Adventure School in Ardmore, in the north-west corner of Sutherland, and I have lived there with my family, in a croft above the mooring in the sea-loch, ever since. My wife Marie Christine joined me for the later stages of the 1970 expedition, but not until we were well down the Amazon; and at that date our daughter Rebecca was only three, so that neither of them had seen the place of which I so often spoke— Osambre.

I struggled to emulate the Bergs' self-sufficiency in our Highland croft, but the north coast of Scotland has neither the soil nor the climate of the Apurimac foothills. Many times I had thought of returning to that little Garden of Eden, but every summer I was running the Adventure School, and expeditions to the Sahara, Patagonia and the Himalayas, and a couple of sailing voyages round the world had taken up the winters. Letters were impossible, for Osambre had no postman. Occasionally I had given talks on our 1970 expedition, and one of our students had actually followed our 4,000-mile route from the furthest source of the Amazon to the sea. I gathered from his report of Osambre in 1974 that all was going well.

In the autumn of 1985 I was anxious to include Rebecca in our travel plans for the winter, as she had just left school and would have the time for an extended trip. Boating, however, was not top of her list for 'our expedition after I leave school'. When she was seven we took her on a sailing voyage from Ardmore, where it rains a lot, down the West Coast of Europe to the Spanish Sahara, where it had not rained for seven years and all the children were black. On the return voyage, in a thirty-two foot sloop with no engine, we were caught in a storm on Christmas Eve, 120 miles off the west coast of Ireland. When a big wave came over the stern, the boat was swamped, and down in the cabin we found ourselves standing knee-deep in icy water. There followed what the child described as 'my horridest Christmas ever'.

Becca's early life in our croft, three miles off the road, where everything has to be carried from the shore straight up a 100-foot hill to the house, gave her stamina and kept her slim. She grew up tall and fair, and at Gordonstoun twice won the cross-country race for girls. By August 1985 she had a temporary job at the Gordonstoun Summer School, and the three of us were arguing, partly by telephone, about whether we should go to the Himalayas or to South America.

I felt that Nepal would be a safer place to take my wife and daughter, but finally decided that it was South America they wanted. Our first idea was to make a cycle trip across the continent, from Peru to Uruguay, but we realised that there was already insufficient time to get bikes organised. Then one evening, after we had finished the washing-up from the Businessmen's Course evening meal, Marie Christine said, 'Let's go to Osambre. You keep talking about Elvin Berg. Why don't we go and see him?'

'All right,' I said. 'We will.' It had been a particularly long day, and I was in the mood for a quick decision. 'We could walk in, from the road between Quillabamba and Cuzco. That would take a week or so. Maybe we could stay a while at Osambre, then walk on down to Villa Virgen, and from there canoe the 100 miles downstream to the Benedictine Mission at Granja Sivia . . .' I was thinking as I talked. 'And we could build a balsa raft, then float right down as far as Atalaya—or even Pucallpa.' I had not so much as looked at the map.

Immediately it occurred to me that our family alone would be a weak team if we had to face up to *los bandidos*, by whom Peru was said to be infested. 'I wonder if Ed would like to come,' I said. 'It would be safer if we had one of the instructors with us.'

The upshot was that both Edward Ley-Wilson, a twenty-one-year-old who was to be our Chief Instructor at the School in 1986, and Justin Matterson, aged twenty-three, who had been Mate on the Adventure School's yacht for the summer, both agreed to come with us.

Ed had arrived at Ardmore in March that year for the month-long Instructors' Selection and Training Course. It was a raw day, with snowflakes feathering down from a leaden sky, as he and his fellow trainees swam out from a fishing boat to an uninhabited island where they had to build a shelter, find food and survive a bitter night before making a raft for their return to the mainland next morning.

From the start, Ed was in his element. At prep school he had been very small, but his father had taught him to box, and he had soon seen off the bullies. At Eastbourne College, besides passing A-levels, he had shone at rugby and, particularly, tennis, going on to compete at Junior Wimbledon. By the time he reached us, his medium height, strong build, bright blue eyes and short-cropped, light brown hair gave an impression of such boundless energy that less energetic instructors nicknamed him 'Action Man'. He was never one to waste a moment, and I felt confident that in Peru whatever he might lack in experience he would make up in effort and cheerfulness.

Justin—tall, long-legged, with aristocratic features and un-kempt brown hair—had also come to us as an instructor, but in 1981. He has an enormous amount of charm, which reflects his privileged background: his family owned a big house in Surrey, with gardener and nanny in attendance to help bring up him and his three brothers. In spite of an exceptional memory, which gave him a marvellous repertoire of comic songs, he was not a success at school, having little interest in academic pursuits and spending much of his time in the roof on illicit chemical experiments designed to produce beer.

His father, a dynamic and successful businessman, died tragic-ally at the age of fifty, soon after Justin had left us at the end of the 1981 season, and the disaster probably affected him more than he realised. He went through a period of not sticking at anything, preferring to travel. Then in January 1985 he contacted me again, saying that he had put on a lot of weight and wanted to come back to Ardmore and sort himself out.

It was a definitely rotund Justin who walked out from the end of the road with his brand new rucksack, but there was still the same spark of fun in his warm, brown eyes. He launched into the business of getting fit with considerable verve, and by the autumn had shed several stone. Although he was inclined to be scatty, I reckoned that his humour and thoughtfulness would be valuable assets in Peru.

This, then, was our team. On 5 September I bought five return air tickets to Lima. We were due to fly from London on 10 October and return on 18 December. The die was cast.

I set much store on the formula propounded by those mountaineering giants, Eric Shipton and H. W. Tilman: 'A six month trip to the Himalaya can be planned on the back of an envelope in half an hour.' There are always so many reasons for not doing something.

This time I intended to travel much lighter than in 1970. Each person would be required to carry in a single rucksack what kit he or she needed for two months. There would be no haggling for mules and guides; we would get by on our own. I had printed a list of essential equipment in my book about the previous trip, so I just copied it. Besides the rucksack, each person would wear emergency belt-order—a webbing belt fitted with four pouches containing medical and survival kit, and a water bottle.

Our local GP, Dr Sunil, sorted out the necessary medical supplies, and we went for inoculations to his surgery in the small coastal village of Scourie, just south of Ardmore. From the posters in his waiting room there is always much to be learned about the dangers of obesity and smoking while pregnant. Typhoid, polio, hepatitis, cholera, rabies, tetanus, malaria—all were apparently still going strong in South America, but at least smallpox had disappeared.

MacArthur Bennie, the travelling dentist from Dornoch, peered into the fearsome box of dental instruments which I have twice carried round the world, and pronounced them rust-free. Then he polished my pegs and pushed me out into the darkness surrounding his mobile surgery.

With three weeks to go, things began to develop, but so gently that I failed to notice. In mid-September I had to drive the 200 miles across Scotland to Aberdeen, the nearest centre, for my yellow fever inoculation. The visit coincided with the publication of the book which Andy Briggs and I had written about our non-stop sailing voyage round the world in 1983–4, and the BBC asked me to do a short radio interview while I was in Aberdeen. A few days later the *Daily Express* ran a couple of inches about our proposed trip to Osambre, which the reporter had picked up from the piece on the radio. This in turn was noticed by the London correspondent of a Norwegian daily paper, and the article which he wrote attracted an immediate response from Berg relatives in Oslo.

During the last days of September, three Norwegian publications telephoned me, but I was too busy to think about them. They were far away. At home we had joiners, plumbers and electricians all working in the house together; 800 salmon were killed by seals over six days in our small fish farm at the foot of the croft, and a BBC television crew was making a film of our last Businessmen's Course of the season.

'When will you be in London?' The Norwegian voice echoed persistently down the line from Oslo.

'Well—October 8 or 9. We fly from Heathrow on the tenth.' I suppose I sounded pretty distracted. I was.

'We would like to send someone over to speak to you. Do you have a telephone number in London?'

I gave my father's number in Wimbledon, wondering what could make it worth a reporter coming so far. I dialled an Oslo number the journalist had just given me, for a cousin on the Norwegian side of the Berg family.

'Alexander Berg.' The Scandinavian voice sounded elderly.

9

We had a brief conversation. I felt Mr Berg was having to think hard to speak his slow deliberate English; but I learned that old Abel had died in 1975; his wife, Esther, might still be alive. Elvin was now head of the Osambre family, and he had written to Alexander quite often until 1980. His letters had come from an address in Huanta, a town near the city of Ayacucho, high up in the Sierra on the west side of the Apurimac valley. I told Alexander that I would try to find Elvin.

All this was submerged in preparations for our end-of-season party. Then, next thing we knew, we were across the sea-loch and loading the Land-Rover for the 700-mile overnight drive south to London, leaving our friends Jenny and Malcolm Sandals to care for Ardmore while we were away.

'Would you and the young lady like to model for us in the window while you're waiting, madam?' Marie Christine and Rebecca were sitting cramped together on the only chair in a rather grim establishment on the eastern side of town, waiting for Ed to come and buy his belt-order and waterproof poncho. Entry is gained only after pushing bells and passing scrutiny through the inspection-hatch. The clients are mostly youngish, short-haired types wanting heavier truncheons or longer bayonets, but the stock of military clothing is unequalled in London.

Ed failed to show. He and his girlfriend had got the wrong address. So as not to waste valuable time, he decided to buy a nappy. (I recommend these for expedition towels.) But his forthright approach failed to impress the shop assistant who, looking sideways at the girlfriend, insisted that the minimum purchase was a pack of one dozen.

Meanwhile, I was closeted with Odd Myklebust in a Wimbledon dining room. Odd was a professional journalist, casual yet persuasive, and clearly enjoying a stay at the Hilton at his magazine's expense. I told him roughly what we intended to, and he showed me some colour transparencies of Osambre taken by a Norwegian expedition in 1972. Half my mind was worrying that Marie Christine had forgotten to put eardrops on her list—

previous experience at altitude warned me to take them. Never-theless, I was thrilled to see the farm just as I remembered it.

Showing Odd to the door, I promised to find out all I could about the Berg family for their Oslo relatives. And, warmed by anticipation of the trip, I agreed that he should photograph us at Heathrow next day, just before his own flight to Norway.

The shoppers came back, only to rush off again for eardrops. Ed and Justin rang in from different parts of London, assuring me they would have everything in time. I sorted through my kit, tried packing the rucksack, and realised I was short of space; a lot of stuff would have to be left behind. Marie Christine's mother was due up from Brighton at six in the evening; then we were going to have a quiet family dinner with my father.

By 4.30 I was sitting at my father's desk, gazing out of the window in grey autumn light, my lists complete. The only British presence with which I am familiar in Peru is the Benedic-tine Mission at Granja Sivia on the Apurimac; with a few spare minutes at the end of the day, I decided to telephone their headquarters at Worth Abbey School in Crawley, Sussex.

'Father Bede Hill,' said a firm voice, which I recognised even after fifteen years.

'Oh, hello. My name's John Ridgway, I don't know if you remember, but I stayed at the Mission on the Apurimac for a few days in 1970 . . .'

'Yes, of course, I remember. How are you?'

'Very well, thanks. I'm flying to Peru tomorrow with my wife and daughter, so I thought I'd just phone and see how things are at the Mission.'

'Oh.' There was a pause. 'The situation is very bad. We handed Granja Sivia to the Peruvian Ministry of Agriculture in 1975. Now there's a terrorist war in the Apurimac valley. Have you heard of the Khmer Rouge in Kampuchea? Their leader was a man called Pol Pot.'

'Yes, I saw the film *The Killing Fields* a few months ago, pretty frightening.' It had seemed chillingly up-to-date and accurate to me.

'Well, the Maoist movement in Peru has the same ideology. It's called *Sendero Luminoso*. That means "Shining Path".'

The Father went on to explain that the movement had been intellectual in origin, formed by a philosophy lecturer at Ayacucho University, up in the Sierra on the west of the valley, where most of the killing has been done.

'Their Maoist strategy is to capture the support of the countryside first. Then, they reckon, the towns will fall when supplies are cut. There follows the complete destruction of established authority. Then they start history again, at Year One.

'At present they refuse to have any dialogue with the democratically-elected government, so there is no communication. They don't announce what they're going to do, and they don't claim anything after they have done it. Blowing up power supplies has been their main weapon against cities so far. The military have responded in a brutal fashion. Mass graves have been discovered—and this brought down the military government. As usual the poor *campesinos* get caught in the middle. It's a dirty war.'

'Sounds awful,' I said. 'What about Julian Latham—the Rhodesian who came down on the raft with us from the Mission? Has he still got his orphanage?'

'No, he had to leave Peru. The terrorists began by demanding medicines, then they threatened to inform the military if he didn't supply a lot more. It became impossible for him. In fact he was inadvertently caught up in one of the first atrocities. In 1980 he suggested that a dirt road should be put in from San Francisco, near the Mission, all the way up the river as far as Villa Virgen. He was helping with the *campesinos'* marketing co-operative when you were out with us, remember?

'Well, a road would have opened up the valley. A meeting was held in Villa Virgen. The *Senderos* were present. They said the road must not be built: links with the outside world were not wanted. Established authority must be destroyed, and, with the Shining Path to guide them, the Indians would be raised to equality and lead a self-sufficient life.

'Anyway, it was voted to go ahead with the road. Next morning the village leaders were found hanged. They'd been castrated and their tongues were cut out. The road was not built.'

'Any news of the Berg family, up at Osambre?' I asked weakly.

'No. But why don't you try the Catholic Institute of International Relations in London? They'll be able to give you the latest information.'

I thanked the Father, and jotted down the number he gave me, feeling numb. I knew that Ayacucho, origin of the Shining Path movement, was close to Huanta, where Elvin's letters had been posted.

The phone was answered immediately by Pat Stocker, a very well-informed and helpful young lady. She quoted from several publications, reinforcing what Father Bede Hill had told me.

'Look,' she said. 'It's five o'clock now, I'll make some photocopies of the cuttings and put them in the six o'clock post. You should get them first thing in the morning.'

I didn't enjoy our family dinner that evening. I couldn't help wondering what I was taking Marie Christine and Rebecca to.

Next day at Heathrow we could scarcely carry our rucksacks as we got out of the Land-Rover. 'Be sure and bring those two safely back,' my father said, shaking my hand.

Odd found the five of us in the terminal, took his photos and said, 'You're a brave man, Mr Ridgway.'

'Don't be too sure about that,' I replied. 'I've found out a bit more about it now.' He smiled, and was lost in the crowd.

Chapter Three

The DC 10 rose heavily from the end of the runway at the start of its 23-hour flight to Lima via Zurich, Oporto, Caracas and Bogota. Impatiently I watched the 'Fasten Seat Belt' sign. As soon as it went out I turned to Ed and Justin on my right, taking the sheaf of cuttings from the already-battered envelope. I practically knew them off by heart.

I had drawn lines beside relevant passages from the *Andean Report*, which Pat Stocker had described as a particularly reliable English language monthly publication for the business community. There were also pieces from *The Catholic Herald, The Tablet*, the *Peru Support Group* and the International Secretariat. They made grim reading.

'I'm afraid the trip isn't going to be quite like we imagined it,' I said. 'The Apurimac seems to be the battleground for a guerrilla war.' Ed read the papers thoroughly, and was clearly excited by the change of situation. Justin read even quicker, but didn't reveal his feelings.

I handed the sheets to Marie Christine and Rebecca; they had already had a quick glance at them in Wimbledon, but now they were much more thorough.

Afternoon tea was served halfway to Zurich. No one said much. We looked at the map of Peru which I had used in 1970. Everyone made a few suggestions, but all we could really do was wait and see what we could find out in Lima.

The plane was full. When it touched down after crossing the Atlantic, Rebecca wrote in her diary, 'People clapping when we landed at Caracas. Thanking pilot and God—Roman Catholic.'

At Bogota Marie Christine noted, 'Abandoned planes line the runway like beached whales. Armed guards in sentry boxes everywhere.' We were no longer in Europe.

Lima is often misty. The cold Humboldt current, sweeping up from the Antarctic along the hot, desert coastline, makes a lot of fog. But it was not too misty to see the lines of khaki helicopters and troop transports standing by the runway; I thought I recognised American, Russian and European designs.

At the airport bank armed policemen kept onlookers behind rope barriers, while tourists changed their travellers' cheques. I remembered getting 100 soles for £1 Sterling in 1970; today I got 22,000.

A battered red taxi rattled us through rough streets on the outskirts of the city. Poverty was everywhere. Refugee families from the interior of a country the area of France and Britain combined were living in makeshift shelters of bamboo and cardboard. Of the eighteen million population of Peru, fifteen million live below the official poverty line. Lima has long since burst its boundaries, with a population of six million.

Graffiti covered most available walls, with the name *ALAN* prominent everywhere. A year before, the Apra government had come into office on the back of sweeping social change, with President Alan Garcia at its head. Polling three million votes, against the 1.5 million of its nearest rival, Apra had made bold promises to build a socialist Peru with respect for human rights. Garcia had made a name for himself with his youthful good looks, fiery speeches and defiant refusal to pay any more interest on Peru's enormous foreign debt than he felt the country could afford. But at home he was caught in a vice. On one side was *Sendero Luminoso*, eager to destroy the system entirely. On the other was the military.

The previous government, under President Belaunde, had turned the military loose in the guerrillas' stronghold of Ayacucho, where some 7,000 people had died or disappeared. Many had been buried in mass graves, their index fingers cut off and their faces mutilated to prevent identification. The few bodies left recognisable were later identified as people who had been arrested by the military.

I was tired from the long flight, and such thoughts made me gloomy. We had ten weeks ahead of us in Peru: what on earth were we going to do? What sort of hotel bills would five people run up in a capital city?

Our immediate destination was a villa belonging to someone called Clara de Guerola, whom Ed's girlfriend Leah had met for ten minutes in the back of a London taxi only three weeks before. A quick telephone call from the airport had found Clara at home and keen to see us.

'Well—here we are!' cried Ed, as what Rebecca cheerfully called 'the paint-free taxi' shuddered to a halt outside a smart modern villa in the fashionable suburb of Miraflores. I noticed the sharp spikes on the extra-high walls of the courtyard. Marie Christine and I looked at one another doubtfully.

A smart lady guest overtook us, looking a little disconcerted at our dishevelled appearance. One rucksack full of kit would never service ten weeks of this kind of life.

Clara could not have been more charming. Warm-hearted and enthusiastic, within seconds she had us seated in a cool, elegant drawing room, sipping lemonade and talking about our proposed journey to find Elvin Berg. I found myself making up a plan more or less as I went along. Luckily I had two useful pieces of evidence as to our intent: a copy of *Amazon Journey*, my book about the 1970 expedition, and a full page article from a Norwegian paper complete with photos of Elvin and myself, which Odd had handed me at Heathrow.

In a few moments the whole of Clara's family had become involved. Her husband Luis, an urbane retired Peruvian Navy officer, was packing to leave for London, to take up a post with the International Maritime Organisation, but he made time to telephone people about the situation in Ayacucho. The daughters, Lily and Mariella, left their studies to call journalists and television programmes specialising in human rights. Clara herself organised lunch and a flat for us to stay in.

All this interest in our plans was just what we needed to shake off the jet-lag. In the late afternoon Clara drove us round to the British Embassy, stopping on the way to buy two huge cream cakes, and to show us an empty apartment, high up in a smart new block, where we could stay the night. She was planning to move there herself when Luis left for London.

The British Embassy in Lima occupies the thirteenth and fourteenth floors of a tall block of offices, largely made of glass, in Plaza Washington. We took the lift to the twelfth and rang a bell for the fourteenth. An efficient, fair-haired, very English senior secretary lady unlocked the heavy steel door to let us into a suite of offices. Coloured photographs of the royal family hung on the walls.

We were led through into the map room, where Jeremy Thorpe, a slight, brown-haired *chargé d'affaires* from Sheffield listened attentively to our plans. His up-to-the-minute briefing was most informative. Beginning with the *Senderos'* first action —the burning of ballot boxes in Ayacucho in 1980—he led us right through the emergency to the present. The relationship between the terrorists and the cocaine smugglers was uncertain, but clearly each hoped the other would continue to divert the forces of order. The final part of the briefing was particularly significant. In the past six or seven weeks at least fifteen incidents had been reported, and some 500 people murdered. The *Senderos* attacked villages by night, killing everyone, Thorpe told us. If we happened to be in a village at the time of such an attack, we would be unlikely to survive.

'I can only conclude by telling you that the Apurimac valley is dangerous,' he finished, 'and we advise you not to go.'

'Well!' I leaned back in my chair, running both hands through my hair. The others looked disappointed. It was a long way to come for this sort of news.

'Why don't you go up to Cuzco and look for something to do in the jungle to the west? There should be no terrorist problem there.' Mr Thorpe smiled in a friendly way. We got to our feet, thanked him for his help, and agreed to let the Embassy know our final route.

Wandering along the streets, in the evening rush hour of a South American capital, I found it hard to grasp where we were. We all felt tired and dirty from the flight, so we headed back towards the apartment.

Marie Christine, Becca and Justin went off to buy food, while Ed and I sorted out our kit on the empty parquet floors. Waiting for the shoppers' return, I suddenly had the idea of ringing Nick Asheshov, who in 1970, as a 30-year-old Cambridge English graduate, had been Editor of the English language *Peruvian Times*. I had got to know him quite well because his sister Anna, a British ski champion, had been a member of our four-person Amazon expedition. 'Asheshov.' The self-assured, rather querulous, high-pitched voice came down the line, and I found myself smiling.

'The unfortunate Ridgway here . . . how you doin'?'

'Fine. What are you up to? I heard you were in town.'

'Lying rat. Listen, I'm here to look for Elvin Berg.'

'Elvin! I haven't seen him since I hired him to help look for Bobby Nicholls. We did find him in the end, you know: he'd been stoned to death by the Amahuacas.' (Nicholls had been one of Asheshov's best journalists.)

'Nick—d'you think Elvin will be at Osambre?'

'Well, that's *Sendero* country—they're a very serious bunch. They burned to death thirty-four of their own men in an argument in the Lurigancho prison, right here in Lima, just last week. They're not your everyday South American terrorist, you know. They really are like the Khmer Rouge . . . Look, I think we'd better meet.'

'OK, when?' I dredged a few reserves. For much of the conversation I had been looking at my sleeping-bag.

'Hop into a taxi and ask him to take you to the Pizzeria in Miraflores. See you at ten. Bring Marie Christine.'

In the flat we ate a cold meal of tuna, bread and an odd sort of Edam cheese, followed by coffee and thick slices of Clara's cakes. The shoppers had bought plenty of food, but then found they hadn't enough money to pay for it, so there had been a lot of embarrassment putting some of it back on the shelves. Then they had difficulty with the security guard getting into the building. All in all, everyone was ready for bed.

'Crazy staying here,' I said on impulse—for I do not like being beholden to people. 'Let's fly up to Cuzco on the six o'clock plane in the morning. I'll wake us all up at four.'

Marie Christine and I took a cold shower and went down for a taxi. The others fell into their sleeping-bags.

The Pizzeria is the cafe for people-watching in Lima; politicians and writers do their talking over coffee or pisco sour, Peru's national drink made from brandy and limes. Nick was there before us; his narrow, handsome face looked drawn, like an athlete at peak—or was it the result of late nights? His spectacles were perched high on his forehead, but fifteen years had turned his curly fair hair to white; and he peered a bit, as if his long-term worry about failing sight had proved justified.

His father had been a White Russian bacteriologist, a contemporary of the fictional Dr Zhivago. Now, after twenty years in the country, Nick is something of an old Lima hand, the Peruvian correspondent for several papers around the world. Although his mother had been an English pathologist, he looks to me more like a rather enigmatic Russian.

On this occasion he ate little, picking at a small spaghetti bolognese while Marie Christine and I sipped strong black coffee. The *Peruvian Times* had been closed by the government several years back, he told us, and he was now co-publisher both of the *Lima Times* and of the paper which Pat Stocker had recommended, the *Andean Report*. His summary of the situation supported the views of Father Bede Hill and Mr Thorpe at the Embassy. He had plenty of horror stories to keep us awake. The Apurimac valley was not recommended.

But Nick went beyond advice: he named contacts in Cuzco, and suggested how, if we did decide to go looking for Elvin, we might get an official covering letter. It was a beginning.

We got a couple of hours' sleep on the parquet floor, but I needed no waking at 0230. We finished most of the cakes as a sort of breakfast. Down on the street, in the dark, we joined battle to find two taxis to carry five people and their kit to the airport: always heavy on the nerves at that time of day, particularly when the driver turns out to be an Argentinian wanting to argue about the Falklands War.

Money-changing was difficult, as the changers did not officially open until the Cuzco plane had gone. Just in time, I roused a blanket-shrouded figure under a counter. There was a crush to buy the tickets: were the little boys who hung around picking pockets?

After the rush there was the usual long delay in the departure area, and I fell asleep. Rebecca was writing her diary: 'Hearing tales of theft and rape on the main roads. I don't know what to think, I have never had to face such terrible things, or such merciless people on both sides—the military are probably just as bad.'

On the flight over the Andes Becca sat at a window/emergency exit. Next to her, Ed said, 'If the exit is opened, the person nearest it is sucked out.' Justin looked out of the window now and then, but he was already making notes from a thick history of China, which he hoped would last him right through the expedition.

'What's the plan, John?' Ed was always asking me this, keen to get up and go, and now enthralled by the great snow-covered peaks beneath us.

'I just don't know,' I replied with a weary smile. 'Sorry, old sprout—I'll come up with something.' The mountains and valleys looked hostile enough, without the people trying to kill us as well. What was I doing, taking my wife and daughter to such a place?

I needed a good long sleep. Cuzco airport was not the place for it. We were badgered by people wanting to carry the bags, go in their taxi or stay at their hotel. Becca saw it more calmly: 'Must move gently, we are at 11,500 feet. Altitude sickness. Mum very tired. I've never been above the height of Ben Nevis —4,000 feet. Quechuan woman: white stove-pipe hat, brightly-coloured shawl and carrying heavy load plus child. Thickly-woven, gathered skirt, bright. Jumper, bare legs and motor-tyre sandals. Lovely face with very dark eyes and high cheek bones. Brilliant smiles and bad teeth. Thick black hair, in two long plaits tied together at the bottom.'

We found a clean, quiet little hostel, and took two rooms on the upper floor, overlooking a peaceful courtyard. The proprietor gave us a cup of tea. I thought it tasted odd, and he told us it was coca tea—to help us with the altitude. Marie Christine, Becca and I slept for a few hours.

'Hallo, hallo!' Ed's enthusiastic greeting rang through the door. It was already evening. I felt sure that, whatever the situation, Ed would allow nothing to get him down for long.

All five of us went out into the dark for a meal. The ancient Inca city—Cuzco means 'Navel of the Earth'—has a charm only slightly diminished by heavy tourist influence. We wandered through narrow, Spanish-style streets, past old houses with carved balconies and ornate, massive doorways of wood and wrought iron. Here and there typical Inca stonework survived: great walls of precisely-fitted grey stone blocks.

We found a cheap restaurant in a back alley, just off Plaza de Armas, the main square. A sticky plastic tablecloth added to the general air of seediness, but the pasta with tomato sauce was filling, if not quite as bountiful as Ed would have wished.

Leaving Becca and Justin to make a tour of cafes playing traditional Peruvian music, Marie Christine, Ed and I walked to meet a nephew of Clara's in a side square. There were plenty of poor people on the streets, but they weren't starving. Strong Quechuan faces peered at us from simple wooden stalls selling bread, sweets, fruit. Primus stoves hissed to warm the cocoa, and braziers cooked doughnuts and kebabs. We kept our delicate English stomachs away from it all, sucking boiled sweets to help with the altitude—which they do by providing sugar and stopping your throat getting dry.

We joined Aldo Chiappe and his friend Guillermo Castro for coffee. Both jungle and river tour-guides in their early twenties, they were dark, strong and vital. They had been contracted to supply logistical support to an expedition of internationally-known canoeists who were trying to follow our 1970 route down the Apurimac, the furthest source of the Amazon. The team was already well down the river, gambling that speed on the water would carry them past any trouble before it had time to develop; but they were taking no Peruvians on the Apurimac, as they reckoned it too risky. Aldo and Guillermo were to meet the expedition biologist, a Costa Rican, and a British doctor later that evening. They planned to leave before first light, taking supplies to the canoeists at a point upstream of the emergency zone.

'Crazy peoples, dirty war,' cried Guillermo, who spoke good English and had already charmed me by describing my *Amazon Journey* as 'a jewel'. Even if you know you're not Tolstoy, encouragement does add a bit of a shine to things when you're tired. His tales of the war were dramatic: a twelve-year-old terrorist boy had confessed to dismembering nine adults; the Air Force had bombed Villa Virgen out of existence. But one incident had occurred even closer to Osambre. I remembered that in 1970 the Rosas, Paullo and Berg families had all been farming quite close to one another on the Apurimac. Guillermo said the Rosas farm had been attacked by night; the *Senderos* had captured Anibal Rosas and hung him naked by his feet from a beam on the porch. While they were inside, ransacking the house and discussing how to kill him, one of the farmworkers had slipped back and cut him down. Both men escaped unharmed, but the *Senderos* burnt the place to the ground.

Even Ed's enthusiasm for the Apurimac was tempered a little by these stories. I also noticed that when Guillermo and Aldo warmed to the subject of the jungle out towards the Brazilian border, or suggested the possibility of making a trip down the Urubamba, both he and Marie Christine looked quite interested. Personally, I felt that anything but a search for Elvin would be something of an anti-climax. Maybe I had only known him for a few days, fifteen years ago; nevertheless, we had seen a spot of drama together, and he was the sort of fellow I felt I could count on. I rather hoped that, if the situation were ever reversed, he would persist in looking for me. Although I did not want to put my wife and daughter at risk, I did not intend to give up.

We got to bed late again. Marie Christine noted in her diary, '*NOT WORTH* taking great risks, but fearful of Ed and Justin's enthusiasm and naiveté.'

Next morning was Sunday, and there was a military parade in the Plaza de Armas. The troops goose-stepped past the front of the cathedral, but it was no church parade. We watched from the centre of the square, in hot sun. A General hoisted the Peruvian national flag, and then the Communist Mayor hoisted the Cuzco flag. When the Peruvian flag was hoisted, two machine guns opened up from among the bushes, to support the anthem and the government. I suppose everyone knew they were firing blanks, but it made the point that military fire-power controlled the country.

There were extravagant speeches by both men and women, and some half-hearted singing. In the march-past of hundreds of civil co-operative workers which followed, three men gave defiant clenched-fist Communist salutes.

An hour after the military parade, a tight group of church people carried a float of the Virgin Mary round the empty square, to the accompaniment of a small ragged band. I wondered how an Inca would have read the situation.

Returning to the hostel, I was surprised to find a note from a Dr Kate Durrant, the English doctor to the Amazon '85 canoe expedition. In it she said she was sorry to miss us, but that she had joined Guillermo and Aldo only just as they were all about to set off for the river. Apparently she had followed the canoeists down from the furthest source of the Apurimac at Cailloma, high on the Altiplano, and she went on, 'Many people remember you, particularly Adam at San Juan.'

'Well, that's nice,' I said. 'Look, why don't we go up to Cailloma ourselves? We could spend a month walking down the river, back towards Cuzco. We could use it as training: Phase One, in fact. There are no terrorists up there.'

I could see the others were interested. Any plan was better than no plan at all.

Quickly I followed my new scheme through.

'The main thing worrying me about going to look for Elvin immediately is the weakness of our team,' I went on. 'In 1970 we were all about thirty years old—two ex-Parachute Regiment officers, a Medical Corps Sergeant who had also been in the Parachute Regiment and swum for the Army, and Anna, who'd been a British ski champion. We found the trip very difficult, and there were no terrorists then.'

I paused, looking round the faces. No one demurred.

'We'd get fit on the Altiplano. We should be able to look after ourselves after a spell up there. If we turn into a good team, then we can think about trying to reach Osambre and find Elvin. That'll be Phase Two.'

Everyone cheered up. We listed tasks for each person so that we could get going as soon as possible. In spite of lingering headaches from the altitude, we took to our boiled sweets and walked uphill to see various Inca ruins near the city. Ed went furthest and fastest; Justin moved at a more gentle pace. Marie Christine, Becca and I were cautious, but, getting caught in a thunderstorm up at the nearest ruins, we ran all the way down, dripping wet, but feeling in much better form. We had been in Peru for two days.

Chapter Four

On Monday morning at last we could get moving. We had a sunny early breakfast in a cafe by the square, then split up. Justin and Ed went to research the route from Cailloma down the Apurimac; and also to get the best maps available. Marie Christine and Becca set off to change travellers' cheques into small-denomination notes for buying food. They also wanted paraffin and meths for the primus cookers, and finally they were to find out the times of trains to Sicauni, on the first leg of our journey to Cailloma.

I was to obtain the letters of permission necessary to get us into the Emergency Zone for Phase Two. The morning was clear and bright, though there was a dusting of snow on the barren mountains round the city. Trotting through ancient back streets with a light heart, I enjoyed testing my new-found acclimatisation to the altitude.

Within the house I had fallen into a sedate walk; officialdom usually has that dulling effect on me. And by half past ten the sun was definitely burning up the optimism a bit. However, spirits rose again when I met Ed, who was carrying an armful of photocopied maps covering almost the entire route of Phase One on a scale of 1:1,000,000. This really was encouraging, for there had been no maps in 1970, and we had had to hire guides. Now, with maps of our own, we shouldn't need guides, and many hours of anxious haggling at the wrong end of each day would be avoided.

After this I began my next call in better heart. A brass plaque on the wall read *LEONARD'S LODGINGS*, and the front door opened just as I rang the bell. A handsome, dark-haired woman of middle age came out.

'Good morning,' I began. 'My name's John Ridgway. I was recommended to contact a Mr William Leonard here, by Nicholas Asheshov in Lima.'

'Ah yes, Nick phoned. I'm afraid Mr Leonard is not here. He's in the country with his wife; but I am her sister, Maria, and I am looking after the place for them just now.'

She spoke clear, studied English, and something in her bearing suggested that she would be effective. 'Nick asked if we would give you some help. Come in, we'll talk.'

The next hour proved critical for the entire project. Maria rapidly typed a letter to the *Prefecto* of the Department of Cuzco, dating it 14 October 1985. The letter asked permission for us to pass through various named villages on the way to and from Osambre, and told how we were looking for relatives of the Berg family. Our five names, ages and passport numbers were listed at the bottom. I signed the document. All the *Prefecto* had to do was to apply his seal and signature.

'But first we shall visit the Secret Police, and ask their permission,' Maria told me. I followed her swiftly down a broad, empty avenue. 'A rich family used to live here, but they sold up and moved to Lima after the big earthquake in the 1950s. And now it belongs to the Secret Police,' she smiled back over her shoulder.

Anybody looks sinister, once you know they're in the Secret Police. Uniformed men with sub-machine guns guarded the entrance; a small front garden sporting a tall flagpole, complete with red-and-white Peruvian flag, led to a nondescript, average-sized private house. Maria put up a fairly imperious show, and we were soon seated in a small ante-room. I felt nervous. An expressionless man in his late twenties, smartly turned out in a grey suit and the inevitable dark glasses, soon came in to see us. Maria wasted no time in handing him the letter.

'That's all right with us,' he said softly in Spanish. 'No permit is needed for this area: there is no emergency now. Things have quietened down.' He looked up. 'Please be seated for a minute.' He walked quickly from the room, turning right towards the back of the building.

He was soon back. 'There were four Berg sons,' he announced. 'Two are dead—one killed in November last year, the other in March this year.' He turned away from Maria and looked me straight in the eye. 'Be very careful. We would like to see you when you get back—we would like to know where the other two brothers are.' Then he smiled thinly and walked away.

The news was a shock: two of the brothers dead. But instinctively I felt that Elvin must be one of the survivors: he was that sort of person.

Maria and I left the building. On our way to the *Prefecto*'s office, I thought of something I had been told in Lima: 'Be careful what you say. You never know who your friends are. Remember, there are plenty of *Senderos* in Cuzco and Lima.'

Did our friend in the dark glasses think Elvin was a terrorist? Why was the policeman so interested in the whereabouts of the surviving Berg brothers? Could he think *I* was a *Sendero*?

We arrived at the faceless building from which the *Prefecto* runs the huge department of Cuzco. Armed guards checked our papers, which we handed over to a clerk before clambering up some steps to the drab council offices. Wide, shallow stairs led us up and round on to a grand landing contained by a substantial wrought-iron railing. Here generations of citizens wait long hours for decisions from their elected leader. The *Prefecto*'s office was on the far side from the head of the stairs; and through its open door I could see a vast, leather-topped desk faced by a single chair whose carved wooden back rose all of six feet above the carpeted floor. Just outside her master's door in the tiled waiting room, an immaculate, middle-aged woman sat behind a typewriter, filing her nails and gazing at a crossword with studied indifference to her surroundings. Peeling beige plaster, a marble-topped table with inlaid cabriolet legs, and an Empress Eugenie couch covered with faded plush red velvet completed a scene of utter stagnation.

We filed into the clerk's smoke-filled little office in the other corner of the landing. The official read Maria's letter, flipped over the page, and compared me with my photograph in the Norwegian newspaper cutting. I produced *Amazon Journey* once more.

'The *Prefecto*'s out. Please come back at two o'clock and he will sign the paper for you. Thank you.' The man nodded our dismissal.

Marie Christine spent all afternoon in that waiting room, and much of the next morning as well. Our letter was always on top of the In tray. Patience and a slight show of distress finally earned a signature. The same procedure was needed for a letter from the Immigration Office on the other side of the city. But 3.45 on the afternoon of Tuesday, 15 October, at last found us on the train for the four-hour journey to Sicuani.

I think we had all been shaken by the weight of our rucksacks and belt-order on the walk down to the station. And now, seeing the giant scale and sheer steepness of the mountainsides through the window of the train as we wound through valley after valley, I wondered just how far we would be able to walk in a day on our own. A rapidly-worsening sore throat lessened my interest in the stream of women and children who passed through the carriage selling avocado pears, oranges, bananas, cakes, bread, newspapers and chocolates. An old crone wailed her way along, followed by two attentive small children: 'Mama's blind, no Papa. Mama's blind, no Papa.' Was this an act? Was it real? It was certainly lucrative.

The railway was built in the 1920s to link Cuzco with Puno, on Lake Titicaca. It seemed strange not to be able to change somewhere for Argentina or Brazil, or anywhere at all. Powerful diesel locomotives pull the five silver carriages. Some of the population see the train as a symbol of capitalism and hurl rocks at it. Everyone ducked as missiles clanged against the metal coachwork, and broken windows marked lucky shots. Darkness came at about six o'clock, and then the lights began to fail, often for several minutes at a time. We had to keep a sharp watch on

JEFATURA DEL CUSCO
MESA DE PARTES
Cusco ....15 Oct....... N° .... de 19 85

Cusco, 14 de octubre de 1985

Señor Prefecto del Departamento
Dr. Julio Jara Ladrón de Guevara
Ciudad.=

Señor Prefecto:
Me permito dirigirme a Ud. a fin de exponerle lo siguiente:
Tengo la misión encomendada por tres diarios de Noruega así
como de los familiares de los señores Berg que tienen una
hacienda en el área denominada "USAMBRE", y que desde el año
1980 no se ha tenido noticia alguna acerca de esta familia,
para averiguar acerca de si ellos se encuentran bien o si han
tenido alguna dificultad seria.
Por este motivo, ruego a Ud. señor Prefecto se digne expedir-
nos el correspondiente Permiso de viaje para esta zona que
abarcaría por el Apurímac desde Caylloma (Arequipa) hasta el
puente de Cunyac pasando Jatumpampa Usambre, Vilcabamba,
Pampacenas, Lucma, Santa Teresa, Machu Pichu y luego Cusco.
La expedición esta conformada como sigue:
- John Manfield RIDGWAY - 47 años - Británico -Pasp.C982681
= Marie Christine RIDGWAY 40   "   "   " G063218
- Rebecca L. RIDGWAY   18   "   "   " M190258
- Justin MATTERSON   22   "   "   " M361164
- Edward J. LEY-WILSON   21   "   "   " N178124 D

Agradeciéndole la atención dispensada a esta petición, me sus-
cribe de Ud. como su atto. y ss. ss.

Cusco, 15 de Octubre de 1985.
Con el adjunto recorte, pase a la Jefatura de la Oficina Depar-
tamental de Migraciones de esta ciudad, a fin de que se sirva in-
formar y emitir su opinión a la mayor brevedad.

P/r/m.

Dr. Julio Jara Ladrón de Guevara
Prefecto del Departamento.

The letter to the *Prefecto* of the Department of Cuzco

MINISTERIO DEL INTERIOR
Dirección General de Migraciones
OFICINA DEL CUZCO

Cusco, 15 de Octubre de 1985.

Oficio Nro.437.Mig(1)Cus.

Señor   : Prefecto del Departamento.-CUSCO.

Asunto   : Sobre extranjeros que se indica.-COMUNICA.

Ref.   : Documento de fecha 14OCT85.

Tengo el agrado de dirigirme al Despacho de
su digno cargo, para poner en su conocimiento sobre el
documento de la referencia, que los ciudadanos "Británicos", John Manfield RIDGWAY (47) con Pasaporte Nro. -
G682681, Marie Christine RIDGWAY (40) con Pasaporte Nr.
G063218, Rebeca L. RIDGWAY (18) con Pasaporte Nro.M190258
Justin MATTERSON (22) con Pasaporte Nro.M361164 y Edward
J.LEY-WILSON (21) con Pasaporte Nro.N178124D, tienen Visa
Autorizada de Permanencia hasta el 09ENE86, por lo tanto
de acuerdo a disposiciones vigentes pueden transitar li-
bremente por todo el territorio nacional, hasta el termi
no de su visa.

Para los fines consiguientes.

Dios guarde a Ud.

RZB/jol

RODOLFO ZUÑIGA BARREDA
yor   P I P
Jefe Inspectoria Migraciones

The letter from the Immigration Office

30

the rucksacks on the seats in front of us. The *ladrones* [robbers] have a desperate reputation on the railways of Peru.

Of course the train was late arriving in Sicuani, and I could not recognise the place at all. Fifteen years ago we had come down to this market town, at 8,000 feet, in a state of near-collapse from altitude sickness, after a too-rapid ascent to Cailloma at 14,000 feet. It had seemed a haven then. Now it felt like another step upwards in an increasingly hard way of life. At 9pm we checked into a hostel, paying the equivalent of £1.40 for a room with four narrow beds. The green walls barely supported a ceiling with a ten-inch sag in it. I was encouraged by a strong smell of disinfectant, which emanated from that dark, extraordinarily heavy blanket, but it did not extend to the lavatory, which lay in total darkness at the foot of the stairs. Using it was a challenge.

With raging sore throat, I shared a single bed with Marie Christine. As Justin turned off the light, we discovered a peephole through to the next room; the Indians there slept fully clothed, across the beds, keeping the light on all night. When we got up at five next morning, Justin found that the chamber pot under his bed had been full for some time.

In the clear, pale light of early dawn we lumbered through narrow streets, past brightly-painted buildings with bat-wing doors. We crossed a bridge over a roaring river and found ourselves by a small market where the trucks load up for their journeys from the railhead up into the mountain country all round. Some urgent negotiations secured £1 seats on top of sacks piled high in the wooden frame of a battered Dodge truck. It was now 6am, and the truck was due to begin the four-hour trip up to the provincial capital of Yauri at 7am.

I urged everyone not to drink much, as there would be no pit-stops on this trip. Ed, Justin and I each had a bowl of vegetable soup and potatoes at one of the clapboard stalls. We saw the saucepans boiling on the primus stove, but we avoided the meat, just in case. Marie Christine and Becca wandered off in search of a cafe with a better loo; to them a bite of breakfast seemed a secondary consideration.

31

The best cafe was scruffy. A teenage boy, leafing through a dog-eared American sports magazine on the dirty counter, was thrilled when Marie Christine read him passages aloud over a dish of boiled potatoes and gravy. She and Becca couldn't face the meat either, putting their lack of gusto down to the initial squeamishness of any expedition. They joined me on top of the truck at 6.30; and together we watched our two boys visiting stalls in the market: Ed erect and all military bearing, Justin sauntering along with hands firmly in pockets. We wondered how they would get on together.

I was pleased at my ability to deal with South American delays —a skill I had lacked in 1970. I felt relaxed and at peace with myself. There were no terrorists here. All we had to do was enjoy each day and get fit for Phase Two. From my perch, up on the sacks, I watched the world of Sicuani go about its daily business. People looked cheerful, and the sun warmed me; it wasn't such a bad place. What did it matter if it was already nearly ten o'clock? We had all day.

Once we did begin to move, the cold breeze made my throat feel sore again. I kept sucking numbing Peruvian throat sweets which listed cocaine in the contents. The truck laboured up a steep, fertile side valley of cultivated fields and eucalyptus trees, and crawled on to the Altiplano. We kept our hats on and applied plenty of sun cream, particularly on lips and noses. A friendly Quechuan woman was among our companions on the back of the truck, nursing a one-year-old baby. Every time it so much as murmured, she gave it a cuddle. I reflected that children must feel very secure, either slung on the back in a brilliant, rainbow-coloured woven poncho, or nursed in the lap. Either way, mother and child are never parted. Rather different from Britain.

The Altiplano was to be our home for a while. I had grim memories of this bitter, bitter plain, two miles above sea-level. The air is thin. The lungs cannot take in enough oxygen. Exertion brings breathlessness, followed by a sharp, persistent headache, which kills the appetite and prevents sleep. Without food or

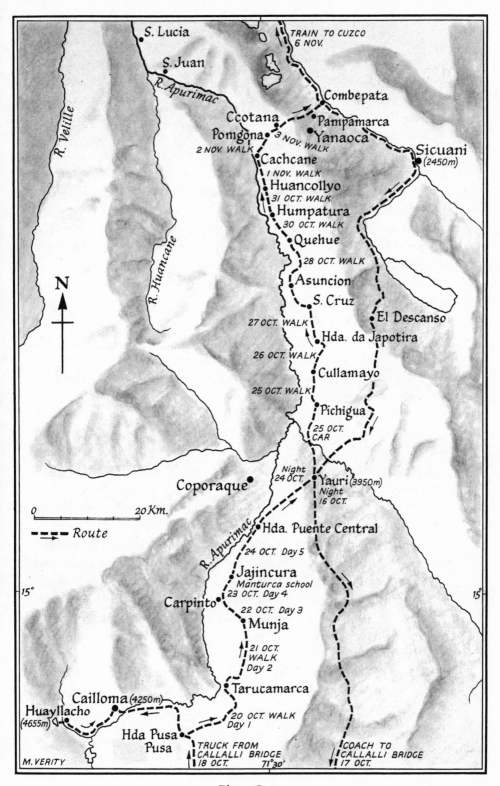

S. Lucia

S. Juan

R. Apurimac

TRAIN TO CUZCO
6 NOV.

Combepata

Ccotana   Pampamarca
Pomgona   Yanaoca
2 NOV. WALK   3 NOV. WALK

Sicuani
(2450m)

Cachcane
1 NOV. WALK
Huancollyo
31 OCT. WALK
Humpatura
30 OCT. WALK
Quehue
28 OCT. WALK

Asuncion
S. Cruz

El Descanso

27 OCT. WALK
Hda. da Japotira
26 OCT. WALK

Cullamayo
25 OCT. WALK

Pichigua
25 OCT.
CAR

R. Velille

R. Huancane

N

Night
24 OCT.   Yauri (3950m)
Night
16 OCT.

Coporaque

0   20 Km.

– – – – Route

R. Apurimac   Hda. Puente Central

24 OCT. Day 5

Jajincura
Manturca school
23 OCT. Day 4

Carpinto   22 OCT. Day 3
Munja

21 OCT.
WALK
Day 2

15°

15°

Tarucamarca

Cailloma (4250m)

Huayllacho
(4655m)

20 OCT. WALK
Day 1

Hda Pusa
Pusa

TRUCK FROM
CALLALLI BRIDGE
18 OCT.   71°30'

COACH TO
CALLALLI BRIDGE
17 OCT.

M. VERITY

Phase One

sleep, collapse soon follows. The only cure is oxygen, and in practice this means a descent to thicker air at lower altitudes.

We had already spent four days at 11,500 feet in Cuzco, and I hoped that the climb to 13,000 feet in Yauri would present no problems. Altitude apart, the Altiplano is a bleak, windswept, treeless, wide open space. Flocks of llamas and alpacas roam the rolling plain, chewing at sparse, yellow-green itchu grass, tended mostly by Quechuan women whose bright clothes splash colour into their drab surroundings. The skyline is rimmed by jagged mountains, often covered with snow, otherwise starkly coloured mineral red, black, yellow or green. Sectors of the horizon are temporarily blotted out by oncoming squalls of rain or snow. At that altitude the sun burns skin more fiercely, combining with a whirling chill wind to split the faces of the Indians.

Homes are built of rough stone, with dirt floors, and roofed with thatch, or, if they are recent, with corrugated iron. There are no chimneys, and respiratory illnesses thrive in the smoky atmosphere: 50 per cent of all reported deaths are of children under five years old.

The homes are surrounded by blackened paddocks, contained within low stone walls, where llamas, alpacas, cattle, sheep and horses are gathered each night—as much so that their owners can collect their droppings for fuel as to protect them from *bandidos*, pumas and foxes.

In mid-afternoon our truck rolled axle-deep through a shallow river, and ground up the gentle hill which is the main street of Yauri, ancient provincial capital of Espinar. Rusty, bent lengths of railway line stuck in the ground beside the dusty street served as telephone poles. Grass was growing between the stones of the old Spanish church tower which dominates the plain for tens of miles in all directions. A biting wind swirled clouds of dust and clanged the tin roofs. This was a commercial town, dealing in the basics of life.

My first impression was of the sheer physical difficulty of lugging my rucksack and belt-order up the street. Thank goodness, we found the only hostel, El Tigre, within a few minutes.

Señor Emilio Beltan Luza showed Ed and Justin to a room upstairs at the back of the courtyard. Marie Christine, Becca and I shared a room overlooking the town square, a large, empty patch of ground which had the effect of diminishing the low buildings on three sides. The fourth side was taken up by a massive stone church, now in such a state of disarray, with its corrugated iron roof, that it looked as if it might serve as a large barn for storing the town's fodder. We had geraniums in our window, and curtains—and a chamber pot, too.

In Emilio's room, lit by a solitary guttering candle, I laid out our passports on the table. While he peered through spotted glasses with one cracked lens, laboriously recording every detail in his register, I studied the religious tracts on the walls.

'Forty-seven, are you? I'm fifty-three.' He clapped plump hands together in delight. To survive fifty-three years on the Altiplano is a real achievement. He recommended a good cafe for a tortilla and chile sauce, but told us there was no chance of a truck to Cailloma for at least another four days.

'You must catch the nine o'clock bus for Arequipa in the morning,' he rumbled. 'Then you'll need to get off at Callalli Bridge at about three in the afternoon. Cailloma is about eight hours from there, by truck—*muy alto, mucho frío.*' I went to bed early, still sucking the throat-numbing sweets.

At three in the morning vehicle headlights were suddenly switched on, blazing at the hostel from the square. They glared right through our lace curtains. Engines revved: shouting and banging on doors followed. They're coming to get us, I thought. I felt frightened, furiously wishing I hadn't got my wife and daughter involved. But when the noise subsided, I quelled my fear and went back to sleep.

At 5am the bumps in the night seemed no more than a fit of paranoia. Emilio's amply-built wife, mother of nine children, gave us half a bucket of hot water. Our washing from the previous day hung frozen rigid from the line in the courtyard. The lavatory, though smelling atrociously and occupying a very public place, could at least be attacked with buckets of water drawn from a forty-five-gallon drum.

We went down the street to a dingy store where we bought tinned tuna, rice, bread and tea. As we walked back up the street to catch the dented coach, people stared and Spanish music blared; a drunk stretched eloquently unconscious on the sunny side.

At first there were no seats for our six-hour trip to Callalli, but after an hour or so we came to the vast Tintaya mine and many people got off. The mine had been first opened for production in May that year, after five years of preparation, and gold was among the metals coming to the surface. The giant modern buildings looked as if they were on the moon, and fifty-ton dump trucks appeared as toys on the waste heaps. I found the armed security force both impressive and sinister: they were prepared for no ordinary robbers.

We got into conversation with a miner who boarded the bus at Tintaya—a pleasant, fat office worker, returning home to Arequipa for a spell of leave.

'Ah! Margaret Thatcher!' he exclaimed as soon as he found we were English. *'Más fuerte!'* [What strength!] He evidently thought we were lucky indeed to come from the same country as the Iron Lady.

The coach ride was less pleasant than the open air of the truck on the previous day, but the scenery was more extravagant. We crossed a couple of mountain ranges, over which the bus climbed higher and higher until we felt short of breath simply sitting in our seats. We also passed through a desert where grotesque cactus plants were just coming into bloom. Formations of huge red blocks of rock were set on the ground like villages. Sometimes we passed so close to the llamas standing like pantomime horses beside the track that their silly faces, with long red tassels hanging from their ears, looked as if they would come right through the window. Above everything lay a great vault of cobalt sky.

At 3.30pm a chant went up in the coach: *'Puente Callalli!, Puente Callalli!'* We had been asking all day to be warned. The driver's assistant helped us retrieve our packs and belt-order from the rack on top of the vehicle. Then the bus was gone, leaving us beside the road blinking in a cloud of dust.

Chapter Five

Callalli Bridge has a high stone arch: that's about all there is to say for it. It is certainly remote, and there are no hotels. We crossed the dirt road and entered the only building—the *cantina*, an adobe mud hut. There was just one customer, a young blood with gleaming black helmet and studded jacket, looking as if he might belong to the Arequipa chapter of the Hell's Angels, and chomping his way through fried meat and chips. A pretty Quechuan waitress, dressed in brilliant colours, complete with a gymkhana-type rosette and white straw boater, looked suspiciously across the low counter at us.

Pointing at the biker's plate, I smiled at her. '*Cinco, por favor,*' I asked, expecting the usual flash of sunshine in reply.

'Si,' came the sullen response. She walked quickly into a kitchen at the back of the building.

Clumsily we heaved our rucksacks across the room and sat round a table by the window. Posters of chimpanzees in various human poses stared down at us from the dark walls, and we practised reading their Spanish mottos, mostly remembering the English version. We were at ease with each other, and the time passed quickly.

Eventually the biker finished his meal, paid at the kitchen door and set off on his Yamaha towards Yauri. Outside, shadows from yellow sandstone cliffs across the river slid towards the cafe under the late afternoon sun. Delicious smells wafted in from the kitchen. We were starving.

'We'll have to get a move on, if we want to find a place to camp before it gets dark,' said Ed, the biggest eater on the team. Already we had been waiting the best part of an hour.

I went up to the counter, and called, '*Señorita*.' Nothing happened, so I knocked on the kitchen door. A sour-looking cook poked his head out and told me there was no food for us: the *señorita* had gone to bed.

'Maybe there's been some sort of misunderstanding,' Justin muttered, trying to be reasonable.

'Not everyone is going to like us,' I replied. 'Gringos don't have much of a record in Peru.' I reached for my rucksack.

We crossed the bridge and turned right, on the road from Cailloma. 'Let's get out of sight of the cafe before we leave the road,' said Ed. 'I didn't like the way they looked at us.'

'Too right,' Becca agreed.

'These cliffs look just like the ones they carve the American Presidents on,' said Marie Christine. I could tell she was anxious.

We must have walked about half a mile, feeling the balance of the weight on our backs, and concerned at the oncoming darkness. The sky was clear, but already stars pricked the velvet blue. The river ran on our right, thirty feet down a scrub-covered bank. On the far side of the river a solitary figure followed a string of llamas towards a small Quechuan settlement which lay further up a valley we had passed in the bus.

'We're out of sight here,' I said. 'Let's get down off the road—by those rocks looks good.' I led the way through the knee-high brush.

'Looks as if this might be some sort of resting-place for travellers,' suggested Ed. The two rocks were all of twenty feet high, and someone had bridged the fifteen-foot gap between them with a low rock wall. There was a pronounced overhang in the angle between the wall and the right hand rock; the ground was covered in mud-dust, talcum-powder fine, but at least it was flat under the overhang.

We leant our packs upright against the wall and set up camp for the first time. The light was going fast. We were tired and a bit tetchy with hunger. Under the overhang we fitted our sleeping-bags inside the bivvy bags, and laid them on blue

Karrimats for insulation. Mine was tight against the wall, then Becca's and Marie Christine's. Becca should be warmest. Justin stretched his bag out a couple of yards further along, under the rock and parallel with ours. Ed laid his stuff out with delightful precision, tight under the foot of the wall.

The cooking did not go smoothly. 'Can you show me how to start this? I've only used gaz before.' Ed was struggling with the delicate pressure-pump on the primus cooker. Already some of our precious meths had been wasted. I felt anxious. There would be nowhere to buy cooker parts, where we were going. There might not be any fuel either. Now, as always, I insisted on leaving everything just a little bit better than we found it. How much kit would be broken before we were all working on the same wavelength?

Eventually some tuna and rice got cooked, and after we had each had a mug of hot, sweet tea, camping didn't seem so bad. It was a clear, frosty night, with a bright crescent moon, and four of us were feeling vulnerable without a tent: the bivvy bags had been Ed's idea. Justin disappeared over the wall and down to the river to wash, downstream of where we had drawn the water for cooking.

'I reckon we'd best get into our sleeping-bags,' I said. 'It must be below freezing already.' I stowed my water bottle in my rucksack, in an effort to stop it freezing during the long night ahead. It was only seven o'clock, and there was no chance of dawn breaking before 5am next morning.

'Well, we'll soon find out how warm the bivvy bags are, Ed,' said Marie Christine, for whom warmth is one of the main priorities in life.

'I used one all last season,' he said cheerfully. 'Sometimes it rained all night, but I never . . . wait a minute. *John!* There's a *fire* up by the road!'

I stood stock still. Flames were crackling only thirty yards away.

'OK, we'll all go up there together,' I said in a loud whisper, forgetting Justin. 'Pick up some stones.' I was already moving up the bank towards the road, which lay in the shadow of the cliffs, in complete darkness.

Ed drew parallel with me as we scrambled up through the brush; it seemed much thicker going up. I was relieved to see that Becca and her mother were falling behind.

'There's no one here,' whispered Ed, stamping out the flames in a cloud of flying sparks. '*Look!* There's another fire!'

Fifty yards further towards the *cantina*, I caught a glimpse of an Indian face beyond the flames.

Ed broke into a sprint. I followed, but with less enthusiasm. Doubt was beginning to wash away my bayonet-charge outlook.

'*John*, he may be *trying* to draw us away from the camp!' Marie Christine called from the dark behind me.

'Yes . . . *ED!* What if he's trying to lead us into an ambush? Let's go back together.' As I shouted, he stopped. In the darkness I heard the frantic flapping of soft shoes on tarmac, panic running like a boy surprised by a policeman in an orchard.

We walked back. I was badly frightened. 'Bring those two safely home,' my father had said at Heathrow. What was I doing? This was our first night out. People were trying to burn us out, even kill us.

'Where've you been?' asked Justin. 'I came back, and you'd all gone. What the hell happened?'

'Yes, well we forgot all about you. The thing is, what to do now?' We stood in bright moonlight by the rocks.

'I think we should move,' Ed spoke with conviction. 'Further down the river maybe, at least go somewhere else.'

'I don't know. If we're quiet, they won't know we haven't gone. This is a pretty good spot. It'll be hard to find somewhere as good.' I felt tired. 'In another ten minutes the moon will be behind the edge of the mountain, and then it'll be very dark indeed. It'd be difficult for anyone to get down through the brush without making a noise.'

We were all cold and tired. I decided we should stay, but each have a pile of stones ready to throw. We could also bang our mess tins to raise the alarm. We probably should have moved. I was just bloody idle.

We eased carefully into our sleeping-bags and lay in total silence, gazing at the wonders of the night sky, made spectacularly beautiful by the thin air of high altitude. I willed the moon to move faster, and within ten minutes it went behind the mountain, shrouding us in deep shadow.

'He's lit more fires, John.' Justin's quiet voice jerked me back from the edge of sleep. 'Up on the rock, the other side of Ed, you can see the reflection of the flames.'

The flickering was unmistakable. But somehow it seemed far away. Surely they wouldn't have lit fires so far from us if they'd known where we were?

'Three out of ten for spotting, old trout!' I whispered. 'Keep an eye on them and let me know if they get any nearer.' I drifted off into a fool's sleep.

Some hours later the cold woke me. Or was it the noise Justin was making? Either way, there was no sign of flames.

Ed was evidently well accustomed to his bivvy bag: he was sleeping soundly, confident he'd be warm enough. He had all his clothes on, including hat, gloves and thermal wear; and he had adjusted the velcro slit at the head so that his nose had just enough space to breathe fresh air. I could just make out his cocoon shape beyond my feet. What a gift to a man with a bayonet, I thought.

Justin had adopted a more carefree approach, and as a result suffered excruciating cold all night. The rustle of his bivvy bag, combined with ceaseless zipping and unzipping sounds, would have been enough to frighten an army. Immediately on my left, my wife and daughter were warm in new alpaca hats and jumpers. Feeling I must remain reasonably alert, I had made the mistake of not wearing a hat and keeping my face exposed to the freezing air; it was something I wouldn't do again.

We awoke at 4.30, after an unsettled, uneasy night. The first streaks of dawn were lighting the sky behind us. The three Ridgways lay shamefully in their sleeping-bags while Ed and Justin hopped around beating their arms for warmth and trying to make tea with water from the river. The water in the bottles had frozen, even inside my rucksack.

Soon golden sunlight touched the tips of the hills across the road, seeping rapidly down the cliffs and over the brush towards us. We waited until we felt its warmth on our faces before crawling out of our cocoons, to sup hot, sweet tea. Within minutes the sun was strong enough for me to try lighting a fire with my magnifying glass, and a few dried leaves from the brushwood on the bank started smouldering almost instantaneously. If we ran out of matches, we could still make fires.

It was a glorious morning. Two pairs of black-and-white geese flew round us while we were having an all-over wash in the river. We all felt terrific, for the first time since arriving in Peru. The bread tasted wonderful, and even the mouse which appeared out of the bank was twitching its nose in approval. The air smelled sweet, with desert flowers just coming into bloom. There were orange and red cactus flowers, and pale yellow flowering bushes, but our surroundings consisted mostly of needle-sharp itchu grass and jagged rock.

The fears of the night melted away with the warmth of the sun. 'It's such a beautiful day, and we feel so full of enthusiasm,' I said to myself. 'Be gone, dull care! Who could possibly come all this way and give up on Day One?'

We decided to brass things out. We would walk straight back to the *cantina*, acting as if nothing had happened, and try to hitch a lift up to Cailloma.

Standing on the middle of the bridge as we arrived at a few minutes to nine was a very pretty Quechuan lady. She was wearing a long pink skirt with turquoise embroidered waistcoat over a matching blouse. On her head was a white boater at a rakish angle.

'*Muy bonito!*' she exclaimed, looking deeply into Ed's blue eyes. Peruvian ladies, being used to brown eyes, are knocked out by blue ones. For the first time on the trip Ed was stuck for words. I think her plan was to head us towards her own little tin stall, rather than have us take our custom across the road to the *cantina*. But her luck was out, because at that very moment a heavy-laden truck lumbered into sight from the direction of Arequipa. As Justin flagged it down, I hurried over the bridge to speak to the driver. He was going all the way to Cailloma, and we soon agreed a price. The journey, which appeared on our 1970 map of Peru as a series of zig-zags uphill, should take about eight hours. I just had time to buy some biscuits from the lady at her stall, and we were on our way, away from Callalli Bridge.

Chapter Six

The biscuits were fine and we wolfed them down—except that the plaster figures on some really were made of plaster, not the icing sugar we craved. But this scarcely affected the delight we felt at being on our way. After an hour we crossed the Colca River by means of a rickety Bailey bridge warped by floods. Turning right, we entered the village of Sibayo and squealed to a halt at the red-and-white barrier pole across the road in front of the Guarda Civil post. While checking our passports, a beady-eyed, bored young officer tried to draw us on the subject of the Falklands.

'Los Malvinas belong to Argentina, yes?' He smiled crookedly.

'Well, I suppose you could say Arequipa really belongs to Chile.'

I regretted the remark as soon as I'd made it. The officer did not seem to find it funny, and for a moment I thought he was going to prevent us going on; but then he cocked his head to one side, slapped the table and roared with laughter. 'Margaret Tatcher, *más fuerte!*'

Back aboard the truck we were joined by Lena, a fifteen-year-old Quechuan girl. In her arms she held a new-born, black-and-white lamb which she fed from a bottle and wrapped in a blanket, like a human baby. By the time we began a zig-zag climb, up and up, the sun was dangerously strong. Halfway up we passed a simple wooden cross on a bend; a memorial for some poor soul who had crashed straight down the mountainside in 1980. Somehow the wooden cross seemed to spread right across that vast mountain landscape: the only human mark, apart from the ancient walled cemetery of Sibayo, which lay far below. It underlined for me the endless struggle the Quechuan Indians have with the harsh terrain which they inhabit.

The old Dodge made heavy weather of the prolonged climb; the cargo of cement alone would have been more than enough for it. The extra sacks of flour, rice and bread, as well as the weight of our bodies, caused the radiator to boil every few minutes, and time soon passed with many involuntary halts. Then we ran into a grass fire, which threatened to cut off the bend in a hairpin.

At 15,000 feet the combination of sun, dust and altitude began to tell on poor Becca. She had seen more than enough snow-covered mountains, condors and vicuña, as well as the by now commonplace herds of llama and alpaca, and the sun had shone all day long. By the time the truck rolled on to the bleak town square of small, dismal Cailloma, she was covered with dust, painfully sunburnt, and suffering from the altitude. 'Head thumping, feeling of failure and holding the others back,' she wrote. 'Feeling like death.'

Cailloma was just as I had left it fifteen years before: grim and squalid, the people wretched. It is on the outer edge of the planet for permanent human dwelling: a high, horribly cold and dusty desert, where snow lies for much of the year.

We managed to get a couple of rooms in the hostel on one side of the square—a miserable place run by a demented shrew of a woman who shouted relentlessly at her staff. We put Becca to bed immediately, and I was relieved to see that she managed to eat a little rice and drink some sweet tea before dropping off to sleep. I was only too well aware that unless she recovered quickly we would have to return to lower altitude in Sicuani.

Justin and Ed were both most helpful and sympathetic; my difficulty was in finding something for them to do. Working on the principle that he who travels fastest, travels alone, I decided to make my own way up to the Huayllacho silver mine that evening. For me the place had such dreadful memories of altitude sickness and cold that I preferred to deal with them on my own.

The *Prefecto*'s letter, the immigration note and the Norwegian article on our search for Elvin Berg all helped win me support at the Guarda Civil post; but the real clincher proved to be the photographs of the mine and Cailloma printed in *Amazon Journey*. It was here that the deathless phrase *quince años antes* was born. I used this 'fifteen years ago' ploy to great effect whenever we needed credibility with officials, who by and large seemed unduly impressed by my ability to compare the present with *quince años antes*.

The police quickly arranged transport, and soon I found myself alone on the back of a small truck carrying livestock and crates of beer up to the mine. What memories the half-hour trip up that bumpy track brought back! In 1970 I would never have dreamed of returning to such a godforsaken place. Now, as the stars shone coldly down on our lonely vehicle, I pulled some old sacking round me with one hand and hung on with the other. Already I was a lot higher than last night, and my head ached with the familiar bitter pangs of altitude.

When at long last we drew near the harsh sounds and lights of the mine, I was feeling desperately tired. It had been a long day. I needed warmth and food, in that order, but both soon. I was rewarded. Within minutes of being admitted through the heavily guarded main gate, I walked into the Manager's office, expecting to bump into Dick Knapp, the friendly American who had been running the mine *quince años antes*.

'This is a Peruvian mine now, and you are most welcome,' smiled Dante Rios, the courteous manager, as I edged closer to the glowing electric fire. 'If you will go over to the dining room, the engineers are having dinner. Perhaps you would care to join them?' I thought guiltily of the rice, onions and curry powder which the others would be having in Cailloma—but at least they'd have my share. I needed no second asking.

With my poor Spanish, I made slow headway with Ramon Castillo, the Deputy Manager; in fact I was concentrating mostly on the plate of steaming hot roast lamb laid before me on the gleaming table. I did, however, discover one ominous piece of information. Nine inches of snow had been lying until recently, and more was expected at any time. Ramon was most insistent that we should make the most of the good weather while it lasted. I decided to collect the others and return to the mine next morning, so that we could try to climb up to Lago Vilafro, the furthest source of the Amazon.

Dante Rios was being driven to Arequipa overnight, and suggested that he should drop me off in Cailloma on his way. The stereo music and heater in his powerful Nissan Patrol made for a much more comfortable return journey to the village, and I was loath to get out when we reached the hostel.

The tail lights of the pick-up disappeared down the alley, into the icy night. Around me Cailloma lay silent, in total darkness. I tried the door in the side wall of the hostel yard: it was locked. I went round to the front: the door was locked. Returning to the alley, I rattled the yard door in frustration. A dog barked, then another took up the alarm. I felt cold, tired and sorry for myself. Our bedroom lay at the back of the yard; I shone my torch on the window, and Marie Christine poked her head out.

'Just coming.' She was laughing and I tried to see the funny side of it myself. A few minutes later a docile maid unlocked the door to the yard and I was able to get to bed at last.

We were up at five next morning. It was cold and bright, and at least there was no wind. Below our window the yard was full of rubbish: lumps of firewood, tin cans, a pile of alpaca skins stretched out to dry. Skinny dogs and chickens searched for scraps.

When at last the sun reached over the yard wall, life began to thaw. We broke ice in the forty-five-gallon drum and drew water for washing, and our primus stoves drummed healthily. Perched on a log, with the sun on my back, and a mess tin of hot shaving water by my side, I supped scalding sweet tea and struggled to steady the uncertainties in my mind.

'I feel much better, Dad, really,' Becca was saying. 'It would be such a pity not to see the source of the Amazon, after all this.'

'OK, we'll buy the stores and all go up to the lake together.' I felt relieved once the decision was made. We could always come back if anyone felt ill.

On the square Quechuan women had already spread out their wares in the dust: the apples, oranges and bananas looked as if they'd come a very long way. Piles of aged vegetables lay among mounds of medicinal herbs. A shrivelled old man sat beside a scattering of rusty spare parts for machinery, but nobody seemed interested. Pigs and dogs nosed about for anything vaguely edible, and the first stirrings of breeze set the dust moving again.

By 9am we were back in the Guarda Civil post once more. The police were friendly, and allowed us to leave our rucksacks in a cell when we boarded the battered coach taking the morning shift to the mine. But the ordinary people were suspicious of us. Mines provide the main source of dynamite for bomb-making, and terrorists had attacked Huayllacho only three months before. They had been driven off without casualties on either side, but a detachment of soldiers had been stationed at the mine ever since. Rifles and machine guns were much in evidence. Wisely, I thought, Ramon Castillo took no chances with us: he would not allow us to see the process for refining silver from the ore, or to photograph the buildings. Even in this barren place, *Sendero Luminoso* posed a silent threat.

A young schoolmistress, Larena Talavera, joined us for the 1,000-foot climb up a rough path to Lago Vilafro. I let Justin and Ed go rushing off ahead, but Larena was unused to exercise, and I used this as a pretext for going very slowly and taking a lot of breaks. Becca, I knew, would gain self-confidence from reaching the source of the Amazon; but to have to give up for any reason might be worse than not having tried at all.

Looking down at the barren valley from my seat on a boulder during one of the breaks, I found it hard to imagine that one could get any sort of pleasure from living and working in such a hostile place. I wondered when the mining had started: perhaps even before the Incas. Certainly the Spaniards were scraping the surface of these mountains by the end of the sixteenth century; they sent the precious metal by mule-train over the Andes to the west coast for shipment home to Europe. The English made impressive achievements here in the nineteenth century, and they were followed by Americans and now Peruvians. But really the Quechuan Indians had done all the work: only their masters changed. Over the centuries the rows of horizontal tunnels had crept down the sides of the valley, from the ridge line to the tenth level, and now they were going in right on the valley floor. Engineers told us the silver, gold, copper, zinc and lead would be exhausted within a couple of years. It was hard to imagine silence here, after all this time.

Birds and flowering cactus could not compete with the thin air for our interest. We walked for ever shorter spells at a time, and headaches were never far away. Larena was weakest, and we used the breaks to practise her English and our Spanish, while sucking boiled sweets.

At last we reached the lake, at 15,275 feet. Its surface was a beautiful pale blue: it lay like a jewel in the vast dry bowl of the Altiplano.

By the time we crawled up to it, Ed and Justin had already been in for a swim. Ducks and geese paddled busily about the weed-beds, but the boys had not stayed in with them for long, as the water was little better than liquid ice with a chill breeze to keep it from freezing over. We declined their kind invitation to a dip.

We were all thrilled to be at the furthest source of the Amazon, but our elation was tempered by a concern lest any of us should succumb to altitude sickness. We made our way, cautiously but fairly quickly, back down the path to the mine. Ramon Castillo treated us to a splendid lunch and arranged a lift back to Cailloma. It seemed that the tide of fortune was beginning to swing in our favour.

Back in the village, we had no sooner collected our rucksacks from the Guarda Civil than along came a big Volvo Turbo truck, filled with sacks of silver ore. We hitched a lift for the twenty-mile trip along the river to Pusa Pusa, an enormous *hacienda*, or ranch, which had been broken up by the agrarian reforms of 1973 into a co-operative for the workers.

At this point the Apurimac river was no more than a grey drain, its waters laden with washings from the mine. There would have been no pleasure in walking its banks. From high on the back of the truck we saw flamingoes clustered round a patch of swamp in the largest stone-walled field I had ever set eyes on. The ungainly pink birds looked hopelessly out of place in such bleak surroundings.

It was still only 5pm on a Saturday afternoon when we clambered down from the truck at Pusa Pusa. None of us was feeling well, but nobody was admitting to anything worse than a nagging headache. Pusa Pusa was a sad-looking place, and had clearly gone downhill since the break-up of the *hacienda*. The buildings were dilapidated, and what had once been a fancy volleyball court now stood in a state of decay beside the road. But the air of decrepitude was more than outweighed for us by the friendliness of the short, stout man who answered my knock on the door. Antonio was the *sanitario* [lay nurse] to the co-operative of some 150 families scattered about the Altiplano, and his air of kindliness took the weight from our shoulders. Showing us across a small courtyard, he said we were welcome to spend the night on the floor in the sick bay.

Our two primus stoves made swift work of cooking the potatoes which Antonio produced, and over hot tea we reached an agreement for one of the *caballeros* to provide a horse and take us on our first stage across country next morning. Becca had developed a cold, and her head was splitting, but she cheered up once we got her into her sleeping-bag. Justin was in a jovial mood, though he too had developed a headache at the mine. Ed was suffering from a skin rash, but he was keeping cheerful as always. Marie Christine and I both had headaches. Our only companion in the sick bay was a teenage boy called Bonifacio, whose left heel had been bloodily crushed by a falling rock the previous day. If he made any move during the time we were there, we never knew it: we simply collapsed in our sleeping-bags and hoped upon hope that deep sleep would take the headaches away.

At dawn there was no chance of water; everything was frozen solid. As Justin went off to a nearby stream with the water bottles, I wondered if it was like this every morning on the Altiplano: surely somebody somewhere had found a way of having unfrozen water in the mornings?

Simeon, our *caballero* guide, was twenty-three, his long, narrow face spoiled by a cleft palate. He wore his sombrero with the chin-strap firmly in place, as if he were about to ride off across the Altiplano at high speed. A gaudy floral hatband added to his carefree air. He was late arriving, and I wondered how long it would be before we were fit enough to manage without help from guides and horses. But, considering how ill we were feeling that morning, I thought we were lucky to be moving at all. Without a murmur of complaint about the late start, we loaded the two heaviest sacks on to the horse. Justin and Ed were confident they could carry the lighter packs belonging to Marie Christine and Becca, and Simeon heaved mine on to his back.

It was a glorious place to walk. The sun shone warmly. There was no hint of snow as we set off across the green Hornillos valley, a mile or more broad at that point. Damp, mossy ground was carpeted with masses of tiny blue forget-me-nots. Black-and-white Andean geese waddled about on marshy patches which were still frozen hard enough for us to cross them without getting our feet wet.

Pushing his sombrero back on his head, Simeon called for a break to adjust the load on the horse. We were nearing the top of a cleft in the mountain, where llamas and alpacas grazed peacefully, occasionally lifting their heads to stare at us with disdain. I noticed that the solitary *alpaquero* looking after the animals had fled, and Simeon told me there was much trouble

Elvin Berg with Campa Indian, near Osambre 1970

The silver mine at Huayllacho, near Cailloma

Above: Morning roll–call at Carpinto School

Left: Florenzio – bully-boy

Below: Llamas (or alpacas!) crossing the stream where we stopped for lunch on the walk from Pusa Pusa to Tarucamarca

with *bandidos*: people just didn't wait and ask questions of strangers, he said.

We were on a high route. I had hoped we would stick to a relatively low path marked on the map, but I long since concluded that Quechuans do not suffer from altitude sickness. Simeon simply took the shortest distance, regardless of the height. The sun grew, and we grew weaker. Again we were walking at around 15,000 feet—and this after we had promised ourselves that Lago Vilafro would be the highest we would have to go. Marie Christine kept admiring the flowers, no matter how tired she felt: white dandelions growing close to the ground, brilliant orange and pink papery flowers from round hairy cactus. Becca struggled on without complaint.

I sensed a healthy competition developing between Ed and Justin as they plodded on ahead, and slowly but surely Justin got the better of it. Perhaps he had the lighter of the two packs. Certainly he suffered nothing like the appalling headache which ground Ed down until he was barely able to shuffle forward. Both gave of their best, but by midday all six of us were sharing the three loads. We took a long break for lunch, eating a few apples and some bread rolls by a crystal stream. Nobody wanted to get started again. A man and a boy rode down to ford the stream with a herd of alpaca, shouting '*Ciao!*' as they passed. We hardly had the strength to reply.

The afternoon became an epic struggle. Stumbling up through a sea of itchu grassland, we wandered across an everlasting series of rolling hills, which gradually turned into semi-desert, with no more vegetation than patches of moss and lichen.

'How much longer, Simeon?' came the cry, with increasing desperation. At last we came down on to the main path which I had spotted on the map, and this was clearly much more travelled. We were joined by a young man from Pusa Pusa who had run all the way along this lower path. Unfortunately he showed no sign of wanting to share our loads, though he was more than happy to walk along at our pace. Later we found out just why he preferred company.

At 3.30pm we came into the *pueblo* of Tarucamarca. With great difficulty we walked in as a team, trying hard not to look as exhausted as we felt. I think we were all wondering how we would ever manage to carry our own kit.

Chapter Seven

Coming in from a death march is probably not the best way of approaching Tarucamarca. We had covered little more than a dozen miles in seven hours, yet I wrote at the top of the page in my diary: 'Pains: Legs, heart, head. Self-doubt.'

The most difficult fact to accept in this sort of situation is that outlook, and consequently judgment, do become warped. Reading my diary six months later, I see still more clearly the harshness of that environment. We all had mental and physical weaknesses, and each of us had to struggle not to let the side down. There was little fun. Allowances have to be made for one's self, as well as for others.

It is probably unfair to describe Tarucamarca as looking like a penal colony in the desert. Huts built of sun-baked mud and roofed with tin stand forlornly in scrubby grassland, backed by grotesquely-weathered sandstone cliffs: this is what I saw, through exhausted eyes, that Sunday afternoon.

Pedro, a *caballero* wearing a clean, bright poncho, met us by the water pipe at the edge of the village. He was clearly the man in charge. He led us straight into the nearby schoolroom; as we stacked our kit against the wall and sat down at little rough wooden desks, jugs of delicious cold apple juice were brought in by Cipriana, one of two young schoolmistresses. Justin slumped on the cement floor, back resting against his rucksack, eyes closed and face ashen: he'd given all he had. Simeon swung himself wearily into the saddle of his long-suffering horse and rode back towards Pusa Pusa.

After Pedro had gone off to organise a meal for us, I produced the letters and book. This helped make conversation, and Indians jostled at the door to catch a glimpse of the first *gringos* ever to visit their village. Both teachers were intrigued, wanting to know simple facts like how many hours a plane takes to fly from Lima to London.

Pedro soon returned with a bottle of mineral water for each of us from the village store. 'This will be the most hospitable place we'll visit on the whole trip,' I said. I had never known such a reception on the Altiplano.

Warmed by so much kindness, we soon recovered. I went up the street to the store in search of tinned tuna or sardines for future lunches. The others went down to the stand-pipe, washing their clothes in the hope of getting them dried by the breeze before the sun went down and froze them solid.

Back in the classroom, I found Becca laying out her sleeping-bag and sorting through her things. Suddenly there came an urgent banging on the door. Pedro poked his head in and said to Becca, 'Can you give medical treatment to this man? He has been attacked by *bandidos*.' Through the open door I saw a slim young Indian, his thick, black hair oozing blood all down the left side of his face.

'Deal with that, Bec. You'd better take the bottle of TCP.'

Picking up the bottle from among the medical stores scattered across a couple of desks, she hurriedly left the room without a word. Only we knew how wrong Pedro was in thinking her a nurse: she dreaded *having* injections, let alone the idea of giving them.

I waited a few minutes before following her into the room next door, not wanting to crowd her. The patient was sitting bolt upright on a straight-backed chair in the middle of the teachers' bedroom. Becca had laid a towel round his shoulders, and was gently dabbing at ugly scalp wounds with cotton wool soaked in TCP. Pedro looked on impassively.

'This is Jesus,' Pedro said, speaking slowly in Spanish for my benefit, with plenty of gestures. 'He is an *alpaquero*. He was attacked three hours ago by four bandits. They robbed him.

Three men pinned him face-down on the ground, while the other man tried to kill him, by battering his head with a rock. Somehow he escaped, and ran all the way here. He is a brave man—yes?'

'*Muy hombre*,' I agreed, looking down at the blood seeping from dents in Jesus's head.

'I think we must shave off the hair round each wound to prevent infection, yes?' Pedro turned to look for a safety razor in the glass-fronted medical cupboard at the back of the room. Rebecca was coping well, and Jesus seemed to be calmed by her broken Spanish reassurances. Then Cipriana came in, a little out of breath, and took over in her capacity as *sanitario*.

Bec and I stayed on, comforting Jesus and standing by to help. He had three wounds: the two above his left ear were still bleeding steadily. The third lay in the middle of the crown, which appeared slightly concave. From the centre of the depression a fleshy red bubble protruded through the skull. No one had a firm opinion about the nature of this bubble, nor how serious it might be.

Cipriana cut off most of his long black hair with scissors, then lathered his scalp with shaving brush and soap and started to shave the wounds. Pedro occasionally poured on to the centre of the wounds a few drops of clear liquid, which fizzed up in a white froth like acid. I stood behind Jesus, with my arm round his shoulders. He trembled only slightly, but occasionally he began to sway, as if to faint.

Marie Christine looked in twice, but each time she had to leave quickly or be sick. Jesus told me he was twenty-one, and married with two children. He was proud of escaping from the bandits, but anxious for his wife now that he had failed to return home at the end of the day. He said bandit attacks were common.

After two hours I began to feel sick myself. I became transfixed by the red bubble.

'Can you take over for me, Bec? Just hold him upright. I'll have to get some fresh air.'

'OK, but don't be long, I'm not feeling too good myself.'

I walked a hundred yards or so up to the top of the street,

where a rough track wound away through the sandstone crags. It was 6pm, fast growing dark and cold. The street was empty below me except for one solitary figure: I could just make out the grey-clad shape of my wife. She was retching against the wall, just outside the surgery door.

A five-minute break made all the difference, and I was able to take over from Becca, who also left for a few minutes and came back again. I was just in time to play an active part in deciding what to do about the bubble. Pedro was into medical experiments: he had already given a graphic account of how he had shot himself in the foot by accident and had tried to estimate his total loss of blood. Now he wanted to see what would come out of Jesus's head if the bubble was burst. Cipriana seemed ready to go along with any majority, but was slightly in favour of Pedro's suggestion.

I was against interfering with the bubble, unless Jesus was feeling pressure in his skull, which he did not appear to be. I felt the bubble might be serving as a plug, and that to burst it might precipitate some sort of geyser. I thought we should keep the wounds clean, as clean as possible, and that Pedro should take Jesus to the doctor at the Huayllacho mine in his pick-up truck.

By then there was one other person in the room—a grizzled old man, whose opinion might carry some weight. He had difficulty making up his mind, but finally agreed with Pedro. That settled it: the bubble was to be burst.

While Cipriana was taking the blade out of the safety razor, I glanced up at the faces of Pedro and the old man. Both were fascinated. I am sure they only wanted to see what would happen when the bubble burst: Jesus's welfare was of secondary importance to them.

Cipriana took a deep breath and leaned forward, placing the edge of the blade at the base of the bubble. I tightened my hold on Jesus's arms. With a quick snick Cipriana severed the bubble and covered the wound with a wad of disinfected cotton wool. Pedro smiled and nodded his head for Cipriana to lift the wad. Gingerly she complied. The root of the bubble was bleeding steadily, but without much pressure. Then she applied a big pad of cotton wool, covering all three wounds, and fixed it firmly in place by winding a bandage right round under Jesus's chin.

I looked at my watch: it was seven o'clock. The whole performance had taken a little under three hours.

Knowing that face wounds do not hurt too much, I guessed that the same lack of feeling might extend to the scalp. I also realised that Jesus could not see what was being done to the top of his head. But I could tell he felt pain from holding him in the chair; he must also have been suffering from shock and loss of blood, and his skull was very likely fractured. Taking all this into account, I reckon he was the most stoical person I have ever encountered.

I helped him up from the chair. He moved across the room a little unsteadily at first, but by the time he reached the door he looked as if he was simply coming out of the dentist's surgery after a local anaesthetic. We walked together up the darkened street and round to some huts at the back. I wasn't allowed into the room where he was going to sleep, but from a glimpse through the door it looked crowded.

By simple candlelight Pedro gave us a fine supper of mutton stew, with plenty of potatoes and onions, in a communal dining hut for senior personnel. The highlight of the meal was a bland white cheese which the people of Tarucamarca export. Later Pedro proudly wrote down the composition of the co-operative: 200 families, 2,300 alpaca, 4,000 sheep, 100 cattle, 100 llamas and forty horses, all living in 58,000 acres at 13,650 feet above sea level.

Despite our exhaustion, we all slept poorly. After the business with Jesus I think that we were still excited by a feeling of siege. We had had some pretty rich stuff in the first four days of Phase One—and that in an area which was supposed to be free from terrorists. On the first night someone had tried to burn us out of our camp; then we had found that after a terrorist attack even the remote Huayllacho mine needed a detachment of soldiers; and now Jesus had nearly been murdered by *bandidos*.

The excitement had worn off by getting-up time next morning. We lay in for an extra half hour, until 5.30—an indulgence which we soon came to regret. For the moment we all felt the benefit of a good wash the previous afternoon, and a hot shave helped get the old machine going again. But the aches and pains from yesterday seemed much worse at the thought of another dozen miles today. I doubted if there would be a friendly Pedro in the village of Munja, and we had to cross a pass of 15,500 feet on the way.

Pedro was most insistent that his community supply two horses and a guide for the day. To see how badly they were needed, I had to look no further than myself. I wondered if I would be able to manage the distance. Ed had caught Becca's cold, and was quieter than yesterday. Justin was trying to come to terms with an expedition which was to last months rather than days: the supreme effort of the previous day was required again today. Becca's cold was not really better, no matter how much she tried to reassure us. Marie Christine was confident she'd be all right, as long as a horse was carrying her kit.

Well, we were still going forward, but I didn't think that any *bandidos* we met would have much to fear. For the first time we all carried our sheath knives in our forward right pouches, ready for instant action. Action against rifles?

Damien, who loaded the horses, was not more than sixteen, but he went about the job in a much more professional manner than had Simeon. Purpose-made rawhide cargo nets held Justin's and Ed's packs on one beast and the other three sacks on the larger animal.

Pedro left the village just before us, heading in the opposite direction, his pick-up jam-packed with Indians standing in the back. Jesus was brought out just before departure and safely wedged in the middle of the cab for the short drive to his home. Although he looked weak, he said he felt all right; but when Justin tried to take his photograph, he anxiously waved him away, concerned perhaps about the consequences of recognition, if the *bandidos* turned out to be real terrorists. We worried about infection, and the possible build-up of pressure inside his skull. If he died, people would shrug and simply say, 'Well, he was killed by the *bandidos*, wasn't he?'

'We head for Ccoccama,' Damien indicated a prominent, round-topped mountain of 16,000 feet. 'If we keep it in sight, we can't go wrong. But we must be very careful: the *bandidos* live up there in the wilderness.'

The early part of the walk was made for us by the handsome Andean geese grazing the water meadows in the green valleys which followed. There were no paths now, and I made it my business to keep the dome of Ccoccama very much in sight. It was not impossible that Pedro might be sending us into an ambush. Wherever we went, our rucksacks and pouches attracted envious glances.

'Look at those rabbits, Dad,' Becca called from just behind me as we wound through a narrow defile between low yellow sandstone cliffs.

'They can't be rabbits. Look at their long tails,' said Marie Christine excitedly. 'They must be some kind of monkey. Damien, *hay mono?*' [Is it a monkey?]

'*No señora, miscatchi, buena comida,*' [No lady, *miscatchi* good to eat] our guide laughed, waving his hands in front of his face like knife and fork.

'I'll remember them all right,' I said. 'Missed catchee—like dropping one in the slips at cricket.' And that is exactly how I remember the scene to this day. Hot sun on our backs, and tens of the rabbit-size squirrels scampering in short, sharp bursts across the cliffs.

Miles from anywhere, on no identifiable path, we came across two small children, hurrying through a huge, empty plain on their way to school in Tarucamarca. A couple of mules carrying a pair of milk churns apiece ambled past under the direction of a young boy with a stick. Women in bright clothes sat alone with their flocks of alpacas, spinning wool in the vast landscape under a giant blue sky. Everyone who saw us coming hurried away, and we thought of Jesus, wondering if he was safely home.

Slowly but steadily the dome of Ccoccama grew nearer. We climbed higher and higher, the carpets of tiny blue valley flowers giving way to the small lupins and orange and pink flowering cacti of near-desert. At noon we were still moving, but not much more. Justin and Damien were well ahead with the two horses; I felt Damien must never be allowed a clear lead on all of us, just in case he decided to ride off with everything.

Ed was back with my family—'something known as the Three Rs'—suffering from altitude sickness and either a heavy cold or a recurrence of violent hay fever. Continual sneezing made his nose raw, adding to the irritation of cracked lips which we all suffered. We put him in front of Becca and Marie Christine, with me bringing up the rear. The barometer of Ed's well-being was the brim of his green jungle hat: as long as it curled up all the way round, I knew he was in good spirits. But now that brim was down, so was he. In spite of his bright little Union Jack, sewn on like a cap badge, Ed looked grim. With his chin on his chest and hands clasped under his belt-order, he just shuffled forward.

Lunch was a miserable affair. We ate clinging to a steep face and watched storm clouds forming over the mountains beyond the Apurimac valley to the west. None of us felt hungry, and now we realised that getting up late had guaranteed that we would reach Munja too late to wash ourselves or our clothes before it got dark and cold. There would be no sun to dry socks, shirts and underwear. Encouraging Damien added another strain; he had never been this way before, and in any case we'd seen his selection at Tarucamarca: youngest gets the job!

I did not want Ed to suffer but all the same I was pleased that he was finding the going hard. It did wonders for Rebecca's self-confidence to discover that she had no monopoly of discomfort: even the fittest and strongest have their off days. I think it was good for Ed, too. Naturally enthusiastic and bursting with energy as he was, he would have found it difficult to resist the chance of taking over the leadership of the expedition if he had been always at the front, the first to meet every new situation, and first to communicate with anyone we met. This practical necessity of working together under stress was just what we needed to weld us into a team for Phase Two. No amount of discussion could do the same job.

Somehow we crept over the western shoulder of Ccoccama, and began heading down at last. I doubted if *bandidos* would have much of a life around the summit of the mountain, though I noticed more than one person glancing back over a shoulder, just to check we weren't being followed.

We were soon below the Quechuan women scattered about the mountainside, brandishing thin sticks and hurling rocks to urge their flocks of llama and alpaca down towards the blackened fields of Munja for the night.

When we arrived the village was deserted, bleak and austere in the first thin flakes of evening snow. It comprised no more than a couple of dozen low stone huts, straddling an almost-dry stream bed. How did people manage to stay on in such a dreary place? It was like the Stone Age.

Damien took his money, said goodbye and disappeared into one of the huts. A bent old man showed us across the stream into a half-built school. He kept peering at the Army green pouches of our belt-order, trying to see if we carried firearms. Unable or maybe unwilling to speak a word of Spanish, he shuffled nervously away towards one of the few huts emitting a haze of llama–dung smoke through the weathered thatch of its roof.

We set about making the best of our home for the night. The thick mud walls and tin roof had been finished, but the doors and windows were simply large holes in the walls, and the floors were piled high with rubble.

'I'll make some tea,' said Ed, shattered but plucky. Soon he had water boiling comfortingly. Supper was a tin of tuna between five, and fair portions of rice. We were unable to buy even potatoes in this poor place, and the next village store might be many days' march ahead.

After supper, in better heart, we went looking for decent water among stagnant pools in the deep stream bed. By then it was pitch dark. Snow was settling around clumps of itchu grass, which tripped us when we tried to climb the bank with mess tins full of water for breakfast.

'*Buenas noches, señores!*' a voice came down the bank, out of the dark. It proved to be Señor Juan Chara Cruz, headman of Munja, with a friend to help his confidence. We lost most of our water on the way up the bank, but this did not matter: we needed a friend more than water. I shook hands with the two Indians and suggested we return to our accommodation.

Back in the school our candle flickered in the draught; I went inside, but the Indians stayed in the open. Through the window aperture, I could see that Señor Juan was no more than thirty. His friend was brandishing a long whip in a rather obvious fashion. Both men were suspicious of us, even a little frightened. They would not be persuaded to come into the building, prefer-ring the shelter of the dark for a quick escape if things turned ugly. I handed Señor Juan the letter of introduction from Pedro, but I don't think he or his friend could read Spanish. We touched briefly on the delicate subject of hiring a guide and horses for the morning, and they said this would be possible. Communication was fragmented at best, and both sides were relieved when Señor Juan said he must return home.

We were all so tired that we found it difficult to concentrate. I knew the best thing would be to leave arrangements until the morning, when we would be able to think clearly. As Ed was frequently quoting from a medical guide, 'Outbreaks of temper usually occur more frequently at high altitude.'

After the men had left the window we lost no time in getting into our sleeping-bags. In spite of our exhaustion, we had learned the importance of applying a liberal coating of Eight Hour cream to our poor noses and lips, and taking extra care with the zipping up of the bivvy bags and the insulation beneath. The air temperature was below freezing.

Chapter Eight

We woke at six—late again. I felt refreshed, but the others, particularly Marie Christine, had slept poorly. Apparently dogs had barked for much of the night, and our meeting with Juan Chara Cruz had hardly inspired confidence.

Breakfast was the usual rice pudding—boiled white rice with lashings of sugar, and a little tinned milk to make it look more appetizing. At least we were beginning to speed up our morning packing and moving procedure. Ed was an example to the rest of us, developing basic principles learned with the Royal Marines. Each morning would see him seated on his immaculate kit, quietly writing his diary, while the rest of us poor mortals scrabbled about stuffing things into pockets too small to cope on the sides of our packs.

Shortly after six the tight masses of llamas and alpacas were released from their stone-walled paddocks. Soon they dispersed across the mountainside, beginning again the eternal ritual of climbing up all morning and coming down all afternoon. By seven o'clock on a hard, bright morning the sun was melting the thin covering of snow, and the village stood empty once more.

Evidently feeling their morning's work sufficiently advanced, Juan Chara Cruz and two henchmen turned their attention to the troublesome *gringos* over in the school. Something in their step told me our meeting would not be fruitful.

At first there were horses available, and at a fair price. Then the price was doubled. Finally, there were no horses and all the men were otherwise employed.

'*Ignominia, deshonor!*' I railed on and on, Langenscheidt's

Universal Dictionary in hand. The Indians looked on impassively, staring at the apparition waving a tiny yellow book and
gabbling a language they could not understand. Then all three
began to laugh, slowly at first, but encouraged by one another,
with increasing mirth.

Ed was not impressed: this was not the Raj he had come
to know and love from books. Quite a little slanging match
developed, with outbursts of temper as prescribed by the medical
tract.

'We'll bloody well show them,' I shouted. 'We'll carry our
own kit!'

The three men left, looking a bit sheepish. We five laid our
rucksacks and sets of belt-order outside the building, swept the
inside clean, and came outside again. We were a long way from
anywhere, and the row of equipment looked every bit as heavy
as before.

'If we could just carry everything for quarter of an hour . . .
At least we'd be out of sight of the village,' suggested Justin,
ever the peacemaker.

'Yes, we must look as if we can manage on our own,' I agreed.
'If we look weak, they might try and rob us.' I polished my
Army lightweight combat boots with extra zest.

'At least it's downhill towards the Cerritambo river.' Marie
Christine was poring over the map with Bec. Ed sneezed for the
nth time, and blew his sore nose on a wet handkerchief, feeling
wretched but looking cheerful.

We loaded up and left miserable Munja without looking back.
In any case, there was no one to say goodbye to.

We managed to carry the loads for twenty minutes. I led the
way, down the side of the stream and across the level floor of a
valley. But when we arrived on the banks of the Cerritambo,
we simply collapsed in a heap. I tried to look on the problem of
keeping going as I had on rowing across the Atlantic: as long as
we kept moving forward, we would get there in the end.

Five minutes soon passed. The small, clean pebbles of the bank
moulded easily to the shape of our backsides as we leaned back

on our rucksacks. Warm sun shone from a clear blue sky: we were at liberty to go when and where we pleased, to stop whenever we liked. There was a lot to be said for being a free agent, I decided: guides and horses were really a frightful tie.

Even though we comforted ourselves with this philosophy, there was no rush to pick up the rucksacks. Eventually we had to move. The boys heaved the Three Rs to their feet.

Crossing a shallow ford without getting our feet wet, we began a long climb up the far side of the valley. There was a good path now, running north-west, parallel to the Cerritambo, which joined the Apurimac some ten miles further on. My legs settled down to take the extra weight fitting snugly against my back and hips. As well as the four pouches on my belt, I had a water bottle in a carrier, slung at the middle of my back, but it was no inconvenience.

For Marie Christine and Bec, things were not so good. Not only was their power-to-weight ratio much worse than mine; their waists were too small and backs too short to accommodate both belt-order and pack. We spent several of our five-minute breaks adjusting their belt-order, and they ended with two pouches each, both well forward of the rucksack and its straps.

The sun grew hotter, but we kept at it, rather pleased to look back and see the hated Munja dwindling into the distance.

'We can do it,' gasped Ed. 'In a few days we'll be able to walk for longer than fifteen minutes at a stretch.' He was still unwell, but I wasn't really worried about him, or about Justin for that matter. I knew they would settle down and carry on without difficulty as long as they weren't injured.

Marie Christine would probably cope, but Rebecca might be a problem. She was bearing up very well for an eighteen-year-old girl just out of school, but there was no taking away the burden of being the youngest and the least experienced. She had to carry a heavy load now, and she seemed always to have a cold. Both she and her mother found it difficult to keep organised: their buttons and pouches were more often than not undone. They wore no belts for their trousers, nor puttees to keep the dust out of their socks. It is little things like these which bring you down over the long haul. I hoped that every day would bring further improvements in self-reliance, but it was going to be a long trip for Rebecca.

With the extra weight to carry, we were all starving by lunch-time. The return of appetite was a good sign that we were acclimatising to the altitude. It was much more fun on our own. We sat under an overhanging rock, eating one of Pedro's fine cheeses with the few remaining stale bread rolls.

By two o'clock we had covered no more than five miles from Munja, most of it uphill, and we were having to point out the place for each break, in order to get us there. Our next halt was to be at a point where a stream crossed the path: we were sweating and drinking a lot of water now, so we topped up the bottles at every opportunity. But the sun had gone and snow was threatening.

'We've done well,' I announced. 'Let's stop for the night. I can't say where the next village will be. It's on the next map, and I think you've got it in your pack, Ed?' I hoped everyone would agree to stop.

'Let's have a drink of water before we do anything else,' said Marie Christine, flopping down beside the tiny stream, and we all followed suit.

We spent rather a long time by the water, but the cold drove us on in the end. M.C., Becca and I left our kit with the boys and walked back towards a village we had seen a few hundred yards below the path. With the first snowflakes falling, we didn't fancy the idea of a night under a rock, or of sheltering in a partly-built hut which lacked not only doors and windows, but also a roof.

A couple of hundred yards down a rough pasture we came to a small mud hut with a wooden cross set at an angle on its thatched roof. A neat row of battered little felt hats set on the bench outside its low door reinforced the squeals of laughter coming from inside to confirm that it was the village school. The *Maestra* soon came out and gave us a warm welcome to Carpinto.

Claudia, a young teacher from Cuzco, wearing a light anorak over a beige polo neck jumper and trousers, looked oddly sophisticated among her primary students. They filed shyly out of the oversized doll's house which served as their classroom, with their wind-cracked little faces and raggedy clothes. We shook hands with all nineteen of them. They had names like Hilda, Pablo, Margarita and Ignacio, and I noticed they were mostly barefoot, though some did have motor-tyre sandals, and there was a particularly lively little fellow with only one shoe.

When I told Claudia our story, she suggested we stay in the tiny other half of the school. I squeezed in through the miniature doorway. It was dark inside, the window having been bricked up. The room was very dusty, and half the space was taken up by animal-dung fuel for the mud oven in a corner. In another corner a raised platform would accommodate the Three Rs, if none of us moved. The two boys would just about fit in the remaining floor space.

A hail squall hit us as we made our way back up the hill to collect Justin and Ed, making our new residence seem particularly desirable. It was tuna and rice for supper again, but Claudia brought along five welcome hard-boiled eggs. When M.C. and Bec went down to the stream to wash the mess tins, they were surprised by a man creeping up on them in the dark.

'We're only washing up!' M.C. cried out in English. The poor man ran off in fright, and in the hut we heard nothing.

Claudia told us she was on a three-year tour of duty in the village, and the nearest teacher was a further two hours' walk down the valley. One of a family of twelve, she found her solitary existence in Carpinto a lonely contrast with the cosmopolitan life of Cuzco. We were very tired, but poor Claudia was desperate to talk to people from the outside world, even if we could only just keep our eyes open. One by one we crept into our sleeping-bags, and it was still only eight o'clock when she blew out the candle and left.

I heard a scratching sound and thought it was Ed trying to find some pills for his cold; but slowly it dawned on me that there was an animal of some sort in the hut with us. I took a firm hold on the hand-powered torch which I always kept with the sheath knife by my head. With a rapid pumping action of my right hand I sent the dynamo whining into life, and a beam of light illuminated a large dog chewing away at the last of the cheeses Pedro had given us in Tarucamarca. It bolted through the half-open door and into the night. I looked out at the starlit sky; there was a dusting of snow on the ground, but it was too dark to see the dog's footprints, and too cold to look for long. So I put two rucksacks against the door and examined the remains of the cheese by torchlight: it was badly mauled, useless for us. I crawled back into my sleeping-bag with a groan. In spite of all the noise, no one else had moved a muscle.

I knew that the dust and darkness would be Marie Christine's idea of a nightmare: when we woke up next morning she felt awful, and her nose began to bleed. Dust from the dung covered everything. Five nights had passed since we had left the comparative luxury of the El Tigre hostel in Yauri, but we were all adapting to our new way of life. Rather surprisingly, we still suffered altitude headaches if we made sudden, violent physical effort.

By 8am we were waving goodbye to Claudia, who was almost in tears. The alpacas and llamas were well up the mountainside, and all nineteen children had arrived for school, anxious not to miss the strange *gringos*. As we slowly picked our way through the meadow towards the path, they chanted their school song.

The sun was shining, as it always seemed to do in the mornings, and swallows swooped cheerfully round the sandstone crags. We knew that the path would run downhill for most of the day, and this decided our new schedule of half-hour walking with five minute breaks. Our ability to cope with this cheered us considerably.

A huge vista stretched far away to snow-covered peaks beyond a great plain, and with my Zeiss monocular I could just make out the church tower on the mound of Yauri. As we descended through weirdly-eroded outcrops of rock, the most remarkable feature was the desert-like appearance of the country ahead of us. It looked as if no rain ever fell. Still, we saw our first tree since leaving Sicuani, and there were several groups of domestic animals, though they did look pretty scrawny. We also saw a great flock of small finches twittering about in a field, and eagles soared high in the sky. Once or twice we passed men pushing bicycles uphill; perhaps they had ridden over the plain from Yauri. We always greeted them with a cheerful 'Buenos días', before they could start wondering about us, and I believe that the presence of M.C. and Bec was reassuring to strangers.

We found that the place-names on our map did not always match local names. We were now aiming for the school at Mamani Huayta, as the teachers there were good friends of Claudia, but we made such good progress on our new schedule that we kept on going. That is another way of saying we got lost. We had seen the bright blue of the school walls from a distance, but the building was some way below the path, so we walked on until we arrived at a few scattered houses at the same time as a break was due. A two-foot wide brook meandered across the path where we sat on our rucksacks, its banks bordered with close-cropped, vivid green grass and moss. Butterflies, moths and dragonflies hovered over the tadpoles in the shallow water.

'Pass them along,' Ed called, handing out the boiled sweets, now mandatory at every break.

The settlement was an arid place, at the end of winter. Huts stood like islands besieged by a sea of wind-blown dust. M.C. and I found a frail old woman spinning alpaca wool among a collection of decrepit shacks. Shaking us warmly by the hand, she led us to where her husband and another old fellow were loading five donkeys with beautifully woven sacks of seed potatoes. They spoke only Quechuan but understood the Spanish word escuela, and told us it was 'cerquita' [close] but we knew that this did not always mean the objective was as near as we might hope. As we turned to leave, the old woman bade us wait while she scurried into the back of a low stone door and returned with a bag of potatoes as a gift. She refused all payment; wrapping them in my polar jacket, I was touched that such poor people should give us something.

The land was flat now, and the rutted track spread out ten or twenty feet on either side. Poverty was everywhere about us. Another three-quarters of an hour of sweated effort brought us to a broken-down school building, lying as if tossed haphazardly by some giant's hand well to the left of the path. We had arrived at Manturca in the lunch break: the fifty-odd children were running wild, in and outside the building, and their teacher, twenty-five-year-old Leonardo, looked like a man at a low ebb. His school had many broken window panes; the blue wash of the walls was splotched by decay, and broken desks lay higgledy-piggledy among drifts of waste paper. His living quarters—a shed-like room on the left hand side of the building— looked more like a garage than a home: cycle parts scattered at random across the floor gave the impression of a desperate man's failed last attempt to escape.

'It hasn't rained here for two years now,' said Leonardo mournfully. 'The children are so undernourished that they can't concentrate in class. They have no future.' In spite of his gloom, he said we could sleep the night on the classroom floor, and we asked him to join us for supper.

We decided to leave the school until classes had ended at 3.30. Leonardo insisted that he lock our gear away in his room to prevent the children from stealing, and we set off to look for the local store. There was no village as such, just isolated huts scattered about the plain on either side of the broad, straight path.

'That might be it.' Becca pointed eagerly at a tall hut with an official-looking tin roof, standing by itself beside the track.

As we made our way wearily up through clumps of dried yellow-green itchu grass, a bitter wind was blowing, though there was still heat in the tropical sun. When we arrived at the hut and found it locked, we lay down in the dust at the sheltered end and fell asleep. By three o'clock there was still no sign of a shopkeeper returning from lunch, so with all the misery of people who have just woken we hauled our stiffened limbs off the dirt and hobbled the hundred yards or so to the nearest building. I felt in danger of an attack of one of the outbursts of temper which occur 'most frequently at altitude', so I was careful to say nothing to anyone.

Arriving at a thatched hovel, we found ourselves in the local shop. The Indian told us we had been lying in front of the district court-cum-church, which was seldom open. He hadn't much of a stock on his gloomy shelves, and most of the floor space was taken up by his bed and living area. Some green oranges lay shrivelled on a dirty table, and the dozen or so bread rolls were stale and hard, but we bought them all the same, chewing into them there and then. The black earth floor was studded with Cola bottle tops, trodden in over the years.

It was not much past three, but already the heat was going from the sun. We bought dusty bottles of Cola to soften the stale rolls and give us a reason for lingering in the store, out of the increasingly chill wind. Our main concern was the lack of canned goods: there was none of the tuna or evaporated milk which had become the mainstay of our diet. Our stocks of rice, sugar and tea were running low, too; but the shopkeeper told us we would get all we needed next day, when we had walked the eight miles down to Puente Central on the Apurimac.

The school was cold and empty when we returned. While the boys set off to look for water, we three tried to stop the wind from howling through the broken window panes, using sides torn from cardboard boxes. We cleared the desks to one end of the room and swept the floor with hand brushes made of itchu grass. Marie Christine and Becca set off on a round of the two or three homes nearby in search of eggs, but there were none for sale.

Leonardo was not an entertaining dinner guest. He had a way of turning every topic to money: his lack of it, and the surplus in the imperialist countries of the West. But at least he showed no envy of the pasta shell and tuna dish we had that evening: his was the only tin not shoved forward for seconds.

We barricaded the door with chairs, and balanced mess tins to raise the alarm if an intruder should try to get in. The school floor was our most luxurious lodging since arriving in Manturca, and we all slept soundly, pleased with our visible progress across the map.

Next morning the sun shone brightly through the windows, and the air outside was perfectly still. For the first time we all felt keen to get on with the walking. After breakfast I went round the back of the building to a patch of waste ground used as a lavatory. As I stood up to fasten my trousers, a skinny dog ran out from behind a wall and ate what I had deposited. This single action gave me an idea what grinding poverty must be like.

Our walk down the dusty trail to Puente Central was most enjoyable. We joined a herdsman taking alpacas to market in Yauri; this was the first occasion on which we had been with the haughty creatures for any length of time, and I found them more easily identifiable as individuals than the Cheviot sheep on our croft at home in Scotland.

Puente Central is a village built around a fine old Spanish stone bridge across the Apurimac. The river at this point is still grey with silt from the Huayllacho mine sixty miles upstream, surprisingly canal-like, it runs quite slowly across that part of the plain in a straight line, and it looks almost artificially confined between vertical cliffs some fifty feet high and sixty feet apart.

The east bank is fronted by a jumbled terrace of a building, partly thatched and partly tiled with terracotta half pipes. This is the main house of the old hacienda, the lands of which had been broken up by the Reforma Agraria only a dozen years before. On the west side of the bridge lies a small square with four shops, each selling exactly the same goods: Camay soap, Gloria milk, Clinic shampoo, Bimbo fizzy drink and delicious crumbly Chomp biscuits.

The hacienda is most decidedly not what it must have been in its heyday. Meeting an old man who looked like a faithful retainer near the black wooden double front doors, I asked what the chances were of trucks passing through on their way to Yauri. With a conspiratorial smile, he signalled for me to follow him, holding his finger to his lips. Inside, I found myself standing in a fine old pebbled courtyard, with a multitude of dead animals hanging in the rafters to dry.

'Mammy! Mammy!' the narrow-faced old man called several times in a stage whisper. Nothing happened for a while; then I could just make out a woman's low voice, asking why she was being disturbed at eleven o'clock in the morning. The retainer replied that *gringos* had come to call, and after a further exchange the door opened. Out swept a woman in her late thirties, dressed in a long, heavy tweed skirt and leather boots, with a grey cable jumper and a jaunty felt hat. She hadn't forgotten her gold and pearl earrings, and her nail varnish looked good as new, after what must have been a monumental party on the previous night. She introduced herself as Dorina.

'Could you possibly come back in half an hour? Pancho will see you then.'

Marie Christine could not resist the opportunity of discovering what Pancho would be like. By the time of our second visit, tables were already being laid between the elegant columns of the courtyard for another party in the afternoon.

'I am a river fanatic,' cried short-moustachioed Pancho, clutching his head, and not realising we hadn't come by boat. 'Come any day but today. This is my birthday!' With that he withdrew, to collapse on an unmade bed. The retainer sadly ushered us out into the midday sun.

We spent a pleasant couple of hours by the river before returning to the square in front of the shops. The timeless sun burned down on a scene which cannot have altered much over the centuries. Little whirlwinds of dust swirled about a few half-built mud houses; the tempo was slow, slow, stop.

Sitting on the edge of the square, I felt good. In spite of a strained left calf, sciatica, cracked lips and sunburned wrists— the sleeves of my shirt were too short—I enjoyed the feeling of moving about again.

I would need to be fit by the time we got to Osambre—if I was to keep up with Elvin. With a smile I remembered the huge, home-made dumb-bells cut from sections of tree trunk that we had found in the Bergs' yard. We could hardly move them, but Abel told us proudly that all his four boys could handle them with ease: he had been training them for years.

Ed won a close-fought catapult competition with the locals, knocking a pile of little stones off a wall. Then a yellow Dodge Ram pick-up roared into the square, and we got a lift right to the door of the El Tigre hostel in Yauri.

Chapter Nine

In the noisy Kana cafe, we took our usual table, the one against the end wall, furthest from the counter. From there I could watch everything in the smoke-filled room without moving my head; and if necessary we could slip through the back door and into the yard. It was another big night in the Kana; four of the half dozen tables were taken by parties of mineworkers from Tintaya, and ranks of brown beer bottles covered their tables like soldiers in a beach landing.

Eight long days of Phase One had passed since we last had supper here. The place seemed metropolitan now. We had each strengthened and acclimatised, and as a team we were coming together well. Over our plates of steak and chips I decided that Rebecca was gaining something from this tough finishing school, even if she was struggling to finish her beer.

As far as Señor Emilio and his wife were concerned, we had been away only a few days, and they were delighted to see us again so soon, making a great fuss over Marie Christine and Rebecca. For us, a five-bedded room with real sheets was luxury indeed, and we slept wonderfully.

Yauri now seemed a fabled city to us, its huge, ancient Spanish church on a mound dominating the whole dry plain, as well as the low mud buildings of the town clustered at its feet.

Next morning, after breakfast at the Kana, we bought some stores and tried to arrange transport to Santa Lucia de Pichigua, which lies on the edge of the plain ten miles to the north. The sun was hot on the main street and the town full of bustle, its silver tin roofs reflecting the importance of its commerce. We saw a black pig bundled from a bicycle into a cafe; there was much screaming, then silence. To celebrate life, we bought fancy second-hand felt sombreros for Marie Christine and Becca at a poky little hat shop down the street. They looked so stylish, and the sunburn had been so fierce, that Justin and I bought one each as well, but Ed decided to stick with his trusty jungle hat.

'*Ignominia! Deshonor!*' Where had I heard these words before? Ed was having a shouting match in the middle of the main street, and quite a crowd of Indians was gathering to watch.

'Outbursts of temper occur more frequently at high altitude,' I murmured, coming up behind him.

'Ten minutes ago, this bleeder was definitely going to take us to Pichigua. Now he says he's changed his mind. What can you do?'

I noticed Ed's right eyelid twitching, a sure sign he was getting hot under the collar.

'This is South America, not Surrey, old top. Just cut your losses and find someone else.'

'Well, there's a fellow with a white Ford minibus somewhere about. Says he's going to Arequipa, but would take us to Pichigua first—for 100,000 soles. I thought it was too much.'

'It'll cost us more to stay in El Tigre for another night and eat in the Kana,' I replied swiftly. 'See if you can find him. We could go in half an hour.'

It was typical of Ed that he managed to find transport to a place that nobody but us wanted to visit. Within half an hour we were on our way. The driver was a cheerful fellow with a pretty wife and a baby to keep him company. We drove north along a bumpy track, across an arid plain to the foothills, crossing stream beds, dry and wet, and passing large flocks of livestock. The trip in the Ford saved us some twenty miles of monotonous flat walking.

Pichigua is a dying town, hardly more than a small village now. Geographically important in the days of the Conquistadores, it has been left behind by the motor age. Its old church is locked up and disused, but we found someone to let us through the vast studded door and into the tall, gloomy building. We stepped into the past. The place was deserted and redundant, neither a shrine nor a museum. Dusty, glass-fronted cupboards held life-sized plaster figures of the agonised holy family, staring across the empty aisle. Still more poignant was the small statue of a Conquistador on horseback trampling on *campesinos* in the fields; I would have liked to find out the date when that was introduced to the church. Just inside the front doors two huge bronze bells lay on the flagstones, with '1700 AD' stamped on them. The towers were too weak to support them any more.

Outside in the sun we sat reflectively on the edge of the empty square and ate mangoes for lunch. Along came a fine-featured old lady in black, who gave us a cautious handshake and spoke briefly in pure Castilian before disappearing down a side lane. I thought she would have fitted perfectly into one of the glass cupboards in the church.

We felt the benefit of our short break in Yauri, and it was just as well, for we were faced with our stiffest test yet: a climb with all our kit and maximum stores up on to a plateau at 13,000 feet. I led the way at a slow, even pace. We sucked boiled sweets constantly to ease the dryness in our throats from breathing heavily in thin, dry air. We were all delighted at the way we soared up, and once on the plateau we found a path on the right compass heading and kept moving easily forward, without seeing a soul.

I found it most satisfying to arrive in the late afternoon without a guide, at the northern edge of the plateau, precisely above the junction of the Rio Collpamayo and the Rio Juyurmiri. Below us lay a delightfully sheltered spot with green, grassy banks clipped short by grazing llamas, where the two shallow streams met at the bottom of a deep valley. It was the sort of place which is always in the mind's eye but seldom found. A little Indian settlement of half a dozen tightly grouped huts, surrounded by blackened llama fields, lay high up on the further side of the valley. I could make out bent figures breaking the ground for spring potato planting.

Arriving at an ideal camp site, we had a quick cup of tea. It was the boys' turn to make the supper, and while they prepared the inevitable tuna and rice, M.C., Bec and I set off uphill on a foray to buy food. We were following a small girl who had come down to the valley floor to herd the animals up to the settlement for the night.

Without our packs, we found the steep climb through tussocky grass surprisingly easy. The hillside was unusual for the three artificial ponds which the Indians had built below natural springs. Humans, animals, agriculture—everything depended on this supply of water.

It was growing dark as we clambered up the last short bank into the settlement. Stone walls and the proximity of some huts gave the romantic impression of a self-sufficient, primitive fortress. Smoke filtered up through thatched roofs, and the few women about were suspicious, denying they had any food for sale. Peering into the huts, we could see grimy babies at their mothers' breasts, and small children with runny noses and dirty faces peeling the skin from boiled potatoes. Chickens also were getting ready for the night, flapping up into special mud oven houses stuck three feet above the ground on the end of the human dwellings.

We were about to leave empty-handed when a team of a dozen men and women, all clad in rough brown and oatmeal clothing made from the wool of their own llamas, returned from the fields. They carried mattocks for breaking the ground, each made of a stone head fastened by rawhide to a wooden handle. Physically tired and relaxed, they greeted us with great warmth. Now it was all smiles and laughter: they wanted us to stay, offered us food, and when we suggested we buy potatoes, they pressed them on us as a gift. We insisted on paying, whereupon they produced five eggs and a dozen freshly-baked bread rolls.

Perhaps it was a trick of the evening light, but as we gazed across the great bleak landscape from the rampart-like walls of the settlement, it was hard to imagine any more cheerful group of families. Walking downhill with our load of stores, all three of us spoke of how happy they seemed, far from the knotted life of Europe.

I recalled old Abel Berg and his theory of 'tranquil' Campa Indians in the deepest jungle, and we agreed that perhaps the basic requirement of life was simplicity, an ability to cope with the grinding monotony of existence and to find a pleasure in simple, everyday things. Education, though essential for development, could only destroy a settlement like the one we had just left. Knowledge of an outside world, where an alternative to hard physical labour exists, must lead at least some of the people away from the land. A system based on the active participation of all the hands in the community must be put at risk when some of those hands are removed.

Perhaps one reason for my being so impressed with the settlement and its inhabitants was my own peace of mind: I felt relaxed, and at one with our own simple life. By the time we approached our camp at the stream, it was really dark. At Becca's instigation we told the boys we had been unable to buy any food at all.

'Never mind,' smiled Justin. 'The tuna and rice are excellent. I've put in some onion as well.' Nevertheless, they were thrilled when we showed them the five eggs and the bread; and they were pleased with all the potatoes, though by now we had eaten a great many.

Safely in our sleeping-bags, inside the bivvy bags with stones and knife at the head of each bed space, we listened with some apprehension to a rumble of approaching thunder. It takes only a couple of minutes at most to settle down for the night. The question always remains, 'What else is there to do?' And when the answer is 'Nothing', I find myself looking at the sky, and wondering, 'What will happen if it comes on to rain or snow?'

Lightning flickered blue-white light into the valley, but never a drop of rain fell on us. Indeed, as the storm faded and died, I realised I was no longer as anxious about terrorists or bandits as I had been. Things appeared much more settled on this northern side of the high plain; we really were going to enjoy ourselves after all.

I awoke at 4.30am and called to Justin to light the stove. But one thing led to another, and we didn't get up for a long time. Justin and Ed gave us a royal breakfast of hot potatoes and hard-boiled eggs in bed, followed by the usual sweet rice pudding. But the tea tasted foul, as it had the previous evening; we could only think it must have been something in the stream water.

We set off up the side of the valley at 7.45, walking parallel with the Apurimac, which was running northwards about a mile and a half on our left. We found the climb much harder, and Marie Christine was soon in trouble. At Ed's suggestion we decided she and Justin should swap rucksacks. Justin's was comparatively small; Marie Christine, on the other hand, at 5'2" and 8½ stone, was carrying the biggest possible pack. She had never fitted it for its size—it was simply one from our Adventure School shop at home, and the mice had eaten a small hole in it while it lay in the mailbox up on the main road.

Already the sun burned hot. The changeover involved emptying and repacking the entire contents of both packs, a tiresome business conducted under the eagle eye of a cruel-looking old woman in charge of a herd of llamas on the hillside close by. To make matters worse, we had difficulty drawing water for our bottles from a slimy seepage in a dried-up stream bed. Then, desperate with thirst, we had to wait a further ten minutes for the sterilising tablets to take effect. I suppose I was rather impatient, and tears followed. Rebecca sided with her mother, but the boys stuck to their dictum: 'Never get involved in family arguments.'

At last we got going again. Good humour returned with the sight of three brightly-clad young Indians swinging down the hill on their way to Pichigua. They were playing a little banjo and singing, and we realised it was a bright, sunny Saturday morning. At home the October weather would probably be dreadful.

Once we gained the plateau, our route took us in a curve, following the course of the Rio Juyurmiri, an almost empty stream now 750 feet below us. Peru is notorious for its devastating earthquakes—we had arrived in Lima only four days after a minor tremor—and now we saw astonishing evidence of their power. The ends of two massive spurs jutting out from the other side of the valley had been split vertically and were leaning drunkenly forward; at their feet lay great black chunks of raw mountainside. The scale of the movement was hard to grasp, but the break was so positioned on our route that for an hour or more we found our eyes continually drawn to it.

By lunch we were exhausted, flopping down in the dry, heathery brush beside the path. Far away on the horizon beyond the valley rose a range of sharp, snow-capped mountains. There was no chance of shade, and the sun and wind burns were a continuous discomfort. I was particularly troubled by sunburned wrists and I had much difficulty keeping them covered. M.C. made sardine rolls for us and the warm water from the bottles tasted strongly of sterilising tablets. I fell asleep while the others chattered on, their voices dimly intruding on my slumber.

I awoke like a bear with a sore head and was unnecessarily sharp with Justin. This altercation rather coloured the next section of the walk, and it was not until we met a young *notario* that the air finally cleared. This fellow was barefoot, but he wore a smart blue beret and carried a satchel on his back. He was moving fast, heading for Pichigua, but he took the time to point out Hacienda Japotira, the place where we planned to stay the night. It lay across a minor valley, no more than twenty minutes away.

We had all imagined another Puente Central, with its own Pancho and Dorina, only this time the occupants would surely have more time to spare. The reality was different. Hacienda Japotira was scarcely recognisable as a house: a jumble of decay frequented by snuffling pigs which had turned the ground into a morass. A fine Spanish arch, supporting a crumbling wall, gave the impression of a ruined dacha a couple of winters after the Russian Revolution, when the tide of civil war had washed over it. The sole inhabitants were a wretched-looking couple who slyly moved their only horse in case we should steal it. This was no advertisement for the agrarian reforms.

Our dreams of a comfortable night dashed, we made our way down to a stream bed, where a trickle of tadpole-infested water appeared here and there among the stones. I felt grim, with a fierce headache, and was allowed to get into my sleeping-bag straight away, with suspected sunstroke. I don't remember much of the night, except that it rained a little and then froze on the bivvy bags. In the morning, M.C. made porridge, but as usual there was not enough food for Ed's prodigious appetite. A couple of young fellows appeared from the direction of the old hacienda. Bringing us potatoes, they looked concerned, as if doubting that we could have survived the night.

By then none of us was faring too well. M.C.'s nose still bled a fair bit; Becca had developed a sore throat; Ed had burnt and swollen lips which bled every time he ate; and Justin had sore feet. I felt a lot better after twelve hours' sleep, but we nursed ourselves along, and the stops each half hour stretched somehow to ten minutes.

Our plan was for an easy day; along the plateau for a bit, and then gently down to the village of Santa Cruz, lying in the valley of another tributary of the Apurimac, the name of which was too difficult to decipher on the photocopy map we had with us. Here we hoped to find a shop and stay the night.

With no identifiable path to follow, we strayed a little to the east of the best way down into the valley, but a group of potato-planters soon put us on the right route. Santa Cruz looked to be no more than a few *campesino* huts, so we stopped a couple of brothers who were herding alpacas towards the Apurimac, and asked if there was a shop there.

'*No hay tienda!*' The negative reply came through lips green with coca. He told us of another village, *cerquita*.

We followed another young fellow who said he would show us the way, but even though he was playing a mandolin as he walked, we couldn't keep up with him. So we gave up and

Dancing with the school at Tucsa

Market-day at Humpatura

Above:
Walking high

Left: Marie
Christine,
Becca, John
and Ed:
keeping a
look-out

John and
friends in
Cachcane

decided to go down to the river for an early lunch. If we felt keen later, when the sun had lost a bit of heat, well, we'd think about going on.

The river was wonderful, meandering along the valley floor; broad and shallow, cold but not too deep, with rounded pebbles and no mud. Ducks, herons, black-headed gulls and eagles patrolled the waters. We sat on the banks watching llamas, alpacas, cows and sheep grazing peacefully under a cloudless sky. Our food was running low—we had little left but potatoes. We ate a tin of sardines, spread on half a roll each. Ed was ravenous, so we went on to eat the remaining dry oats with sugar. We would have to find another shop, so we must press on to the next village. Unfortunately we had been unable to get a map for the next few days of the route, so we had no idea where, if anywhere, we might buy food.

But first we could swim. The boys went upstream to a pool on a bend. M.C., Bec and I bathed in the shallows. We washed all our clothes and laid them out on the bank to dry, then dozed in the sun for an hour. All the while we were watched by a young shepherdess with only one shoe, dressed in rags and wearing a black hat; as is the custom, whether walking or sitting, she was always spinning wool.

Becca wrote in her diary that I said this was the best part of the trip so far. Perhaps it was—but our euphoria evaporated abruptly when we began to climb up the cliff on the further side of the valley. We did very well to reach the plateau in one fierce effort, but once there, without a map, we were confused. We could see a long way; there were many houses, many paths and many patchwork fields, but no blue-walled school. After a discussion we turned left on the path, though at least one of us wanted to turn right.

The walk turned into something of an epic. Ed found a piece of what looked like cornelian, the barley-sugar stone, to add to the collection he was taking home to his girlfriend. We met a tiny old man in a homespun, oatmeal-coloured garment, who directed us on to another path, assuring us that the school was in Asuncion. '*Cerquita! Cerquita!*' he grinned. I wondered how much *chicha* [maize beer] he'd had to drink.

As we set off again, Becca and I began to chant a poem which she had learnt as the only pupil at Ada Bell's primary school at home at Ardmore:

"'Twas a misty, moisty morning, and cloudy was the
    weather.
I met a little old man, clothed all in leather.
He began to compliment, and I began to grin,
With a "How do you do?" and a "How do you do?" and a
    "How do you do?" agin.'

We kept on across the plain, and at 4.30 began a long descent to the village. The blue walls of the school made a grand sight, deep in the valley, close to the banks of the Apurimac itself.

Halfway down the mountainside, we met a man who introduced himself as Benito Roca, outside his thatched home, and he accompanied us down to the school, where his brother Saturnino let us into the building and made us welcome. Both brothers were charming, gentle fellows; they told us that for the 150 children there were four *profesores*, all away on this Sunday evening. The school was less welcoming: wobbly floor-planks covered with litter, broken window panes blocked by tables, the green wash on the inside walls all chipped, ceiling sagging badly. 'The upsetting thing is not the state of the building,' I wrote in my diary, 'but the mental attitude of those responsible for allowing their one symbol of hope to decay. The community quite clearly is not interested in maintaining its school. It speaks volumes for the future of Peru.' Such were my thoughts—maybe rather harsh—at the end of a long, hard day.

Becca and I went up with Saturnino to his home on the hillside. He had a number of little outhouses for livestock, and we were astonished to see him fiddle for a different key to unlock a padlock on every one of them, even the most trivial. He reached into all sorts of inaccessible places, behind doors and up in roofs, and in the end he had ten eggs, as well as a great pile of potatoes, to sell us. When a woman nearby sold us a piece of mutton, we went on our way rejoicing.

We had just got back to the school when a giant thunderstorm rolled down the Apurimac valley. Lightning bathed the bust of the revolutionary hero Tupac Amaru out in the school yard, and we felt very grateful to be in a building for the night. Marie Christine made a fine stew of mutton, rice, onions, potatoes and red peppers. Even Ed had had enough to eat. Then the door burst open and in swaggered Florenzio Bonito Condore, apparently the *Presidente* of the community. He had a cruel Red Indian sort of face and he was wearing a brilliant red and green poncho and two dramatic hats: a bright woollen head-warmer with ear flaps, and on top a sort of Paddington Bear sombrero.

Florenzio cut quite a dash, and he was a bully. He told us he had no difficulty in getting elected every two years. We gave him some of our stew and he barked out questions for an hour or so. We humoured him—after all, it was his village, and I think he was suspicious we were military or miners. There was an old gold mine near the village which had been closed some years before. Florenzio was expecting a Swiss engineer by helicopter the following morning and he hoped to start negotiations for the re-opening of the mine. He couldn't get out of his head the idea that we might be going to interfere with his plans.

We were clearly exhausted, so Florenzio boasted he slept only between twelve and three each night: he said we were sheep. Ed and Justin were beginning to look cross. Then he wanted our primus stoves and our walking boots but of course we refused. Finally he said we couldn't go to sleep until we'd sung him a song!

Short of starting a fight, in which Florenzio might well produce a knife or a pistol, there was little for us to do but sing. We gave him 'ZippedeeDooda', 'Good King Wenceslas', 'God Save the Queen', 'Rule Britannia' . . . and he was gone!

Still we felt nervous. Florenzio might well return with a lynching party. We stacked all the chairs against the door, with the mess tins arranged so that the slightest move would waken us. Then we drifted off to sleep.

El Presidente did not return until 7.30 next morning, by which time we were all packed and ready to go after Ed's fine breakfast of hard-boiled eggs and hot potatoes. In the daylight Florenzio was more like a joke Mussolini, strutting about blowing his bugle, apparently to call the children to school. But he was still as offensive as ever, and when we pulled out of Asuncion we felt we were leaving behind a little dictatorship.

Chapter Ten

We were getting fitter, and a lot thinner. Knowing Florenzio was watching our progress, we set out to climb the cliff out of Asuncion in one straight pull, with no break. The path zig-zagged up the crumbling sandstone face, but after half an hour we crawled out of a gully and on to the plateau. Poor Becca's cold was now so bad she nearly burst into tears. At least we were on our own again.

Without a map, we had only the compass to give us rough direction. As a check, we asked everyone we met if we were on the right route for Quehue, a large village which Saturnino had told us was within a day's walk to the north.

The first people we questioned were a whole family of *campesinos*, breaking up new ground with their mattocks and planting seed potatoes as fast as they could go. They were so full of smiles and laughs that we dished out sweets for everyone. We were very relieved to find we were indeed on the right path, and to celebrate this minor triumph we moved a hundred yards from the potato planters and sat down on our packs for a rest. A wrinkled old Quechuan woman came across and from her poncho produced a pile of tiny hot potatoes, half of which were purple. She was cackling with pleasure as she handed them over, and we thanked her profusely. As we got out some salt, she showed us how to remove the skin with finger and thumb of one hand; then she gathered her things and hobbled back to watch the planting.

It is generally believed that potatoes originated in the Peruvian Andes, and that the purple variety is close to the original, which was being grown here 1,800 years ago. The Spaniards brought them to Europe in the latter half of the sixteenth century, and by the end of the seventeenth the Irish economy was dependent on them. In living mainly on potatoes, we were on a fat-free diet. We were eating much less than we were used to at home, while burning many more calories in physical effort; the result was a considerable loss of weight for each of us, and—apart from the discomforts of altitude and sun—a much greater feeling of well-being. Without the fear of attack by terrorists or *bandidos*, life would have been nearly perfect.

We walked on all morning, enjoying the magnificent scenery all the more because we had no map to pore over. We were heading a little to the east of north by the compass; rolling plainlands lay ahead, and the straw-coloured stubble of winter made us feel that we were plodding across the steppes of Russia. One little place of no more than half a dozen houses had a walled field for a cemetery; there were few graves, and they looked forlorn in that great, arid, windswept place. Although we were sweating under the sun, it seemed the sort of place in which everything is naturally stone cold.

As usual, we were done in by midday. Lunch-time found us at the bottom of a valley which had taken us an hour or more to reach from the plateau above, the path angling down the valley side as we dropped towards the stream. It was very hot now, so that the impending climb back on to the plateau was not a pleasant prospect. We shared our few remaining potatoes with a Quechuan horseman who was going in the opposite direction; he had a horse and not much else, but he produced a hard, white cheese from a grubby cloth, pared away the rind and gave us each a piece. Again we found that someone with the least to give was the most generous with what little he had.

The lunch hour stretched on, long after the horseman had led his mount over the hill we had come down. We fell asleep in the sun, and only raindrops from a purpling sky got us on the move again. At least the shower cooled the air, and we went well up the hill. Thunder rolled down the valley early that afternoon, but luckily no heavy rain fell; if it had really begun to pour, we should have been soaked, as there was nowhere to take cover. Up ahead we could see the blue walls of a school standing all alone on the open moor, and we consoled ourselves with the thought that at least we would find temporary shelter there.

Nearing the school, we found it stood next to a large, square church with two towers. Soon some of the children ran out across the compound to see our strange procession, and they were joined by a couple of male teachers. We rested on the school wall, talking to the men and asking how far it was to Quehue. Soon all 100 children were out staring at us. A third teacher appeared, but he was unable to shake hands because his fingers were covered with butter-oil, which he had been doling out to the pupils from a big gold-coloured tin. This butter-oil, alongside milk powder, was a gift to the school children of Peru from the government of the United States of America.

We told the teachers what we were doing in Peru, and the man in charge of the butter quickly sent two of his fellow *profesores* off to fetch their guitars while he got all the children lined up. When everything was to his satisfaction, he made a short speech to us, their honoured guests, thanking us for visiting them and making this such an occasion for them. Elaborately he gave out the name and address of the school: Escuela Primaria de Menores, No. 56129 TUCSA.

We were glad of the rest. The sun had come out again, and it was burning hot once more. Soon we were all swaying to the insistent beat of Quechuan music. Watching the children sing their school songs, with the mountains stretching into the distance, I compared this welcome to Florenzio's performance of the previous night.

Everything was going swimmingly, but after a rest I thought we should push on to reach Quehue before dark.

'Now we would be honoured if you would dance,' said the teacher. I looked at him in stunned silence, hoping that perhaps my Spanish had let me down again. But then I saw one of the girls coming out of the crowd towards me, and I got to my feet with a forced grin. Thank God, it wasn't only me—M.C. and Bec were already twirling their walking boots around the bare feet of their partners, while Ed and Justin looked a little too adept for my liking. Unluckily my partner was extremely reluctant and shy, and this did nothing for my own lumbering performance. But there was worse to come: by the time we were allowed to rest, it seemed I had danced with every girl over the age of six.

'Would you please take a photograph of whole school, and send us a copy from *Escocia*?' asked the butter-handler. We nominated Justin as best cameraman and all got to our feet again, crossed the yard and arranged the children in front of the school bust of Tupac Amaru, a national hero famous for his martyrdom in driving the Spaniards from Peru. Singing broke out again, and the butter-teacher explained that while *Gran Bretaña* and Margaret Thatcher are well known in his country, *Escocia* is also remembered—for a scoreline in the 1978 Argentina World Cup. '*Escocia*–1, *Peru*–3!' he chanted, with a roar of laughter.

Again we had to dance and sing our medley of songs. The children looked on astonished. Then they brought us hot potatoes in a large enamel bowl, and a thick, malted drink like sago pudding which I suspected also might have come from Uncle Sam.

Rain was again threatening, and it wouldn't have taken much to persuade me to stay at the school for the night, but the others were for pushing on, in spite of the excellent chance of a drenching. So off we went, with many expressions of mutual esteem.

The walk took us three hours. Becca was happy to take the lead, and I found I had to ask her to slow down for me. I was worried about her sore throat and never-ending colds, but she went well enough that evening. The country was a little greener now, and there were even a few trees. We crossed two deep gorges, referred to by the locals as '*torrentinas*', which in the rainy season would no doubt be an awesome sight. The gaily-dressed people we met along the way were all a little more prosperous, and without exception friendly and eager to help us.

Quehue is a small town, founded only in 1917. We came winding down a newly-built road which now connects it with the outside world. Like Pichigua, it is not much more than a village, centred round a Plaza de Armas town square. The long, low school building flanks the upper side of this square, and a massively built church with two square towers dominates an adjacent side. A third side is mostly small village shops, while along the bottom of the square lies the Guarda Civil post.

Ed and Justin made a dash for the only shop still open and began to gorge on paper bags full of animal-shaped biscuits. I gathered the passports and went to see the Guarda Civil.

The walking-holiday atmosphere was dispelled immediately I entered the austere police station. The policemen were of a different breed from the local Indians—young, slim, smart and weapon-carrying. With the town generator out of action, the only illumination for the examination of our passports came from a single candle held in a human skull on the officer's desk. I soon learnt these men had served in Ayacucho, the centre of terrorist operations. They carried themselves with that careful directness which comes from recent acquaintance with violence. Dynamite attacks on isolated police posts are the terrorists' main means of getting weapons; the Prime Minister claimed that 341 posts were attacked by *Sendero Luminoso* between 1980 and March, 1985.

Formalities complete, a well turned out young policeman showed us to a small, windowless room next to the church. In daytime this overflow schoolroom was illuminated only by the open doorway, which gave directly on to the square. We stacked the desks against the back wall, swept the floor, and soon had our stoves roaring under the supper pots. Justin brought in sardines, bread and tea from the shop, and the thunderstorm which had threatened all afternoon finally broke over the village. No matter the strong smell of wood preservative from the floor, or the dangerous sag of the ceiling; we were in the dry.

I had learned the importance of rest days on the 1970 expedition; and when I heard that the school was closed for the whole week, to celebrate a religious festival, I decided to spend the next day in Quehue. The police were keen to play volleyball with us in the square, and there were clothes to wash. Becca's cold was no better and, as we were still above 12,000 feet, I was concerned lest it turn to bronchitis or pneumonia. We were all suffering from swollen and cracked lips and burned noses, and this nagging discomfort was a drain on morale. Altogether, a rest day was called for.

The Plaza de Armas had a statue of Tupac Amaru in the centre, and a sullen old gardener was tending the flower beds, which were protected by barbed wire. Sheep, pigs, donkeys and at least six stray dogs snuffled around in ceaseless search for food. The surrounding buildings had shiny tin roofs, and walls liberally daubed with political slogans dating back to the April elections, 'Alan 85' being the most common.

There were ten policemen in the almost empty town, posted there to discourage the *bandidos*. They were crazy about volleyball; so were Justin, Ed and I, and we had the advantage of between six and twelve inches in extra height—invaluable at the net. 'Justin, Dad and Ed got really carried away,' Becca wrote in her diary. The same could not be said for her or her mother; but we won the five-a-side match 3/2, after two gruelling hours in the midday sun.

The game did nothing to ease our sunburn, but a great deal to ease our relations with police and villagers. Ed sketched out our route from a good map in the police station, and we were allowed to use the washing lines in the back yard.

After the match, Marie Christine felt sick, and poor Bec was feeling pretty rough as well. After a heavy lunch of tinned pilchards and bread rolls, with beer and Bimbo lemonade, Justin fell asleep in his usual lotus position, and I read a book. Ed, still full of go and quite unable to sit still, went off for a walk on his own to investigate a shrine on the summit of a small hill. M.C.

and Becca crawled happily into their sleeping-bags. It was a real holiday.

In the evening an even bigger thunderstorm rattled the building, making our candles flicker as we scoffed Marie Christine's splendid stew of mutton shoulder, potatoes, rice and onions, cooked in a big saucepan borrowed from one of the shops in the square. Soon afterwards we got back into our sleeping-bags, dozily arguing who should make the morning tea.

Next day Rebecca felt awful; her cold had gone to her chest, and her throat was still sore. All the same she had to get going. We had two policemen take us out of the village and put us on the road to Humpatura, which was well marked on Ed's sketch. Our first half hour took us well above Quehue, and during our five-minute break we looked back on what could well have been an Elizabethan village in England, except for the few tin roofs on the square.

As always, that morning was fine and sunny. We wound our way through gradually softer countryside, with different flowers and more grass, and saw our first snake—small and dead—lying on the path. By eleven o'clock we were looking for a break when we came to a group of old farm buildings beside the track. '1937' was carved in stone above a stylish portal, and as we rested in these unfamiliar surroundings an old lady wearing a felt hat in the Spanish style and spinning pink wool invited us into the courtyard to sit in the shade. Having disappeared into her house, she came back with her husband, as well as with two rugs for us to sit on. I noticed an old whisky bottle and an empty Harrison's tea caddy on the ground. For a while we sat in the cool shade and listened to the old couple talk of their beloved Quinta; impoverished but proud, they had probably lost a lot in the agrarian reforms of a dozen years before. When the time came for us to leave, the old man led us through his rocky property to ensure we took the right path for a short cut.

Humpatura is at the end of the dirt road from Yanaoca, a small town further east. The six-teacher school serves a large area, and the friendly man in charge during the holidays gave us the impression that it was organised quite separately from the village. Unfortunately, he was on the point of leaving for Yanaoca with four engineers who were putting in an irrigation scheme for the village, but before he went he showed us into one of many classrooms surrounding a small dirt square or playground. The room was distinguished by a grisly mural hanging above the blackboard, featuring Tupac Amaru: this time the gallant Quechuan was being hung, drawn and quartered by the Spaniards. The illustration did nothing to foster good relations between the Quechuan villagers and *gringo* visitors like us, and from the outset we felt their resentment.

Perhaps there had already been some trouble between the villagers and the engineers. The chief engineer came in to talk to us while his colleagues were packing their equipment—a big, overweight fellow from Cuzco, clearly proud of his Castilian background. The jarring disdain he showed the Quechuans could only foment trouble.

I felt that the villagers wished we had left with the teacher and the engineers. In fact no sooner had they gone than we received a delegation from *El Presidente* of the community. He and two friends trooped in with a sheet of paper covered with almost as many rubber stamps as written words. The missive demanded cigarettes, alcohol and money in return for the community's 'collaboration'. Justin offered them his pack of cigarettes, which they snatched from him without hesitation. We weren't in a mood to be pressurised and so I refused their other demands. Justin asked for his cigarettes back as they left, and they tossed him one from his pack as they went through the door. He looked hurt.

Heavy rain battered the school room that night, increasing the atmosphere of menace. We felt more than a little besieged, and anxious to move on. After supper Marie Christine kindly held a hair-cutting session for Justin, Ed and me, and this helped occupy the time. Then we barricaded the door once more, got into our sleeping-bags, and discussed the possibility of the troubles in Central America spreading right down the western seaboard of

South America. Civil war wasn't hard to imagine, and we agreed that it would be wise to keep clear of towns during the Tupac Amaru celebrations of the following week.

We were up early the following morning. Marie Christine and Becca found it difficult to dress under the fixed gaze of the janitor. We swept out the room and set about packing for the move, but the sun was slow to shine, and our washing was still damp from the previous afternoon. We decided to spend the morning in the weekly market which was getting under way outside the school compound: people were coming through the fields from all directions.

Soon we were glad we had stayed, for the Wednesday market evidently provides the major social event in the district. Ranks of strongly-built Quechuan women dressed in brilliant, multi-coloured clothes seat themselves on the ground with their wares: their embroidered waistcoats, contrasting full skirts and petti-coats all help set the scene. Their sharp, dark eyes, alert under chalk-white stovepipe hats, miss nothing as they bargain for every sale. Disagreement brings a fierce toss of the head and sets their waist-length black plaits flying. Babies lie tightly swaddled amid sheeps' heads and trotters. The school janitor's wife does good business, frying small trout from the river over a primus stove, and she keeps a live chicken trussed to her stool ready for a change in the menu. Wool traders stretch their goods between sticks driven into the ground. Piles of dried coca leaves are carefully weighed on crude wooden scales, eagerly watched by women with eyes bright and lips coated green from chewing the drug. Chicha beer brewed from maize gushes out of tall, grubby jugs, and the event warms to life. Parading *señoritas* and flashy *caballeros* turn the occasion into a marriage market.

When a lorry rumbles in from Yanaoca, a bartering element is introduced. At the back of the vehicle the slick driver-salesman with his pinstripe suit and fat Spanish-looking wife exchange their rice and flour for carcases of mutton, while Indians queue for the fresh bread rolls being sold over both sides.

M.C. bought eggs, a wet white cheese, onions, much bread

and some fresh oregano; and by this time all our kit was dry. We heaved on our rucksacks and picked our way through the throng. I realised I was at least a head taller than the locals.

The hubbub of the market died behind us as we left the line of horses and llamas hitched to a rail outside the school wall. We were walking north, along the eastern side of the Apurimac valley now, with the river out of sight far below us. We climbed a steep hill and on to a high plain, then deep down into a valley where we found a thatched hut among some trees beside a clear stream. We were just thinking how grand it would be to stop here for the night when a young fellow ran up to meet us and pointed out the way to Huancollyo. Of course it was up—750 feet up the far side of the valley we had just come down. At the top we found a neat blue school in a tidy little *pueblo*, but as there was no teacher, and Becca seemed to be beating her cold at last, we kept on walking.

As we entered Huancollyo we were greeted by a delicious smell of baking bread. Cheery waves from the villagers in the narrow streets made a welcome contrast with the surliness of Humpatura. Was it coincidence that hospitality seemed to increase with distance from the end of the road to the outside world? Places on the road always appeared seedy and run-down, as if the inhabitants wished themselves away in the cities.

We were ushered into the empty school by the friendly young *Presidente*, well wrapped in his poncho against the chill breeze of approaching evening. Shooing away a crowd of children, he left us to sort ourselves out. We soon made friends with the inhabitants of a small field in front of the school: a horse and foal and a donkey and foal. From the back of the school I could see over a stone wall, straight down to a footbridge crossing the Apurimac, 2,000 feet or more below, and on the far side of the valley a few scattered communities like Huancollyo. Jagged bolts of lightning slashed through black rain clouds further up the gorge, and I hurried indoors, glad to be once again under cover for the night.

The chief returned with a friend, right in the middle of the thunderstorm. He told us that pumas lived in caves on the cliffs overlooking the river, where they couldn't be reached by man. A pregnant woman had recently been caught and eaten by one while walking to the bridge. We stacked the chairs against the door before going to sleep.

Snow on the ground gave the mediaeval village a look of Christmas next morning, Friday, 1 November, and steam rising from the thatched roofs, pale grey against the deep blue of the sky, turned our thoughts to home.

We set out early for the walk to Cachcane, pausing to sing a few songs to the villagers in return for their kindness. Our path was poorly defined, and about an hour after the start we had to make a hard, nearly vertical climb to an upper path. Each of us was doing his or her best. Although we found we could walk further each day, we were certainly getting thinner. Violent exercise and poor food were exacting a toll. Ed now felt fine again, and he wanted to step up the pace a little. He asked if I would mind him going on ahead, and I half-heartedly agreed, preferring to avoid a clash. The result was a general increase in speed—the very thing we should have been avoiding at this stage. An expedition stretching into months needs delicate handling; usually at least one person is feeling under the weather, and holding back when you feel good is one of the hardest things to do. Rebecca was not feeling at all well; being the youngest and least experienced walker, she was determined not to complain, but it was significant that she ceased writing her diary on this day.

The snow soon melted but the air kept cooler than usual, and this helped us keep a faster pace, even though we had to cross three ravines. Now that the first shoots were showing, llamas and alpacas were being kept off the potato patches by alert herdswomen; and it was one of these women, dressed in red, who kept an eye on us as we ate our lunch directly above Cachcane. The bread rolls from Huancollyo were all the better for a filling of pilchards, and we enjoyed them in the knowledge that we had only to go downhill to reach our destination. But then we heard the woman shout and saw a stream of men coming up towards her from the village. When they reached her, we were alarmed to see them switch direction towards us. Though they appeared unarmed, they greatly outnumbered us, but we felt we had nothing to hide. While we sat waiting for them to reach us, I got out my dog-eared book and letters.

They had a few sticks and catapults, and they were a little cautious in their approach over the last few yards, but never aggressive. When I explained who we were and what we were hoping to do, they led us down to the village. We were dazzled by the green vegetation; thatched mud huts surrounded with eucalyptus trees and tiny fields with the first maize we had seen. Women and children peered at us through doorways and over mud walls crowned with spiky yellow flowering cactus, where Europeans might put glass. The women had big, creamy, trumpet-shaped flowers in their hats, which they gave to M.C. and Becca, while children dashed to pick roses.

A growing procession of villagers led us to the school, a beautiful place perched far above the Apurimac. Two buildings formed half a square on a ledge overlooking the river. There was the regulation green bust of Tupac Amaru but also some eucalyptus and fir trees, swaying gently in the hot breeze. The village water point was some 300 yards away across the fields. The school was as clean as any we had seen in Peru, and we were sorry the teacher was away on holiday, for he seemed an enterprising fellow: his children had the benefit of models to help with geology and biology, and there was even a stage with a Peruvian version of Punch and Judy, all set up to perform.

While Becca was making tea, four men came in with parcels of food. They were led by a sprightly ancient called Andresquispe, who at seventy-eight was clearly held in esteem as the oldest person in the village. He was the same age as my father, I realised; as I looked at him, I thought how completely different the two men's long lives had been, and yet how much they would enjoy swapping experiences—which in theory they could easily do, if one or other were to buy an air ticket between the continents. In their youth any such meeting would have been impossible; now it would be simple.

With a huge smile the old man handed us a large, cloth-covered enamel bowl containing steaming, spicy broad beans, maize and rice. His companions gave us *chuño*, a Quechuan delicacy of small potatoes which are left out in the frost overnight and then dried. Perhaps *chuño* is an acquired taste: to us, it was like a mixture of schoolboy ink and unripe walnuts.

Our walk up to Pomgona next day was made easier by cooler air resulting from the nightly thunderstorms. Sometimes our path was strewn with white, star-shaped flowers like crocuses; at others we seemed to be walking on a carpet of brown and black caterpillars. Again Ed was keen to lead, intoxicated with the beauty of the mountains and the gorge. I felt an inevitable clash approaching. The physical struggle with the mountains, the mental struggle with the monotony of our daily routine, the discomfort of sore lips and sunburn—these things chew away at the nerves.

Pomgona is at the end of the road, bleak, dusty and decayed. Raw sewage lay in the street as we walked down past ruined mud houses and broken walls that Saturday afternoon. The few people about were mostly drunk, for it was the beginning of the Tupac Amaru celebrations—in fact the great man had been born in Tunga Suca, just down the road. The school was locked and the teacher away. Through the window of a store I saw dust-covered pieces of complex commercial Singer sewing machines scattered about the floor—uncared-for gifts from the United Nations. We sat in the sun, watching a scrappy football game and keeping an eye on a funeral further up the empty valley. Several mourners threw themselves to the ground, overcome by grief or alcohol.

Hours passed and nothing much happened. Bec fell asleep in the sun, her cold worse, and the sun burned her face still more harshly. For whatever reason, the people of Pomgona were suspicious of us. We slept in two ends of a tiny mud hut, divided by a partition, which looked as if it might be for livestock. It was a miserable, lowering night for Becca, and we weren't sorry when dawn came. Pomgona could get anyone down.

Chapter Eleven

'Becca's got earache, John,' Marie Christine called up the line. I stopped and turned. The poor girl was in tears. We had come barely 400 yards from Pomgona, across a field and over the stream. Everyone was keen to push on.

'Listen! This is not Europe.' I was furious. 'If Becca develops pneumonia, there's no doctor. She might die. These things come on very fast up at this altitude. That funeral yesterday—it was probably a child, dead of a respiratory illness.'

'What are you saying?' Ed interrupted impatiently.

'What I'm saying is this: unless we're very careful, Becca may get seriously ill. And that might mean the end of the trip.'

'I'm sure it's not that bad, John.' M.C. was trying to cool things down. 'Let's keep going slowly and see how she feels.' Becca nodded silently.

We walked on up the broad, grass-covered road. I could almost feel Ed's disapproval radiating from his position three places back in the line. He was wishing he was on the snow-covered peaks to the north, or kayaking down the rapids in the gorge: anywhere but with this plodding team.

After some ten minutes the road bent away to the east; our route lay north across a shallow grassy valley towards Cochapata, a village in which I had stayed on the 1970 expedition.

'You take a break,' I said. 'I'll nip down and intercept that fellow coming down the valley with the cattle. If he gives me the route, I'll wave you down.'

The herdsman and his young wife were eager to help. Cochapata was best reached by a track running from Ccotana, the *pueblo* at the head of the valley, they said. I thanked them for their courtesy and waved the others on. While they kept on along the road, east to Ccotana, I walked along the valley floor, parallel with them.

I used this time alone to clear my head of the unspoken struggle with Ed and concentrate on what our plan should be. By the time our paths crossed at the edge of the village, my mind was made up.

'OK. I've decided to stop here for a rest day. We'll try and find somewhere comfortable for Becca to sleep. Let's hope Ccotana has a school.' I spoke as decisively as I could, knowing Ed's frustration would be hard for him to bear.

'Maybe Justin and I could go down to the Apurimac for the day,' he said. It was more of a statement than a question. I could see his eyelid beginning to twitch with annoyance.

'Well, let's see how we get on here first. It's a long way, and a hell of a drop to the river.'

Before things could get worse we arrived at a gate in the school wall. Children were playing in the yard, while a couple of adults kept an eye on them.

'I'll do the talking here, Ed.' In this critical situation I didn't want anything to go wrong through a misunderstanding.

'I'm not going to be told when I can talk and when I can't!' he muttered rebelliously.

Villagers directed me on down the street to the *Presidente*'s house. I left my rucksack with the rest of the team in the schoolyard, and set off.

Ccotana lies in a shallow bowl, high on top of the Sierra, surrounded by rocky hills which have been dug over for potatoes wherever possible. There is little grazing for the llamas, alpacas, sheep, cattle, horses and donkeys. The *pueblo* is a *comunidad*, the lands having been divided among the villagers by the agrarian reforms of 1973. But families producing ten children since that date have seen no increase in their share of the land to feed the extra mouths, and the place has the same distressed appearance as Pomgona, where a cow had kept us awake by eating the straw thatch of our hut.

The *Presidente* lived in a low mud hovel down a walled side lane, at the far end of the village from the school. His family were in high spirits and the holiday was evidently in full swing that Sunday morning. They sat me on a bench in the hot sun against the wall outside the front door, and produced a foot-high vase of *chicha* for me to drink. I could feel their grinning faces willing me to join the party spirit.

Apparently there would be no trucks coming until after the holiday, but the priest was expected at any minute. He didn't come more than a couple of times a year, they said, but this was a big day. The church would be opened, and after the service, why, surely the priest would help the sick *gringa*. The teacher was away until Tuesday, but of course they would try and find a key for us.

Walking back to the school, I felt weighed down by the responsibility of having brought Rebecca to such an isolated spot. The previous afternoon, as we watched the funeral party straggle home from the cemetery along the track by the Pomgona school, a young Quechuan mother had asked us for help with the baby daughter on her back. She had said the child wouldn't eat, and was dying of a breathing problem. Now I remembered how, in a moment of stress before leaving Ardmore, Marie Christine had shouted at me, 'I don't want my daughter killed in South America!'

I walked the few yards up to the church. A bit of slack in a thin black chain fastening the padlocked double doors allowed me to peer inside. It was empty. I hurried on back to the school.

Back in the schoolyard, I found Ed and Justin keen to walk the five miles to Tunga Suca for stores, and to see if they could find any medical help for Bec. After they had gone, M.C. and I laid Becca on her sleeping-bag in the shade of the wall and waited for someone to bring the key to the school. An hour later we moved her into a hut in a corner of the compound. Not much bigger than a dog kennel, it had shafts of sunlight filtering through the balding sooty thatch, and I could only just squeeze through the tiny plank door. Much of the floor area, eight feet by seven, was taken up by a broken mud stove in the far corner, and the rest was uneven dust, broken glass and animal droppings. Indian parents kept a vigil over the school wall, wondering if the *gringa* had something contagious. In the yard children played a frenetic game of football with a ball of polythene bound with wool.

At 2pm Bec woke up. She was deaf in her left ear, and the pain was so fierce that she had to sit upright to ease it. Marie Christine gave her two aspirins and a tot of whisky, and she went back to sleep for another two hours. When she next woke, her mother gave her two more aspirins and started a chart of symptoms and treatment. One of us sat in that filthy hut holding her as she moaned softly in agony. The other stayed outside watching the kit. I'll not forget my feelings as those huge, frightened eyes stared at me, silently pleading with me to stop the pain. She thought she was going to die.

We waited all day. The *gobernador* of this and the *Presidente* of that came down to meet us, but nothing was accomplished. The key never arrived, and the priest never came to the church, but I saw I would achieve nothing by making a fuss. We didn't expect the boys back until the following morning—they had taken only enough kit to carry stores back with them, so we moved all five rucksacks into the hut with us, laying our sleeping bags on either side of Becca. During this operation a crowd of women and children gathered round the door, and finally M.C. had to shout at them to go away. We shut the door on the world and blocked the window holes with stones to prevent children peering in at us.

When M.C. began cooking supper by the light of a candle, the drumming of the stoves providing some warmth and comfort at an awful time, a narrow-faced Indian called Eusebio looked in on us for a second time, clearly worried about the situation. He and I went to his house for a twist of salt, which he wrapped in a piece of religious paper called *El Evangélico*. On my way back I filled the water bottles from the village supply—simply the drain running across the main street, the haunt of pigs and dogs. A human skull stared down from the wall.

Becca managed to eat a hard-boiled egg and two potatoes, and I began to hope she was better. We were just giving her two Paracetamol when there came a gentle tapping at the door. It was Eusebio again, this time bringing something covered with a brown woven cloth. He stooped to enter, and unwrapped a plate of fried sheep's intestines. While he sat down against the wall at Rebecca's feet, Marie Christine tipped the meat into an empty mess tin and reheated it over a stove. From under his poncho Eusebio produced a small paraffin wick lamp and another cloth containing a pile of small purple potatoes, still hot from his fire. In return, we gave him a tot of our precious half bottle of medicinal whisky.

I believe we had to think back over the previous weeks really to appreciate Eusebio's action; a poor Quechuan Indian with eight children of his own, a bitter night in a broken-down village two miles high, on the edge of existence. His precious understanding of our predicament made our hardship worthwhile. Our hearts went out to him.

He left us at 7.30pm. We got into our sleeping bags on either side of our daughter, taking turns to hold her in our arms. At midnight we gave her two Paracetamol. At 2.30am her ear began to discharge a pale liquid tinged with blood. Marie Christine and I were each stuck with our own thoughts in the dark. With no telephone, no vehicle, no doctor, it was hard to see what we could do. The altitude must have something to do with Becca's illness, but she might become even worse if we took her down, for the pressure would increase as the air grew thicker. Marie Christine had seen the skull on the wall, too; she kept thinking how far we were from Lima and proper medical help, and dreading the idea of an amateur *sanitario* poking dirty instruments into Becca's head.

At 4am we tried some eardrops, but what Becca wanted most was someone to hold on to. The discharge from her ear was at least a clue as to what was wrong and Marie Christine consulted our paperback *Traveller's Guide to Health*. She found a passage linking sudden changes of barometric pressure with the common cold, and this seemed to fit:

'*Otitis Media*: infection spreads up the Eustachian tube to the inner surface of the ear-drum, and the tube closes as a result of swelling, when the ear-drum is partially sucked in by the development of a vacuum. The drum may protrude again by the formation of pus, indeed pus may burst through to the exterior canal or spread to the air spaces of the mastoid bone. Onset is usually sudden, with discomfort in the affected ear rapidly increasing until pain is severe, and deafness increases.'

The book recommended 'expert attention'; we couldn't supply that, but we did have a course of antibiotics, in the form of Amoxil. We began a full course of one tablet every eight hours for five days. We gave Paracetamol for pain, and aspirin if the pain wasn't too bad, as we were short of Paracetamol.

At 8am Justin and Ed returned with the stores, and were horrified to discover Bec's predicament. In Tunga Suca they had found a *sanitario*, who had told them the patient should have antibiotics, but not eardrops. He also recommended we walk to the hostel in Tunga Suca, but I decided that it was unwise for Becca to walk anywhere. We stopped the eardrops forthwith.

I went in search of Eusebio to thank him again for his kindness, but his wife told me he'd gone to Yanaoca for the Tupac Amaru anniversary and would not be back for several days. By 8.30am we had a crowd of thirty children at the door of the hut, all waiting for the school to open. Each of them carried a piece of sun-dried dung, which they had to pick up on the way to school to fuel the fire which cooked their lunch.

At 10am, when no teacher had arrived, some of the children went home, but others began playing football. And when they tired of this, there was always Justin to play with. Justin invariably made friends with children, and this morning he conducted a search for keys: sure enough, one of the little rascals had a key on a string round his neck. It fitted one of the classrooms, and Justin was the fellow to persuade him to use it—in spite of his mates warning him not to. Within ten minutes we had Becca laid down in a clean, bright classroom, well on the way to being convinced that she felt better.

Reassured that she was getting the right treatment, the two boys set off on their travels once more. Ed was still pretty abrupt, and I felt it would be good for them both to get away from us for a while. This time they hoped to walk to Yanaoca for the festivities, and planned to return on the following morning.

Marie Christine and I spent a pleasant day, vastly relieved to have come up with some realistic diagnosis and treatment. Unless Becca suffered a relapse, we could be optimistic that she would soon recover. It is indecision that grinds you down worst. We slept part of the day and just relaxed. Two problems occupied my mind. First, I had to decide whether or not to declare an end to Phase One of our trip and prepare for Phase Two. Second, there was the niggling worry of coming to terms with Ed's natural impatience.

Phase One had accomplished its aim: to build a team fit to deal with Phase Two. We were now self-sufficient, capable of performing effectively without assistance from guides and mules. Rebecca's health should improve with a period of recuperation in Cuzco.

Ed's impatience was only a minor irritation, springing from his hyper-active constitution and the relative inexperience of his twenty-one years. We needed an old-fashioned air-clearing session, something I had encountered on all expeditions when times were hard. The best time for such a discharge of tension is after a good meal, when people are relaxed and at their most reasonable.

I decided to hold a briefing for everyone together on the first suitable occasion, next day. This should deal with both the plan and Ed at the same time.

Just before dark I went to fill the water bottles and mess tins for the night. Walking back along the empty main street, I reflected on how different everything was from the previous evening. How lucky we were. As I came along the street the sun was setting in front of me. The mellow light would have graced a Constable painting; herds of livestock were winding up the gentle hill out of a broad vista of empty mountain and valley, with small boys urging them on in place of sheep dogs.

I took great pleasure in cooking supper for the three of us. Becca was putting a good face on things, gaining confidence in her recovery. By the following morning she had needed only one Paracetamol in fourteen hours, and although her ear was still leaking, the antibiotics seemed to be taking effect.

The school children arrived bright and early. We felt particularly grateful to the little boy who had unlocked the door for us, and this made the scene which followed especially uncomfortable. His mother stormed into the classroom in the sort of towering rage which I have only ever encountered with Quechuan women. She grabbed her son by the left ear and started belting him with her right hand, bumping him round the room. With the harridan screaming abuse and the boy howling an awful, high-pitched wail, other parents glared at us disapprovingly. I felt embarrassed and weak. Becca felt responsible for all the trouble. Marie Christine felt outraged. I am ashamed to say we did little but utter a few half-hearted words of protest. It was not a performance of which the Ridgways could be proud.

Things did not calm down until Justin and Ed arrived on the scene and created a diversion. The crestfallen little boy seized his opportunity to flee to the far end of the playground. The mother clearly expected the imminent arrival of the teacher to bring about some fearful retribution for her son's actions, and she correctly blamed us for having led the boy astray. We busied ourselves with Ed and Justin.

Sharp on 8.30 the dapper figure of Francisco Suma entered the playground; everyone fell back and the noise died. Pulling the peak of his baseball cap firmly down on his brow, he strode across to us—and shook hands. Welcoming us to Ccotana, he apologised for the fact that he had been away, and hoped we had been made comfortable in his absence. Smiling, he suggested we move our kit to another classroom, not then in use.

With the formalities over, he dismissed the parents and paraded the whole school on the playground, and the morning roll-call and singing began. We stood on the sidelines, and then, realising we were no longer involved, prepared our kit for the move. Our boys, meanwhile, had met a nun in Yanaoca who was also a trained nurse; from their description of Becca she too had diagnosed *otitis media*, saying it was very common on the Altiplano. She had kindly sent us a course of antibiotics, but we decided to continue with the Amoxil as we were already into the second of five days with it.

I felt awkward when I realised Francisco was amalgamating three classes into two so that Becca would have somewhere to sleep. Two more teachers had arrived, a man and his wife, and they were organising the move of books and cleaning the classroom, with the help of the whole class. We thanked them all and moved Becca straight away. She felt pretty grim, with a return of her earache, so we put her to bed, and she managed with an aspirin in place of Paracetamol. While the boys went off to wash clothes, I took the opportunity of discussing my ideas for the rest of the trip with Marie Christine.

We had a good lunch together in the empty classroom, and Bec got up for a bit. At the end of the meal, as we sat at the desks, I outlined my plan.

The date was now 5 November. Twenty-two days had passed since we had left Cuzco. I decided we should end Phase One—the High Walk—now. Our flight from Lima to London was scheduled for 18 December. If we devoted thirty-five days, from 6 November to 12 December, to Phase Two, we would still have six days in hand for contingencies.

In Phase Two—the Emergency Zone—we would start by trying to walk to Tunga Suca on the following morning. If Rebecca was fit enough, we would try and get a truck down to Combepata station and catch the afternoon train for Cuzco. After a few days there, we would take my 1970 back-door route to Osambre, stay a few days with Elvin, and then follow the mule-train route back over the mountains to Lucma, Quillabamba and Cuzco.

There was no adverse comment, so I set about trying to restore harmony between Ed and myself. I explained how subtle and complex I found the day-to-day dealings with the villagers. On this, my fifth visit to South America, I still felt it was a vastly different place from Europe. I pointed out that this was the first time Ed, Justin and Becca had been in South America, and that was why I needed to do the talking whenever we met people for the first time.

'Believe you me, Ed, I'm only too familiar with the power struggle that develops in a closed group like the five of us,' I said. 'It's pointless and negative. I lead my expeditions, Ed. There can be no racing ahead. The speed on a trip lasting months, rather than hours or days, must be the speed of the slowest. Anything different means trouble, or even disaster.'

Ed looked astonished. 'I'm sorry you feel this way, John. Honestly, I was only trying to help, by going ahead. It does get rather boring at the back.'

I was delighted by the positive effort he made to see my side of things. To his great credit, there was no whingeing. The air was cleared.

In the late afternoon, Ed, Justin and I turned out with a couple of visiting teachers and one of the children to play volleyball against the school and its staff. The match was billed as *Los Visitantes v. Escuela Ccotana* and greeted with fervent enthusiasm by the rest of the school. On this occasion we seemed just over twice as tall as the opposition. The girls formed a choir on the sidelines, and, reading from a book, furiously chanted songs of loyalty to *Escuela mía,* while the lady teacher chalked up the scores on the base of the Tupac Amaru statue.

After a narrow victory by the home team, the teachers asked us to supper in the school office. It turned out to be more a case of sharing our supper with Francisco, when the married couple were called away to their digs in the village. Before they left we gave all three a tot of our medicinal Johnny Walker Red Label whisky. Francisco told us he was married, with a wife and family in Sicuani. A compulsively neat little man in his mid-thirties, with a short-sighted, peering gaze, he lived a solitary life. I shall never hear the BBC World Service again without thinking of Francisco, tuning in to the South American edition in Ccotana, high in the Andes.

He said he was *muy triste* to see us leave, and asked us to stay another day, but we had to push on. He came in early in the morning with pieces from a haunch of pig, which M.C. fried for breakfast. The children lined up to give us a cheer as we filed out of that square-arched gate. Rebecca would never forget Ccotana school.

Nearing the end of the village, we spotted the little chap who had unlocked the school room door for us. He was late for school —something of a tearaway, I reckoned. I walked over to the bridge where he was lurking and gave him what must have seemed a substantial sum of money, to make amends for my cowardice. He let out a whoop of pleasure and hurried off to show his fainthearted mates—but I didn't feel much better about it.

Becca found the walk, most of it downhill, very hard going. I worried in case the increased pressure might cause her more pain as we descended, but it was a feeling of weakness which bothered her most.

Tunga Suca was much as I remembered it from 1970—a little market town packed with people. We soon arranged a lift on a truck down to Combepata, which would leave the square at 1pm. Waiting for the truck presented the boys with the difficult problem of restraining themselves from eating too much from the market stalls, whose curiously cheap and sweet cooking chocolate was to prove Ed's downfall. Marie Christine and Becca spent the time trying to entice six ginger piglets with bits of bread; M.C. was longing to pick one up and hear it squeal with outrage. It took a lot of doing: the piglets of Tunga Suca have to be street-wise to survive.

Chapter Twelve

Two thousand feet below Tunga Suca, the Vilcanota river rushes between the neatly ploughed fields of Combepata village. As if to keep the torrent in order, man's single-track railway follows its course in grand, sweeping curves.

Our old truck was heavy-laden; the Indians jammed in with us on top of a layer of cargo used our rucksacks as stepping stones so they could see over the high timber sides. We juddered across railway tracks and pulled up near the station platform. A high wind swirled dust in our eyes. The driver was a man in a hurry, with little time to waste on unloading *gringos*. Five rucksacks, five sets of belt-order, a couple of stuff-bags of food and five waterproof ponchos which we had worn during the rain showers in Tunga Suca—all had to be passed quickly from hand to hand, with women cackling and drunks tugging while the driver checked my money against the sunlight for forgeries.

Once everything was settled, we heaved the kit on to our backs and stumbled across the road towards the platform, belt-order in one hand and poncho in the other. There was one other person in sight: a short, dark, squarely-built girl, standing beside the tracks. Her brightly striped leg warmers and yellow scarf contrasted oddly with the ragged traditional clothing worn by the Indians, which was all we had seen in the past few weeks.

'Aha!' I said cheerily, but mistakenly. 'She likes the look of you, Justin!' She moved towards Rebecca, who looked a sorry sight, with a khaki head-warmer covering a bulging pad over her sore ear, and began to help her with her load.

The girl's name was Elizabeth Paullo, and like us she was

waiting for the Cuzco train. She was beginning four days' holiday from her job as teacher at a primary school near Tunga Suca. Her mouth had lines of bitterness unusual for a girl in her early twenties. Withdrawn and introspective, she exuded unhappiness. If impulse had not driven her to help Bec, we might never have got into conversation, and our lives might have been different.

We sat on either side of her, waiting for the train on the platform seat, our dusty navy blue thermal jackets zipped up against the wind. She spoke no English, and our Spanish relied heavily on enthusiastic gesture. Inevitably the talk came round to what we were doing in Peru, so I got out the dog-eared copy of *Amazon Journey*, thinking the photographs would speak for themselves.

Suddenly her face lit up. 'I know this man!' she cried, stabbing a finger at the picture of Elvin. We stared at her. I let the book fall to my knees in astonishment. How could she? The odds against finding someone who knew Elvin here in Combepata must be millions to one against. This empty platform was many days' journey from Osambre; the jungle seemed to belong to another country. It was one more of the extraordinary coincidences that seemed to be pushing us on—as if a stranger we had met while walking in the middle of Wales had known a neighbour of ours in the Western Highlands of Scotland.

Like other solitary people I have come across in remote places, this lonely girl felt a compulsion to talk. Normally her background and social position as teacher would keep her apart from the villagers; now information flooded from her like water pouring through a broken dam.

She had been born at Hatumpampa, a village close to Osambre. To my amazement I remembered I had stayed a couple of days with her brother, Humberto Paullo, in that village on the 1970 expedition. Now she told me that he had left the sugar cane plantation years back, first to study and then to become a lecturer in anthropology at the San Antonio University in Cuzco.

Elizabeth went on to say that the land-owning families of Paullo, Rosas and Berg were good friends in that part of the

Apurimac valley, but that bad times had come. The farm at Osambre had been destroyed; so had the Paullos' sugar cane business in Hatumpampa. Only a year ago her father had been with the head of the Rosas family, staying in a friend's house in the village of Vilcabamba, three days' walk from Osambre. The *Sendero Luminoso* terrorists had taken them by surprise at night in the house and savagely murdered the two old men.

I looked along the bench at Marie Christine; I could practically hear her thinking, 'We're not taking Rebecca *there*!' The familiar, leaden feeling returned to my stomach: what on earth were we doing, stumbling about in this Godforsaken, tortured place?

'Things are much better now, though,' Elizabeth went on. 'Your friend Elvin is living in Lucmahuayco, about half a day's journey from Osambre. Everything has quietened down. There are soldiers and police posted there to keep things peaceful.'

'You're sure Elvin's alive?' I asked.

'Yes, of course. Why not?' She shrugged, making light of my doubts.

I leaned over and kissed her on the cheek. Everyone was astonished, including Elizabeth and me. Kissing is not something I do a lot of—but it was an immense relief to hear Elvin was still alive.

We all cheered up. Children began to gather round us, not wanting to miss the excitement, and we matched them song for song. The train rolled in, only ten minutes late, and Elizabeth talked non-stop for the four hours to Cuzco. Since the awful business of her father's death the family had broken up, and her mother had moved away to Lima, a forty-eight-hour bus journey from Cuzco. Whenever she got holidays from the Siberia-like isolation of her school, Elizabeth stayed with cousins near the middle of Cuzco: and for us she recommended a cheap hostel nearby.

A great mob of people milled about the train when we arrived after dark. Elizabeth was catching a bus, but it was easier for our team to carry the kit up through the city; so we parted, agreeing to meet for lunch next day. We all felt a good deal fitter than when we had last been in Cuzco, acclimatising for Phase One. We seemed to soar up the gentle hill from the station, jostling through the busy evening crowds, and satisfied with the self-sufficiency of carrying our own little world on our backs.

With the start of Phase Two imminent, and because the rift with Ed was healed, I decided to maintain the hard routine we had established on the Altiplano, all the time trying to build the team by keeping us all together and inter-dependent. We booked into the Hostal Familiar, as Elizabeth had suggested, and took a room with four single beds, getting a special rate of roughly £1 a night each, because the hot water system was broken. M.C. and I would share a single bed between us.

While we changed to go out for a late supper to celebrate the end of Phase One, I looked round the room to gauge how everyone was bearing up at the end of a long day. Becca and Ed had both complained of feeling sick on the train; Justin was phlegmatic as ever, and M.C. was her usual buoyant self. I felt encouraged by the strong feeling of unity. So far, so good.

Supper was no great success. We stopped at one of many little tourist trap places on a narrow, cobbled side street off the Plaza de Armas. The heaped plates of greasy fried meat and chips were too much and too rich for us, and one by one we made our excuses and left. Justin went off for a walk in the night, looking for cigarettes, while the rest of us scuttled back to our room. Ed lay groaning with pain in the bed nearest the door, and we were about to put out the lights when Justin came in. Assessing the situation with commendable speed and compassion, he brought a red plastic dustbin from the lavatory in the nick of time, and Ed was violently sick into it. Rebecca only just managed to avoid following suit by staring fixedly at the ceiling: her deafness and the wrapping round her head at least spared her unsettling sound effects.

M.C. and I found our single bed particularly narrow, and we did not sleep well. For us it was Phase One (a). Nevertheless, we managed to lie in until seven next morning, and then took turns to have a cold shower behind the three-quarter ceiling height plywood partitions which served to separate the ablutions from the sleeping area.

At noon M.C., Becca and I sat on a green bench in the Plaza de Armas, waiting for Elizabeth. We had left Justin and Ed behind, feeling that perhaps a ratio of five to one would overpower our new friend. Thunder clouds threatened rain as she arrived, and we hurried through narrow streets lined with massive Inca stone-work buildings to a simple restaurant with a few tables set around a leafy courtyard.

I could not believe it was simply the thundery atmosphere which had caused the change in Elizabeth's mood. She looked really low, and hardly spoke at all. I wondered if her relatives, perhaps fearing the terrorists were on their trail again, had warned her against saying too much to people she did not really know. When I asked for her brother Humberto's telephone number at the university, she told me he was unobtainable, and I dropped the matter.

We ordered fried guinea pig, to see how the Quechuans liked to cook their favourite dish. It arrived looking as if it had been killed with a giant fly swat—a flat, fried rectangle with feet stretched out off each corner, front teeth and whiskers still intact. Elizabeth brightened a little with the arrival of the food, and even Becca started to giggle as her mother began to tackle her unfortunate rodent.

Towards the end of the meal, as if almost against her better nature, Elizabeth suddenly blurted out that she'd heard on the radio that the terrorists were in Lucmahuayco, and we shouldn't go there at all. If we decided we really must go, we should take a rifle with us. We could buy one in Cuzco for 300,000 soles (about £15), and we could get a licence from the *prefecto*'s office.

Having said her piece, Elizabeth volunteered nothing more. She seemed to go into retreat. I thought maybe she was suffering from depression caused by the tragic break-up of her family and the isolated nature of her work. She seemed embarrassed or even frightened to be seen with us. After leaving the restaurant, we walked back towards our hostel in uneasy silence. We found she was staying no more than a hundred yards down the street, but as we said goodbye I realised she had no intention of seeing us again. When she said she would leave a letter at the hostel for us to take to her relations in Lucmahuayco, none of us really believed her.

Back in our room we found Justin asleep, lying on his bed flat on his back with his feet tucked up in the lotus position. Ed was busy planning a three-week course to teach himself Spanish and make use of any spare time there might be on Phase Two; he'd found a second-hand instruction book in the market.

We told the boys about Elizabeth. It had been a depressing meeting, and it placed the weight of responsibility firmly on my shoulders. The situation was not far different from the worst scenario painted for us by Jeremy Thorpe at the British Embassy in Lima: Osambre was no place to be taking wife and child.

The difference lay in us, the team: there was no talk now of not wanting to go into the Red Sector of the Emergency Zone. We all felt that the hard, team-building weeks on the Altiplano must not be wasted. Our confidence in our self-sufficiency encouraged us to believe we should be able to cope with most situations. I certainly had everyone's support, but I knew that in the end I was responsible for everyone's safety.

'At least nobody knows we're here,' said Ed.

'That's right,' I said abruptly. 'That's the key!' Heads turned towards me. 'Obviously the situation on the Apurimac has changed for the worse. But we got our letter from the *prefecto* a month ago. We'll try the old back-door trick!'

My team stared at me as if I'd gone crazy.

'Well,' I explained, 'if nobody knows we're here, and we have the *prefecto*'s letter of permission, we can follow our 1970 route into the valley—rafting across the river from the south, instead of coming down the coffee trail from the north, where the Guarda Civil posts are. That way we'll get in: there'll be no one to stop us!'

I threw up my hands with delight, thrilled with the cunning

of this new scheme, and ignoring the fact that it did not lessen the danger one bit. It was a way forward.

'I think we should rest up first, Johnny,' said M.C. anxiously. 'We must get Bec's ear right before we go into the wilds again.' But I could tell she was keen to give it a go. Bec was nodding too. The more dangerous it was, the better it would suit Ed, and Justin had shown us all he wasn't easily left behind.

'Okay,' I said. 'This is Thursday. We'll give it till Monday: if we're all fit by then, we'll catch the bus for Lima.' I was developing the plan as I talked. 'After about eight hours, we'll just ask to be put off the bus, right in the middle of nowhere. From there it should take less than a week to reach the raft we used to cross the Apurimac in 1970.'

Friday, Saturday and Sunday passed gently by. M.C. and I made unavailing efforts to contact Elizabeth's brother Humberto Paullo, and spent much of our time sitting in Trattoria Adriano, a long-established corner cafe at the top of Avenue Sol, sipping cups of *café con leche* very slowly and watching the world go by. The massive dark timber counter and linings lent a warm feeling of continuity, as if we were still in the 1920s. Compared with our complex existence at home, life seemed beautifully simple: we were dealing with one problem at a time. The sun warmed us from clear blue skies every morning. I had lost two stone, so there was no worry about getting fat. It was wonderful, and we loved it.

The others were not as fortunate. Becca sank into a feeling of permanent ill-health when she was hit by a severe stomach upset on top of the declining earache and never-ending head-cold. 'I'm always the one who's sick, Mum. I hold everyone back,' she sobbed one evening, when Justin, Ed and I were out getting something to eat. But bit by bit she did begin to recover, and I felt sure the whole struggle would stand her in good stead for her secretarial course in the London jungle when she got home. Justin also felt queasy for a couple of days. Ed fought back, however, to make several visits a day to an amazingly cheap back-street restaurant where he devoured vast helpings of a dish called *Americano*, though he was never certain which animal the 'beef' came from.

On the Sunday I telephoned Nick Asheshov in Lima and left details of our proposed route with his daughter Tammy, just in case. Elizabeth never did leave a letter for us to take to her relatives in Lucmahuayco.

We decided to start Phase Two on Monday 11 November— Remembrance Day—and we spent several hours packing our kit. The two ladies running the Hostal Familiar had been particularly helpful, and they now agreed to keep our passports, travellers' cheques and cold weather gear while we were away. We took only photocopies of our documents and passports, and carried what money we needed in small denomination notes, spread among all five of us. At three in the morning I woke up in the dark, as so often before, worrying about what I was letting everyone in for: there had been plenty of signs of trouble, but I had simply chosen to ignore them.

Chapter Thirteen

We left the Hostal Familiar at 6.30 in the morning. Ed was doubling up with stomach cramps, so we hired a taxi for him and Justin, with as much of the kit as the battered machine would hold. M.C., Bec and I walked down the hill towards the bus station.

It was the sort of pearly, fresh morning you might yearn for on your death-bed. The streets were already quite busy: the mountains ringing the city had a fair covering of snow, and the sun was bright yet not hot. Justin appeared precisely on cue, guiding us off Avenue Sol and up to a small, dreary terminal building. There was no sign of any transport, but a notice read 'Bus leaves promptly at 7.30'.

'I'll be all right, John,' muttered Ed, sitting hunched on a low garden wall, his face a luminous grey. He was conveniently positioned to lean over the garden if the worst happened. I don't think any other member of the team approached Ed when it came to stoicism; he seemed to have been practising it all his life, with his interminable hay fever and fragile skin. Yet he has an immensely cheerful manner and seems impervious to discomfort: given the option he would cheerfully drop dead in harness rather than cause five minutes' delay.

There was a sizeable queue by the time the dusty coach pulled into the kerb. Justin swung his hairpin-thin frame up on to the roof to help with the luggage, the red band round his black felt trilby lending him a Noel Cowardish air. Ed dragged himself into the bus to secure our numbered seats against the tickets we held. We knew that if a battleaxe Quechuan woman once got her broad stern on one or two of our places, the fiercest authority in Peru would melt into nodding approval. I hopped about the melée, moving the rucksacks with M.C. and Bec, arguing the toss on overweight. But I wasn't too busy to notice the tattered state of the tyres.

We weren't the strongest of teams that morning. Rebecca's eyes were already closed by the time the coach had ground its way up on to the mountain pass above the city. Ed was hardly enjoying the view, either, and Marie Christine and I were in dispute: there was some uncertainty over the nature of the fluid which dampened the window seat I'd offered her. Even Justin slept, anaesthetised by the sawing Quechuan dirge from the coach tape system. When we stopped for fuel, Indian women crowded aboard, trying to sell cheese, onions, fudge, leaf-wrapped hot corn snacks and *chicha* maize beer by the glass from big enamel jugs. None of our team bought a thing.

Marie Christine adored the journey, her spontaneous enthusiasm for every changing view as fresh as when I had first met her twenty-three years before. She was thrilled by the yellow broom of the Altiplano and the sharp, snow-covered peaks. But the change in vegetation when the road swooped down into the fertile Pampa valley, the blue of the jacaranda trees, the scarlet blossoms, huge white roses, bougainvillea, geraniums—all this was the stuff of the South America which she had come to find.

Avocado trees, bananas, sugar cane and thudding heat awaited us at the Guarda Civil post by the rusty low Puente Cunje bridge across the Apurimac. The river flowed like milky coffee in the bottom of a gigantic canyon, with rapids like lace necklaces every half mile or so. The coach only just fitted on the bridge, with the driver's assistant walking ahead as guide.

On the far side, I was dismayed to find armed and businesslike Guarda Civil demanding inspection of all passports. I watched the checking procedure with interest, hoping to find a way of keeping our destination secret. I realised we should have bought tickets to Abancay, a Provincial capital a few hours further along the road from where we hoped to get off. But our tickets were for the small town of Curahuasi, and this could prove suspicious, as it was no sort of destination for *gringos*. We were able to create a diversion by making a fuss about clambering up on to the roof of the coach to find our photocopies among the luggage. The heat and dust became our allies as we joined the tail end of the queue, and the policeman cast only a perfunctory glance over the tickets and five sets of papers, eager, perhaps, to join his off-duty colleagues who were splashing about in the shallows to cool off.

I was relieved when the monotonous Quechuan taped music began once more, and the bus started on a two-hour grind back up on to the Altiplano. We stopped for lunch halfway up, at Curahuasi, where we bought avocados and tangerines from a stall. I became so incensed by a little boy who was tormenting a green parakeet which he'd caught and was trying to sell that I all but lifted him off the ground by his ear. Ed sat pale and silent.

I discovered that no one on the coach had heard of the turning off the road which led to Huanipaca. But I knew it existed, because we'd used it in 1970.

'*Gringos* off!' shouted the bus driver at 4.30 and we piled out on to a bleak mountainside world of potato patches and rough yellow grassland. The other passengers looked astonished, peering through the windows, first at us and then at the advancing snow showers. We had stepped out of civilisation and I shuddered at the thought of it. Ed said he felt better, but it was imperative we find somewhere to sleep, especially since a couple of Quechuan women waiting by the roadside with sacks of maize were adamant that this was not the turning for Huanipaca at all: it was further up the road, they said.

The only hut in sight was firmly padlocked and, the two crones told us, the widow who owned it was not expected back until late evening. Looking through a crack in the door, I saw it was seething with guinea pigs; they sensed my presence and began a chorus of 'cooing', from which they derive their name in Quechuan, *cooi*.

Marie Christine and Becca saved the day. They returned from a tour of their own with excellent news of accommodation

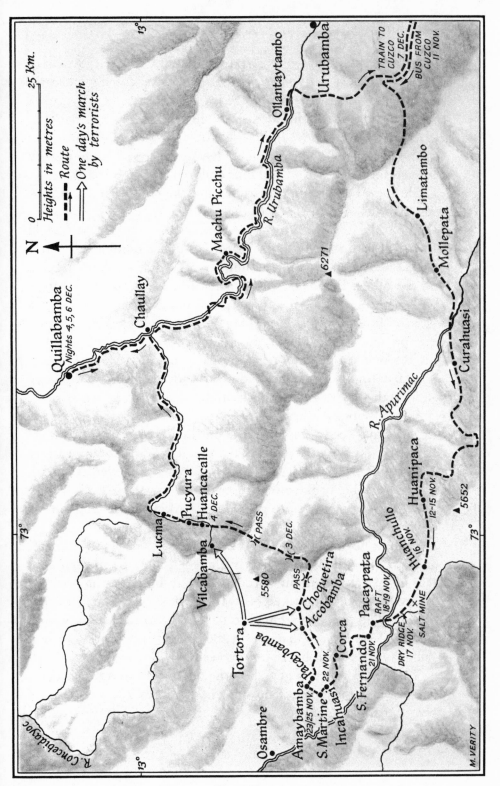

N

Phase Two

available in somebody's porch over the hill. Snowflakes swirled around us as we arrived at the first and only other hut. Clearly financial inducement had prevailed: the Indian family hadn't enough room for themselves, let alone for lodgers. Our smoke-blackened, mud and bamboo lean-to, eleven feet by six, was open to the snow on two sides. It was where the wife usually cooked for her husband and four children. Now she had to cook inside the dark sleeping quarters, and the whole family had to step over us to gain access to their home.

The fruits of Phase One were immediately evident: M.C. and Bec swiftly got the stoves roaring and the familiar potatoes, onions and rice were soon boiling on one, while black tea brewed on the other. Ed, Justin and I managed to seal out the weather with a series of interlaced waterproof ponchos, and we found a way of fitting five sleeping-bags and a cooking area into the bumpy space available. It was done without fuss; this was the life we were used to. When survival becomes a way of living, mental confidence returns, and making-do seems easy. We were all in high spirits. Ed and Bec both looked much better.

All the same, it was a disturbed night. We were warm inside clean linen liners, sleeping-bags and bivvy bags on Karrimats. Each of us knew how to work the zips for the right temperature and ventilation. The barking dogs and crying baby were standard; but real trouble broke out at three in the morning.

I was woken by shouting and dogs barking somewhere in the darkness, apparently quite close. The man of the house trod on my legs as he burst out of the family quarters, across the lean-to, and out into the night. Quietly I opened the zips and felt cold rain on my face, coming through the gap between the ponchos where the man had pushed his way out. I whispered to the other four, but no one else seemed to be awake, so I lay quietly with torch in one hand and knife in the other. I was fully dressed, with my basketball boots by my head.

There was more angry shouting, then the sound of a truck starting and moving off up the road towards Abancay; then a few mutterings and the odd bark marked the end of the trouble.

Our host stepped carefully across me on his way to bed. I wondered if I'd imagined it all, but in the foggy, damp morning, muddy footprints on my bivvy bag showed where he had stumbled on his way out in the night.

The Indian family looked miserable, paddling about in cold mud, and we found they had suffered a major loss. *Bandidos* had come in the night with a truck, and although surprised in the act had still managed to load a bull on to the lorry and make off for the Abancay market. Alive, the beast would be worth something like three million soles, but its brand marks would prevent the rustlers from selling it intact; they would chop it up in the back of the truck and sell it in the market half price.

Clad in our green waterproof ponchos, with hoods up, we left the wretched family at 7.40am. It looked as if the rain might be set for the day; the countryside was shrouded in mist, just like on a wet summer morning in the Scottish Highlands at home. It took us only ten minutes to reach the place where we'd been dropped off the previous afternoon. It was in fact the Cachora junction, no more than a point on the mountainside where the track from Cachora village joined the dirt road to Lima.

We came across a solitary, sorry figure draped in a sheet of thin clear polythene against the downpour. 'Two men were killed by *bandidos* on the road to Huanipaca last week,' he told us. 'I saw the bodies being packed away on the road here.' This was hardly cheering news. Apparently the *bandidos* had been rustling cattle, and they simply murdered the two unfortunates who tried to intervene.

The man offered to show us a short cut to the Huanipaca junction. The road took a large hairpin bend to the left up ahead, and there was a path which cut straight across. As we followed behind him in the mist, I wondered if we were wise to trust him not to lead us into an ambush; it would have been easy to set one up while we slept in the lean-to. I mentioned the thought to the others, and we all kept our knives handy. But what would we do if they had rifles?

As we came to the top of a ridge, the mist cleared a little and we could see the road bending in from the hairpin below us. Our friend pointed out the Huanipaca junction, told us the village was thirty-two kilometres to the north-west, and wished us good luck. There should be a truck coming through from Abancay at -some time during the day, he said, but it was not certain. Anyway, he was returning home; it was too cold and wet to be going to Abancay.

With legs soaking from the undergrowth, we sat at the junction beneath our hooded ponchos like khaki cones. But the rain was easing up, and Marie Christine optimistically filled mess tins with foaming yellow water from the edge of the road. At 9am the Cuzco coach, forty hours out from Lima, dropped off a couple of piratical-looking Indians from Abancay who were heading for Huanipaca. The driver glanced up the track and then, looking grimly down at me, drew the index finger of his right hand slowly across his throat.

The rain stopped and the land began to steam as the sun came out. As the mist cleared, for the first time we could see where we were, high on the side of a deep tributary valley well to the south of the Apurimac. Through a saddle to the north, beyond the river gorge, vast snow-fields rose towards the 20,000-foot peak of Sarkantay. In the foreground waves of livestock rippled across the dun-coloured mountainside, herded by two gaily-clad Indian women. First came sheep in arrowhead formation, then ponderous cattle in line abreast, followed by a few horses, cruelly hobbled against straying. Black pigs brought up the rear, driven by the women, who appeared as moving red and black dabs on the landscape.

When our two rascally companions told us they expected a truck for Huanipaca from Abancay sometime in the early afternoon, we settled down for a long wait. M.C. boiled some potatoes in the yellow gutter water. Ed became absorbed in his *Teach Yourself Spanish* book, bombarding us with requests for questions on the text of Chapter Three, mysteriously entitled 'Francesca has a surprise visitor'. Unfortunately Ed had heard little Spanish spoken, and the book could hardly help him with this snag. Phrases like *quince años antes* much used when describing the 1970 expedition, could be mispronounced to mean 'fifteen bottoms before'. But Ed is nothing if not persevering, and no amount of hilarity from his audience could affect his dogged persistence to master the lingo.

While Becca and I spent much of the time out of the sun, under our ponchos and fast asleep, Marie Christine, unable to resist the chance of sunbathing, painfully burned her face. Justin took a downwind position so that his cigarette smoke would drift away from us. He shaded himself with his black trilby and dug into his Chinese history, jotting notes in a special book.

We gave our two companions some of our potatoes, and although the younger one was drunk, they were a cheerful pair and we developed something of a bond with them as the day grew longer and longer. They were hoping to buy fifty-kilo blocks of red rock salt for cattle-lick in Huanipaca, and then go on to a salt mine where we had stayed a night in 1970. The mine was only a few hours above the rafting point on the Apurimac, and we agreed it might be useful to both parties if we travelled together.

At 4pm we began to think of finding somewhere to stay for the night. Our companions said they would sleep just as they were, huddled under their ponchos, but Justin set off up the track looking for a suitable jumble of rocks to provide shelter and keep us out of sight of unwelcome observers.

An hour later we loaded our rucksacks on to our backs, bade farewell and good luck to our companions, and set off up the track to look for Justin. We'd only been going a few minutes when we saw a decrepit truck pull off the road on to our track; and we could scarcely believe our luck had changed. We saw the two Indians climb up into the back; then the vehicle started up towards us.

'Where's Justin?' cried Becca.

'I've got his rucksack. I'll stay here and find him,' Ed volunteered. 'Then we'll come together in the morning.'

'No.' I felt sure it would be unsafe to split up. 'Let's all get on. We can get a lift along the track a bit. If we don't find him, one or all of us can get off.' Once apart, we would have no means of communication, and I pictured the bus driver drawing his finger across his throat.

The new driver was a friendly fellow, and we were soon clambering over the tailboard to join our travelling companions: men, women, children and a crate of chicks were crammed together on top of sacks of cement, foodstuffs and timber. Justin got a shock when he saw the truck, and began running to head it off; this wasn't too difficult, as we were moving slowly across a series of axle-deep, water-filled potholes, and all the men had to keep getting off so as to lighten the load on the springs.

We were in for a long journey. When we got a puncture, within an hour, we were then treated to a display of real Quechuan ingenuity. In a country where tarmac roads hardly exist and spare parts are especially hard to come by, few vehicles have a jack; so as soon as the shout went up, the owner-driver stopped on a gently sloping bank, overlooking a magnificent sweep of glacier-laden valley and forested mountain. Everyone was ordered off. The burst was in the inner wheel of the two on the back right-hand side. The guard, whose job was to watch the cargo in the back of the truck, gathered some flat rocks and began jamming them under the rear axle. Once he had it firmly supported, he began swinging the pick with fine precision and speed, digging a pit under the punctured wheel. With the tyres well clear of the ground, both outer and inner wheels were removed and the bald spare fitted on the inside, followed by the outer. Then we all got back on board and continued our journey in the failing light, fully aware there were no more spares.

The track was spectacular. In 1970 we had been stopped by an avalanche some five kilometres short of Huanipaca; this time we lurched crazily onward, precipice to the right and overhanging mountainside to the left. Conversation in the back of the truck was carried on as much to distract the passengers from their fears as anything else. The dominant figure was a fat young man who claimed to be half-Japanese and dressed in Western style, with a snappy new ski jacket. We took to calling him Humberto, though it's doubtful if this was his real name.

It was cold in the back of the truck, now the sun had gone, and I curled round some cement bags right back against the tailboard. Marie Christine and Becca were next to Humberto and a school teacher, with their backs to the cab. Between us lay several Indian women and children, and a solid stench-barrier of passenger vomit and dead chicks in a crate. Justin and Ed perched high on the sides, their noses in the air, carefully ducking passing rocks in the dark.

Humberto was a bully and a show-off. He set his cap at Rebecca, offering to buy her, to impress the others in the truck. I felt my jaw tightening with an increasing enthusiasm to smash his face. But gradually he lost his audience as everyone concentrated on hanging on and keeping warm.

Above us stars pricked the moonless velvet of the sky with that peculiar brilliance found in clean, high air, and the glaciers slithered luminous-white through a black land uncomforted by lights of human habitation. Conversation died. The passengers simply endured. Now and then we were able to ease our numbed limbs when the driver had us all dismount, so that he could nurse the vehicle through a *torrentina*.

When we began the descent into Huanipaca, I had vivid memories of a model village where things were so well organised as to detract from the character of the place. I'd written, 'We were very much surprised by the comparative affluence of the people, as against the almost passive plea for existence which we had seen on the Altiplano.'

The moment we arrived, something about the atmosphere in the small square warned me that things were not as they had been on my last visit. Struggling stiff-limbed from the truck, we were immediately surrounded by a crowd of cheeky children who pushed and pulled at our kit. Surprisingly, it was Humberto who offered us accommodation in his new house, and, in the absence of any better idea, we accepted. He led us a few yards to a bare, windowless adobe structure, with a rough roof over its two storeys. There was no door, and the floor was typical of a building-site-cum-latrine. Humberto smiled wolfishly, no doubt thinking he would teach the *gringos* a lesson. How was he to know that we had slept in far worse places?

It was past ten o'clock, and tempers were short. We shared a tin of pilchards, laid our bivvy bags among the puddles and went to sleep. I was woken by the sound of pigs grunting and squealing in the yard at the back of the house. It was raining hard, with water coming through the roof and dripping on me steadily. As usual I had my knife and torch to hand; and this time I gathered a pile of stones by sweeping my hand slowly across the ground by my bed space. Rebecca and Marie Christine were sound asleep between me and the corner of the room.

I could sense that the pigs were inside the house and working their way along the corridor in the pitch dark. Soon they'd surely reach the doorway into our room, and my sleeping-bag was the first thing they'd encounter. From the snuffling I could tell that they were big, and I felt unusually vulnerable with my head right on the ground.

I suppose I must have dropped off to sleep. Next thing I knew, I was sitting bolt upright in my sleeping-bag. Something like the trumpet of a stampeding elephant had blasted in my ear. Luckily for us all, the pig turned and bolted back through the doorway. I flashed the hand powered torch and just caught a glimpse of a bristly black body tearing down the corridor. I threw my stones after it, and a few fresh ones I could now see with the aid of the torch. Collapsing on to my back in the darkness, I realised that once again the rest of the team had slept right through the drama.

Justin was up with the sparrow on a rainy morning. His hot, sweet tea and rice pudding, brought to us in bed, helped dispel the squalor of our surroundings. Marie Christine told us that, as usual, she had been dreaming of luxury. One empty doorway in our room opened straight on to the street, and M.C. and Bec were unhappy at the attention they received from the village children while they were dressing. We noticed the children were

The villagers of Huanchullo. Jesus on horseback

The horse which couldn't carry the load. Huanchullo

Above left: Cutthroat saltmine. Cachicunga

Above right: Tarantula on Dry Ridge

Left: Half-way down from Dry Ridge to the rafting point on the Apurimac River

much prettier here, not quite so bluntly Quechuan-looking as on the Altiplano. Perhaps Europeans had worked in this fertile valley —or maybe it was just a result of trading in a big market town like Abancay. Again, the cause could have been a better diet.

Huanipaca stands on an island of land high above the south side of the Apurimac. Only two good days' walking from here, the Pachachaca joined the Apurimac, and our aim was to cross the Apurimac on a raft a short distance upstream of the junction. In the old days the raft had ceased to operate each year with the onset of the rainy season, at the end of October, and it had started again only in March. But now I was pinning my faith on an all-year-round wire cable strung above the river, which had apparently replaced the *balsa*, as rafts are called in Peru, being made from balsa logs.

The Three Rs, dressed in green waterproof ponchos, hopped across the puddles in the square and headed for the village office, hoping to arrange mules for our onward move to the Cachicunga salt mine. A high ceiling accentuated the bareness of the office: an out-of-date calendar for Coca Cola looked down from whitewashed walls on a couple of typewriters set on dusty tables; these were attended by a young secretary in horn-rimmed glasses, who looked as if she really ran the place. The office occupied the middle room of a tall, ramshackle building, adjacent to a large locked white twin-towered church, which had been re-roofed with corrugated iron, as if to put it into mothballs.

I didn't anticipate difficulty over hiring mules. Each animal carries two fifty-kilo blocks of salty rock down to Huanipaca, whence it is exported by truck. The mules return unladen to the mine for another cargo, and I reckoned that carrying our kit could prove a nice windfall for some muleteer.

'The mine is closed, señor,' said Sylvestre, the slim, young *gobernador*. 'The rains make the path too slippery for the mules, you see. What falls as rain down here makes snow and ice up there.' He nodded in the direction of the mountain pass in the mist above. An easy-going, take-it-or-leave-it sort of fellow, he then admitted that a few mules were still operating 'now and then', and that the next day or two could see a team coming in with salt.

We decided to wait, and Sylvestre suggested we stay in the village hall, next to his office. 'Dusty wooden floor, pale grey walls, and high, whitewashed ceiling,' I had written fifteen years earlier. 'The long room was completely bare save for a large wooden table under the big window at the far end, an old Empire sofa, and a Peruvian flag on a long wooden pole propped up in one corner.'

Now the Peruvian flag had been removed and two hydro-powered light bulbs hung naked from the ceiling, but otherwise the room was much as it had been all those years before. Like the village as a whole, it looked less tidy, with corrugated iron sheets coated in cement dust piled in one corner. To us, however, it had great possibilities: for a start it was ordure-free, and a deal better than the accommodation of the previous few nights.

Walking round the village with M.C. and Bec, I was struck by the misery of it all, the rain, mist and mud serving to intensify the squalor of the place. The children's bare feet were clogged with yellow mud, and they all seemed to have runny noses. Pigs, cows, turkeys and chickens were scattered everywhere; they rushed to eat most things, but tin cans and plastic were too much for them, so that the spaces between the smelly open drains were littered with rubbish. Lush hedges grew pink, yellow and white roses, and there was a fair sprinkling of red trumpet flowers and huge white waxy bells; it was like walking through Devonshire lanes on a wet day in high summer when the Council had been on strike for several months.

We came across a young female schoolteacher, feeding her tots their maize-bean lunchtime gruel from a black pot on an open wood fire at the end of their school building. The children were having a great time, rushing about getting the wood and tending the pot. After squatting to taste some of the gruel, I stood up and found myself almost collapsing with dizziness. We'd all commented on this problem, which was a much exaggerated form of what we normally felt at home. We attributed the trouble to altitude.

Far from being prosperous, the village appeared to have gone to seed since the agrarian reforms. The valley is fertile, but the people looked drunk and disorganised. Raw alcohol, such as we used for starting the primus stoves in place of meths, was being dispensed from a forty-gallon drum in the street, to beaten old men whose hands trembled so much that their tins clattered against the tap on the drum.

As we'd found out, trucks came infrequently from the outside world; and several people, like our salt-buying friends, spent days hanging about the square, waiting for transport to get them away from the place. Abandoned stand-pipes bore witness to the breakdown of the water supply. The compact little hydro-scheme wasn't functioning properly either, and dead street lighting wires sagged from post to post. How much foreign aid had been wasted here? There was no pride left in the place; people lived only from day to day, earning just enough to subsist—no more.

By the time we'd got back to the hall and met the two boys, we felt exhausted; so all five of us set off for lunch in one of the tin shacks lining the opposite side of the square from the church and hall. We chose a particular stall by the size of the *mama* running the place: we reckoned she must be a good cook to maintain her own enormous proportions. She cooked on a wood fire with several black iron pots and lived behind a partition in one end of the tiny hut.

Her steaming soup was a delicious mix of potatoes, cabbage, pasta, parsley, and a local herb which added a slightly tart lemon flavour. Sitting on benches at her bare wood table, we lingered as long as possible over enamel mugs of hot sweet black coffee. Through the open front of the shack we watched rain falling steadily on the muddy grass of the square.

In the afternoon we went shopping and a woman in one cavernous store provided dried broad beans, potatoes and a litre of paraffin. When we asked the price, she insisted it was a gift in return for some kindness we had shown her in 1970. I couldn't recall the occasion, but it was more than likely she received medical treatment from Mac, our Army medic, who had carried a large stock of medicines and usually tried to hold a surgery wherever we went.

In the late afternoon the rain stopped and the sun came out, revealing a magnificent panorama of snow-covered mountains on the far side of the valley. A teacher asked us to play volleyball, and while we waited for school to finish for the day he pointed out an area of forest below the glaciers coming down from Choquequira. There were apparently unexplored Inca ruins in the trees, and I thought of returning some day to look for them.

The volleyball drew a large crowd, and we made several new friends among the villagers, who loved a laugh. We won the hard-fought match, largely because we were lucky enough to have three of the best teachers to make up a team with Justin, Ed and me.

To our surprise Humberto showed up for the game, under the eagle eye of his wife, a tall, handsome teacher who wore high leather boots and dark glasses covering a poisoned eye. We saw that Humberto was popular for his legendary idleness and flamboyant manner, but we were never really sure of him.

We slept well in our spacious new surroundings until, at 6am, Ed sprang up to answer a hammering on the door. It was our two friends, the salt buyers, come to tell us a mule-train was leaving for the mine within the hour.

'If that's true—I'll blow me brains out!' I said. And it wasn't. No mules were going to Cachicunga. We settled down for another day in the rain at Huanipaca. We were getting bogged down, losing our momentum.

Chapter Fourteen

There must always be a balance—a balance between pessimism and optimism. I like to prepare for the worst. But those around me in Huanipaca urged me not to be too pessimistic, and I was coming round to their way of thinking. We were in Peru for a holiday; we had no compelling reason to risk life and limb; and, after all, if we felt like it, we could simply catch a plane and fly home.

Marie Christine complains that every holiday with me has to turn into a drama. The village of Huanipaca showed no signs of drama, but I forced myself to calm down and accept things for what they were: the fate of the world did not depend on what we were doing at all. Besides, Rebecca's health was improving with every day of rest.

While we were finishing our breakfast, a young teacher in a dripping blue anorak called in for a red plastic bowl which he'd lent us for washing up. I told him our plight: no guides and no mules. He smiled that beam of sunshine they all do so well and told me it was *no problema*—in fact, he'd fix it before school started for the day. Ten minutes later he returned with Jesus, a rather cocksure seventeen-year-old schoolboy, whose soaking shirt clung to his chest.

We soon concluded a deal. Jesus would supply three mules to carry our rucksacks and guide us to Cachicunga salt mine (the third mule was in case Becca had to ride). Our start would be delayed until dawn on Saturday, as the boy could hardly say he was going to play truant in front of his teacher. We thanked both teacher and pupil, and they set off in the rain for the *colegio*, or secondary school.

The noise on the porch outside had been rising for some time, as little children from the primary school gathered before lessons to stare at the blue-eyed, fair-haired *gringos*. These children found us a source of constant fascination and were forever trying to get into the hall or peer in through the windows at us. In particular, they loved to play with *La Rebecca*. Now they persuaded us to go to school with them, but when we walked into their dark little classroom we found the teacher had yet to arrive. So, while we waited, we gave a spirited rendition of 'Zipedeedooda' and 'Good King Wenceslas' and the children responded with '*Escuela mía*'.

When at last the young male teacher arrived, he straight away insisted we write our names and addresses on the blackboard, and I realised he was drunk. This made us all a little gloomy, and we returned to the hall feeling low.

We passed a miserable day in a miserable place. In fact it was so cold in the afternoon that Becca crawled back into her sleeping-bag. Ed and Justin did their best to amuse themselves by promoting catapult competitions against the locals, trying to knock tiny piles of stones off distant walls. M.C. and I spent much of the time drinking mugs of coffee at a wretched little stall where a skinny mother cooked and served, and in the intervals tended her sick baby which lay bawling on the dirt floor.

The evening was much better. After supper we were just thinking of turning in when three teachers arrived unexpectedly. They had come through heavy rains in the dark to entertain us: so we sat them down on the Empire sofa, against the end wall in the huge bare room, and by the light of three candle stubs the concert began.

Walter, who sat in the middle, was the most versatile of the trio. On a simple bamboo flute he played sad, haunting Quechuan music which reminded Marie Christine and Becca of Bach, Tallis and Byrd. Now and then the other teachers supported the flute with songs, but Ed and I had to battle against our drowsiness. From our side came our familiar little repertoire of songs, and although the Peruvians were polite enough to clap, it was a little like the Hammersmith Palais trying to challenge the Wigmore Hall.

It rained again on the Friday, and Jesus missed school for the day on the pretext of helping us with our packing. He even told us we would be leaving at two o'clock that afternoon, but in the end he couldn't get the mules, and so we found ourselves back on the volleyball court when the rain finally cleared at five.

We heard little mention of terrorists in Huanipaca. In their remote valley, surrounded by high mountains, the villagers seemed pre-occupied with their own problems. There was, however, just one hint of the troubles which lay ahead. When I went to try to persuade Humberto to turn out for the volleyball, he was standing in front of his new house, calling up to his young son, who was trying to lay clay tiles up on the roof.

Humberto was reluctant to play—and then abruptly he changed the subject. 'Señor Juan—*no hay balsa!*'

'*No hay balsa?*' I joked. '*No hay problema!*' I wasn't going to let him think I was worried.

Humberto's eyes hardened. '*No hay cable! Nada!*' [No cable—nothing at all.]

That stopped me in my tracks: no raft and no cable either? How would Humberto know that? No one else in the village had made the slightest suggestion we might have problems crossing the river. But the street was not the place for cross-examination, so I made light of the whole business. Humberto did not show up at the volleyball, and we never saw him again.

On the day of our departure, Jesus got off to a bad start. Crashing into the hall at five in the morning, he ordered us to get moving, and we could see he had all the makings of another bully. Justin had lent his new playing cards to Jesus's school friend, on the understanding that the friend was coming with us to the salt mine. Now it was clear Justin had been fooled: there was now no friend and no pack of cards. There were no mules either, but Jesus told us they were waiting on the outskirts of the village. So we had to scramble up the mountainside behind our new-found Hitler, who made no offer to help M.C. or Bec with their loads, and I could see Ed's eyelid beginning to twitch with annoyance.

'This is my wife,' said Jesus, nodding at a bright-looking, fifteen-year-old Indian girl in cardigan and green army trousers, who was standing patiently beside a small white horse and a rather stronger mule. 'She is coming with us.' I mentioned the lack of a third animal, but Jesus just shrugged arrogantly. He surprised me by showing little idea of how to load the beasts, and once we got going up the hill on equal terms, it was he who fell behind.

After half an hour we paused for a break, waiting for him. Below us, grey smoke filtered thickly through the thatched roofs of the village, and with the snow-covered mountains in the background the view was every bit as grand as the memory I'd carried over the years.

It took us one and a quarter hours to climb up through bushes and trees to the clear grassland on the pass; luckily the ground wasn't too slippery in the deep gulley cut by thousands of mule trains. Jesus was far behind with the animals, and Justin and Ed were sticking with him to see there was no funny business. M.C. and Becca were going well. Jesus's wife's name was Emilia, and she was a deal fitter than her husband of a few months, who was already complaining of a sore stomach and being described accurately by Ed as 'a bit of a wimp'.

When he joined us on the pass, Jesus suggested we stop for a meal further down the trail, and we agreed a price with an old man who walked on ahead to warn his wife of our arrival. After the green of the valley, the pass was bleak, and we weren't sorry to dip down into the bushes again. Fifteen minutes' walk brought us to a primitive stone hut beside a stream. Inside, a tough old woman gestured us to sit on ponchos of black and red llama wool, which she spread on the beaten earth floor. As she began counting potatoes from a sack, I ran my forefinger down the glistening brown neck of a plump hen which had snuggled against the wall behind some sacks.

'I expect we'll soon be eating this,' I joked—and sure enough the woman turned and picked up the bird. Holding it firmly under her left arm, she closed her right hand over its head, as if to comfort it. Then she peered out through the front door, and we thought was waiting for her daughter to come back with more vegetables.

'I think it's dead!' exclaimed Bec, as the woman suddenly put the inert creature on a pile of sticks by the fire.

'She must have suffocated it with her right hand,' said Ed. Certainly the bird made no move when the woman plunged it into a pot of boiling water on the fire to loosen the feathers for plucking.

After a good chicken stew, and several mugs of camomile tea, we set off in high spirits. I remembered the journey from Huanipaca to the salt mine as one of the longest days of the 1970 expedition; which was why I had been prepared to wait for guides and mules. But now, I realised, Jesus was taking us along the wrong side of the valley for Cachicunga; and when Emilia asked us for medicine for her husband's sore head, she let slip that we weren't going to Cachicunga at all, but staying the night in her home village of Huanchullo.

This disagreeable diversion apart, we had a glorious walk, down through increasingly jungly vegetation. As we descended there was always a sense of anticipation; and the day was made all the more enjoyable for me by the pleasure that Marie Christine found in the great variety of wild tropical flowers. Orange lilies and catmint both appeared for the first time; humming birds were quite common now, and we were on the look-out for the flocks of green parakeets which I knew couldn't be far away.

Emilia was greeted warmly as she entered her village with her new husband; people flocked out from their houses, and this suited Jesus's ego very well. A slim, dark teacher called Stanislaus made us most welcome. He showed us to a clean and tidy classroom in a well-run, shiny tin-roofed school with blue doors, and the glassless windows even had neat orange shutters. We laid out sleeping-bags on the wooden floor and read the motto written in copper-plate script over the inside of the door: 'Children are the Springtime of Life'.

Stanislaus invited M.C., Becca and me to join him for a little *dragi*, which we took to be something like a Scottish 'drammie'. So we walked across a field and sat waiting on a log, while he directed a group of villagers who were energetically building a massive log stile in a fence that kept cattle from straying on to the school football pitch. There was evidently some disagreement over design, so we took that opportunity to have a good look at our surroundings. Huanchullo lies in a fertile valley, a day's walk from the nearest motor vehicle, and we were surprised at the abundance of livestock and neatly ploughed fields. Everything looked peaceful and well-ordered, and yet I could see from the map that we were getting close to the emergency zone. Mountains and valleys are on a vast scale in Peru; and in this case there was the added barrier of the Apurimac river, imposing a natural border between the departments of Apurimac, where we were, and Cuzco on the north bank. More and more we had the feeling that, by crossing the river, we would be going into a foreign land.

Eventually Stanislaus resolved his difficulties with the stile-builders and apologetically offered us some of the same fierce *aguardiente* the workmen were drinking. By its taste, it might well have come from the forty-gallon drum in Huanipaca. Wobbling a little, we separated: M.C. and Bec to try and buy stores from the villagers, and I to bathe in the stream.

Mother and daughter visited several huts, some with gardens of pinks and pansies and a few bushes of heavy white hanging bells, but nobody would sell eggs or potatoes. Eventually they found a kind old lady who said she could provide something. She claimed she had a hundred guinea pigs running about her hut; with paper-thin hands she drew four eggs from a hanging bowl and a few potatoes from a box. Stanislaus also brought us some potatoes and carrots, and Ed cooked a giant meal of boiled vegetables. A middle-aged couple and two little children knocked on the door with a bowl of warm, cooked maize, and we asked them in for coffee and a chat.

Next day was Sunday, 17 November, and we wanted to reach the rafting point by nightfall, so we were happy to go along with Jesus's plan to move as quickly as possible to the salt mine. He needed to be back in Huanipaca for school on Monday morning, and hoped to return by another route, loading his animals with fruit on the way to ensure a good profit when he reached home.

There was a bit of a scrum at the start. Emilia and another girl were riding horses, and our kit was all on Jesus's horse and mule. With mounting excitement we set off towards an area which looked like Conan Doyle's Lost World. We soon passed out of Huanchullo, its neat little properties fenced with wicked barbed sisal leaves. Our side valley was running west into the deep, deserted gorge of the Pachachaca river. Keeping to the high ground, we headed north, with the desiccated Pachachaca on our left and the mighty rain forests of the Apurimac on our right. The mountains across the Pachachaca looked arid and unforgiving—slabbed cliffs falling sheer for thousands of feet, unvisited by man but patrolled by sinister condors.

Jesus had often told us there would be no water at the Cachicunga salt mine, but we forgot to drink, so engrossed were we with the grandeur of our surroundings and the physical demands of keeping up with the girls on horseback. Around noon we came upon a solitary hut set in a desert plateau on top of the ridge, and Jesus tried to tell us this was the salt mine. I knew different, and we began a blazing row, which petered out only when he left us at the mine proper, a further hour along the trail.

With Jesus gone, I took stock of our situation. Dizzy with reaction and fatigue in the midday sun, I realised how I had fuelled my progress with rage. We slumped on our rucksacks, peeling tiny boiled potatoes for lunch and bemoaning our lack of drinking water. The mine was not more than a small hole in the red and white rock, and an Indian miner and his ten-year-old son were hacking away with axe and shovel to cut one fifty-kilo block an hour. There was nothing else—no building of any kind. When I scrambled down into the hole, the miner looked anxious, and I guessed he was thinking the odds were five to one against him. Running with sweat, and covered with salt, he tried to find out what we wanted to know: then he gave us the answer most likely to get us on our way. Our communication was limited to place names, grunts and gestures, since we spoke no common language.

He told us the cable was not operating, but the raft was. We should be able to reach it in two hours, maybe an hour and a half, if we moved *rápido*.

Rejoining the others, I felt stiff and dehydrated. We sucked on a shrivelled orange each and nibbled a few grains of cold boiled maize while the first few biting black-fly nibbled at us. There was nothing to be gained by waiting. The Apurimac might be the first place for water; a check revealed two-thirds of a bottle with M.C., and about the same with Ed and me, but none with Becca or Justin.

The packs were heavy, yet oddly reassuring; we were on our own again, five people moving as one, towards the back door.

Retracing our steps up the steeply-rutted path for a quarter of a mile, we found a good route through cactus and thorny bushes to the spine of the ridge. From this splendid vantage point we were able to plan our route. I fished out my Zeiss monocular and we each had a go at spying out the land; it was important that we should all agree before we started walking.

The dry, dusty ridge pointed like a finger into a narrow U-bend in the river, some 5,000 feet below us. On the far side, perhaps 3,000 feet above the water, we could clearly see our destination, the village of Pacaypata.

We could spot no definite path down to the raft, and the only practical way forward seemed to be along the spine of the ridge, where there was least vegetation.

Thirst got us moving once more. We found the going easy at first, downhill through sparse cactus and bushes, though the sun was hot. When the spine narrowed into something approaching a knife-edge, we followed a steep but reasonable path, which was marked here and there with old animal-droppings, and this gave us hope of a track all the way to the raft. We even came upon signs of a fire and camp site, though they could have been months or years old.

I led all the time, keeping the pace down, and the thicket grew steadily harder to penetrate. With collar up and cuffs fastened, I went head-down, crash on, bullocking my way through dry branches. Once or twice we retraced our steps, hoping to find a better route. Then we reached the first of the small hills on the ridge, and progress became still more difficult as we had to force a way through the bushes while scrambling up crumbling cliffs of dust.

Compared with the men, M.C. and Bec were carrying disproportionately heavy loads for their own body weight, and they found the clinging undergrowth claustrophobic; the dense bushes and uncertain footholds made keeping their balance even more difficult.

We tried altering formation to clear a better path for M.C. and Bec. I led, with Ed and Justin behind me, then Bec and finally M.C. I was annoyed to see that my shirt and trousers were torn, and the coating of dust was an irritation. Our heavy sweating worried me too, as we were so short of drinking water.

Sinking back on the bushes, we stopped for a break halfway up a short cliff. Ed caught my eye; nodding his head back towards Becca, he rubbed his cheek a couple of times to show she was in tears. While the rest of us lay back and rested, Becca was too frightened of falling to try and sit down. I realised I'd better come up with something.

The outlook was grim. We'd left the salt mine at 1.15pm and it was already 5pm. The river was still at least 2,000 feet below, and both sides of the ridge were densely overgrown precipices. It would be dark in another hour. Like it or not, we must stop for the night—without water.

We kept on along the ridge until we came down on to a

narrow, level saddle, and here we started looking for somewhere to lay out the bivvy bags.

'Becca—tarantula—photograph!' I stopped in my tracks. The black, hairy spider was about six inches long and a foot from my right boot. Bec came forward and took photos from as close as eighteen inches. I decided there was not much wrong with her.

'You'll be glad of the puttees now,' I said. 'There'll be snakes in here as well. They like dusty places, don't they?' My insistence on the old fashioned leg-wrappings had been something of a joke with the others.

'Only certain species of tarantula are deadly poisonous, you know,' Justin called up the line as we continued along the ridge.

'Yes, but how do we know which ones?' asked Ed.

A hundred yards further, we found ourselves at the foot of another steep little cliff.

'Well, this is as far as we can reasonably get from the spider,' I said, tramping down the brush. 'Let's find the best space we can for five, close together.'

'Here's another, John!' Marie Christine couldn't quite keep the quaver out of her voice, and we all moved cautiously towards her. This time it was a ginger fellow, fully as big as the other. Justin nudged it with the end of a stave he used to steady himself on the steep sections, but the spider darted only a short distance.

'Let's hope they're not a courting couple, meeting halfway by moonlight,' I said, as we retraced our steps to a piece of level ground.

This bit of excitement was just what we needed to take our minds off our predicament. Only after we had laid out the bags did we begin to feel sorry for ourselves. We were all exhausted and suffering from sunburn, and our toes were sore from the sharp descent. Our urine had turned the deep yellow which comes with dehydration, and our mouths were gummy with thirst. Water was our greatest need.

The biting black-flies had got us all, and they would continue biting while we remained below 6,000 feet. We all had little spots of blood on most areas of naked skin, so far the only trace of their painless attack. The inflammation begins some hours after the bite and swells into hard, intensely itchy lumps which last for days and sometimes weeks. Scratching in sleep often leads to infection, which can soon become disabling in the tropics. For the first time we had mosquitos buzzing round us. These insects have caused more damage to the human race than any other creature, and I knew there were many cases of malaria in the upper Apurimac valley.

No one of these irritations is too bad, but it is their cumulative effect over a lengthy period which can bring a team down.

We were now less than a mile from the northern end of the ridge. It was a poor view for the thirsty. The yellow-brown band of the Apurimac lay below us on both sides and round the northern end of the ridge, the rapids generating a continuous roar from deep within the gorge. Crystal waterfalls traced brilliant white lines against the succulent greens of the tropical rain-forest which clothed the mountainsides to the north of the river. Even the tops of the mountains were covered with water—great caps and glaciers of snow and ice surrounding our position on three sides. But we to the south of the river were barren dry, the mountains stark red, brown, yellow and black.

For supper we divided a tin of sardines, a small tin of evaporated milk and two-thirds of a pint of water from Ed's bottle. We also sucked every last drop of moisture from a small raw white cabbage. I was now particularly glad we had spent the weeks training together on the Altiplano.

By seven o'clock we were all zipped up in our bivvy bags to avoid the mosquitos. But my feet were burning after the long downhill trek, and by eight I was out of my clothes and lying on top of the sleeping-bag, though still zipped in the bivvy bag.

Rebecca was jammed in between M.C. and me. 'Stop fidgeting, Dad!' she muttered.

I unzipped my bag and felt the cool night air on my face. I couldn't hear a single mosquito. 'I think it may rain. The thunder's much closer to the lightning now,' I said, reaching out with my hand to check that my mess tins were ready to catch any of the precious stuff that fell.

Chapter Fifteen

I woke at midnight, my leathery tongue scraping about inside my mouth. I reached out and rattled my mess tins: there had been no rain. The thunder and lightning had ceased; perhaps it never rained south of the river. Everyone else was sound asleep.

Two hours later I awoke in a tropical downpour. With only the thin Goretex bivvy bag between my skin and the drumming rain, I couldn't believe I wasn't getting wet. Then I realised I was. A tiny trickle of water was finding its way through the zip by my head: that was what had woken me. I tried stemming the rivulet with a handkerchief, and turned on to my left side to deflect the flow.

Everyone else was awake, and, with the exception of Ed's, which was a different design, all our bags were taking water. Over the noise of the rain we discussed ideas for keeping the flood out, but mopping it up seemed the favourite. At M.C.'s suggestion I tried sucking my handkerchief for the moisture. Unable to sleep, I lay cocooned in the bivvy bag, wondering what on earth I was doing, risking the lives of my wife and daughter in such a place. As an adopted child myself, I worked out that Rebecca was my only blood relative: how could I have brought her here?

The rain cooled the air, and I began to shiver. By 3.20 I was so cold that I had to wriggle into the linen sleeping-bag liner during a lull in the rain. We shared the collected rainwater, fishy from the sardines in the mess tins, and metallic in the saucepans. Glumly we realised that we could have collected much more if we'd set up the waterproof ponchos.

At 4.30 I slid into my sleeping-bag, trying to warm up. It was wet from the leak, and I felt sticky and dirty. Half an hour later Ed and Justin sprang into life and began to make breakfast. It had not been the best of nights.

'I'm soaked, I'm getting up,' muttered Bec. It was just light, and as we sat up and began to dress I saw that both Bec and M.C. had their hair slicked down on their heads by the rain. Neither had been keen to open their zips in case a tarantula crept in.

Ed made an important discovery when he found water trapped in sisal leaves where they joined the stem of the plant. If you bent them down, the water trickled back along the leaf and into your mug. He rapidly filled a water bottle, and his enthusiasm helped us all. Justin was quietly cooking the breakfast, sympathetic and kind as ever.

I felt dreadfully stiff and immobile, and there was the familiar dizziness which came with standing up too suddenly. But an almost-dry shave, with the help of Justin's badger brush, and a good effort at polishing my boots helped get me going again. In spite of the water shortage, M.C. insisted we all clean our teeth; we needed to brace ourselves for a long day.

We drank the last bottle of water between us, shared a bit of hard, white cheese and cold maize, and set off along the ridge. The sun was already heating and drying, brewing a regular steaming jungle, and a large flock of black swallows looked as if they were surfing on the billowing banks of mist which filled the valley around us.

After an initial stiff pull up on to the knoll on the ridge, we were faced with a steep descent through slender saplings set in crumbling, dusty soil. The ground fell away sheer on all sides. M.C. pointed out the white, scented lilies growing out of the dust: they looked like the kind you find on coffins. Becca found it hard going, and it was all she could do to blink back her tears, but Justin was a great support, using his stick to steady them both.

When we stopped for a break on an open, level patch, masses

of huge ants began crawling over the rucksacks. Brushing away insects was to become part of our life. We were now desperately keen to get down to the water, but could not see a way. Worse, I could not remember exactly where the rafting point was, and unless we reached the water's edge close to the right place, we could easily find ourselves hemmed in by cliffs at the bottom of the gorge. A vivid green burst of about fifty parakeets screeched by, mocking our plight.

After separate recces, none of us had been able to see the path that Marie Christine was firmly convinced she had spotted. If she was correct, we had only to make a straight descent of the eastern side of the ridge to cross the track on its way to the raft.

It was 9.30 in the morning, and we still believed we would reach the river in a couple of hours at most. The ten foot high sisal plants were not too difficult to negotiate, once we'd got the hang of pushing 'with' the barbs, which faced in towards the central stem. We had gathered quite a bit of water from them so far, but now the sun had opened the leaves like octopus's arms and they had mostly shed their water.

I led the way, and thirst became an all-consuming topic as we bashed down through trailing, clinging brush. Once through the sisal, there was nothing for it but to lean on the brittle scrub until it gave way.

'Jesus Christ!' My left leg felt on fire. Had I been bitten by a snake? I jumped back, uphill. The rucksack felt quite weightless. Falling into the bushes, I looked down at my leg. Tell-tale prickles reassured me: this was the giant stinging nettle about which Elvin had warned us in 1970; he had always insisted we keep our sleeves rolled down, and now I knew why. Once I knew what it was, the pain seemed to recede a bit. The plant had a stem like a leafless Brussels sprout stalk, but covered with a fine down of glass-like splinters.

'Make sure you keep clear of those things,' I muttered, hauling myself to my feet. I wondered how much longer I should keep leading: it was taking a lot out of me. The heat, dust, sweat and above all the thirst were damaging my judgment. An hour and a half after leaving the ridge we reached a ravine; we could either go back up and round the top, or try and get down the cliff into the bottom. Foolishly, I decided to try the cliff.

It was now 11am, and the route called for mobility and confidence. M.C. and Bec had neither. Their packs were too heavy for their strength, so that they could only lurch from one difficulty to another. Rocks and stones fell with every step, and the only security lay where slender tree trunks emerged from the ground here and there on the nearly-vertical, crumbling slope.

While Ed and Justin encouraged M.C. and Bec down the easiest route available, I cut off to the right in an attempt to speed things up, hoping that once I reached the bottom I would be able to come up to meet the others. I moved swiftly and easily across the face—too swiftly and too easily. I reached a point where I was hanging with both arms round a tree, unable to go on or back, my rucksack pulling me out and over the edge.

My strength ebbed fast. A fall would mean injury or worse. I decided to drop the rucksack while I could, aiming it for another tree some fifteen feet below. After severe wriggling I had one arm round the tree and the rucksack hanging from the other. The rucksack fell, bounced off the tree and cartwheeled into space, down and down: the sound of its crashing lasted some time after it had gone from sight, leaving a trail of its contents for us to follow. Guiltily I thought about what I would have said if someone else had committed this act of folly, but at least I lived to fight for the rest of the day.

I felt my colours were fast running dry. Without the rucksack it didn't take me long to reach the bottom of the face, but I had little strength to help M.C. and Becca, who were both terrified. Ed looked ashen with fatigue, after making heroic efforts to help, and Justin, who had joined us by a lower route, was also feeling the strain. One slip could be fatal. Rocks and stones kept roaring past me. It was like being on a cliff in the middle of a gigantic hedge. There was no sign of water, and the river seemed as far distant as ever.

I passed up a safety line and presently, exhausted, thirsty and very frightened, M.C. and Bec at last reached the bottom of the ravine. This little saga of a couple of hundred feet took us three hours, from 11am until 2pm. We were now all completely done-in. A desperate search for water produced a quantity of stagnant liquid from an old sisal plant; stained deep brown by rotting leaves, it made me retch.

After a rest we continued our slow descent through the thicket, picking up hats and finally coming to my rucksack. I'd been lucky: one of the two flap-securing straps had been torn from the bag, but the frame was only bent and I soon twisted it back into shape. Apart from the odd shirt and other articles of clothing, which marked the route to the pack itself, the stuff-bags containing my few possessions were intact inside. My blue Karrimat was torn, but nothing was broken or lost.

Of the path there was no sign. Our paramount need now was water, so, with under four hours of daylight remaining, we agreed on a straight line approach to the river. Occasionally we caught glimpses of it, enticing as fast-flowing iced coffee. The undergrowth grew thicker, with more and more bamboo, the giant stinging nettles more numerous, the vegetation greener and less brittle. We decided to take turns at breaking the trail. Justin led first. He looked extraordinarily thin now, like a stick insect with a red-banded black trilby, and I wondered if he would have the weight to force a path. But he used his long stave to good effect, and I found the going much easier. I had time to look back up the massive slab of mountainside: what would happen if we had to return all the way back up to the salt mine?

Once more we found ourselves on a spur, once more we were uncertain which side to descend. Justin roved ahead, while we sat on our rucksacks.

'I'm on a path!' Justin's muffled cry of triumph came up through the jungle. It seemed like a miracle, but a path it was—or rather, it had been. Slumped in the undergrowth beside a foot wide strip of red-brown earth, we could see it stretch no more than fifty feet in either direction. So overgrown was the route that we could easily have stepped across it without ever knowing it was there.

I led the way, zig-zagging down the path, praying it would not peter out. Now and then it was blocked by a fallen tree, or I lost it on a sharp hairpin bend, but always we came back on to it. The roar of the river grew louder and louder. Desperate as we were with thirst, it seemed as if by some cruel trick the water was retreating before us. But at last there were no more zig-zags to negotiate, and we emerged from the undergrowth, out on to the steep, rocky bank.

'The rock puddles'll be okay. We can drink them without sterilising,' shouted Ed, his voice almost drowned by the solid roar of brown water, some forty yards wide. We dropped our gear and knelt, gulping handfuls from the little clear pools of last night's rain.

Our initial thirst slaked, we paused to think out our next move. There was absolutely no sign of raft or cable. The sheer power of the flood seemed to rule out any question of us crossing on our own. Had we missed a fork in the path, perhaps a couple of hundred feet above the water? Marie Christine was still convinced the path continued down-river, at least to a point directly opposite the village, which was now out of sight and high above us. Coming from the original discoverer of the path, her views won much credence.

We had just two hours before nightfall. Justin and Ed agreed to have a bathe in the river and then make a short recce, to try to put our minds at rest. Bec, M.C. and I bathed and set about lighting a fire on the shore to cook supper. There was plenty of driftwood—and plenty of biting black-fly, too. We set up both Milbank bags, and the silt-laden river water slowly filtered through the canvas into a mess tin. I wasn't feeling well, whether from dehydration, too much sun, the brown sisal water, or just plain old-fashioned worry, I don't know. I was sick six times in the river, and then crawled into my bivvy bag among the rocks on the bank.

I lay half-awake, a water-bottle and a packet of Dextrosol at my head, with knife and torch. How nice it was having Marie Christine and Becca along with me. There was none of the homesickness of my non-stop sail round the world a couple of years before. The river thundered along by my side, the roar reverberating in the gorge; even though I was wedged in the rocks, I did feel a little anxious about rolling over into the water in the night. I just wanted to sleep.

'No sign of a path, John,' Ed's voice cut into my drowsiness. 'We had a good look down the shore . . .'

'What about the raft or cable?'

'Nothing.'

'All right, let's get some sleep. We'll make an early start and work our way down-river, before the sun heats the gorge in the morning.' It wasn't the best news to go to sleep on, but at least everyone had survived the day. I took one last look upstream: the salt mine mountain reared high into the cold night sky. Anything to avoid climbing back up there.

The night went well. I awoke once or twice for a sip of water and a Dextrosol tablet, letting the lemon glucose fizz sweetly on my tongue. Although it rained quite heavily, I managed to escape any leaks into my bivvy bag. Bec and M.C. were both up at five in the morning, but I felt tired and turned on my side, planning to sleep on until breakfast.

'*Aiieee!*' Becca's scream jerked me into a sitting position. 'There's a huge tarantula by Ed's clothes! It's crept into a crack in the rock. It was bigger than the ones on the ridge.' Her voice returned to normal as she spoke, but we all looked nervously around to see if any other furry friends were crawling about nearby.

There was further alarm when Marie Christine discovered a collection of six-inch stinging millipedes under her Karrimat. But they, too, scuttled to safety among the rocks.

The whole team was tired from the exertions of the previous couple of days, and tempers were short. The black-fly were biting, and I was worried about the number of bites Justin was taking on his unprotected skin. He had yet to realise the irritation they would become. I felt weak, and my stomach was telling me it was allergic to the chlorine water-sterilising tablets. Bec and M.C. took over cooking the breakfast from Justin; the fire lit best with small twigs and seed pods, but cleaning the blackened mess tins delayed our departure. Just packing our kit was exhausting in the trapped heat of the chasm.

We didn't get away until ten o'clock—pretty slow going, considering the breakfast-makers had been up at five. But we all felt it couldn't take long to cover the half mile to the river bend. Ed was in the lead, as he had done the recce, then came Justin, Becca and M.C. I brought up the rear. It was terribly hot. The sun seemed to vibrate within the walls of the canyon. Skirting round house-sized boulders, we soon came upon a simple bamboo frame and a few ancient horse droppings. It was probably a fishing shelter, and it must have been used since the floods of the previous winter. But had the fisherman crossed the river, or had he returned up the long hill to the salt mine? Surely the former: no one could be so keen to fish that he would make a special trip to this place, unless he was going to use the raft or cable.

Further along the shore the boulders became progressively harder to negotiate with our heavy packs, and frequently we had to swing out over the boiling, muddy waters to work round a difficult corner. Becca's imagination began to get the worst of her, and we had tears. Justin's stave, stretched across the gap and held at either end by M.C. and Ed, solved the problem. But things wouldn't have to get much worse.

At the far end of the bend, high on the opposite bank, a two-storey mud hut came into view. I had the feeling I knew it, yet somehow I couldn't quite make it fit my memory of 1970. My mind was absorbed with the boulder problems and we constantly scanned the bank for a path, which M.C. was still sure must exist. Justin left his pack with us and scrambled up a landslide, disappearing into the jungle, but after ten minutes he came sliding back down in a cloud of dust, having had no luck.

We sat in the sun for a while, feeling shattered by the heat. A flock of bright-green parakeets flew screeching up and down the river: we counted more than fifty, and wondered if they were the birds we'd seen the day before, on the other side of the ridge.

We dragged ourselves to our feet and set off, scuffing our feet in the sandbars, the black-fly nibbling away at every chance. Ahead lay a cliff: starting off as an unstable bank of clay, it stretched downstream into a sheer rock face. As Ed had predicted, there was no way round the end.

'The old back door trick, eh?' I muttered to myself. 'You silly twit!' It was 11am. We'd been going for an hour. The bottom of the canyon was like an inferno. The river had risen in the night, and I knew it would go on rising for months, as the rains set in. It was 19 November, and I remembered the salt mine manager in 1970 telling me the *balsero* never operated his raft between the end of October and the beginning of March, as the river was too dangerous.

I plodded along at the back. A couple of hundred yards to the cliff, and another battle with Ed would begin. I was feeling weak and helpless.

Chapter Sixteen

Then came a miracle.

'There's the raft—over there—behind the rocks!' Marie Christine shouted, pointing across the river. The others could not have heard—they kept shuffling on. I peered along my wife's arm: the opposite bank looked featureless, a continuous tumble of vast rocks, gouged, polished and rolled by the racing torrent.

'Look—just in that little bay, downstream of the big rock.'

I looked again, and then something happened, as if I were watching a frozen, trick camera shot in a television quiz. In an instant I saw everything: not only the ends of the balsa logs which made the raft, poking from behind the end of a tiny, natural rock harbour, but the entire scene. It was as if I'd failed to answer a question and the film had been rolled on, to bring the pieces of the puzzle into focus. I hadn't realised how memory can fade after fifteen years: on my own I would have walked past the place.

I kissed my wife. 'Pretty good! The path yesterday, the raft today—and I always thought I had better sight than you!'

I recognised the rock, the logs, the harbour. I even recognised the position of the lone two-storey house, way above and to the left of us on the bend in the hillside on the opposite bank. Someone's words in Cuzco came back to me, 'The *balsero* is no longer there. He was dispossessed after the Reforma Agraria. It's someone new now.' Of course. The new man must have put up the fine, two-storey mud building in place of the shack I remembered.

'I've got it. I've got it!' I shouted, waving my arms with

excitement. 'It'll be in the book.' Ed and I checked the rock-face, crack for crack against the photo in *Amazon Journey*: there could be no doubt, we were at the raft crossing.

Ed's face lit up. 'I'll start a fire, get some green leaves on it for maximum smoke. We can flash my steel shaving mirror . . .'

'We can turn the sleeping-bags inside out and make a yellow square,' Becca suggested. Her look of frightened exhaustion was gone.

We all got to work. Ed and Bec flashed mirrors at the two-storey hut. M.C. got a smoky fire billowing, Justin arranged the sleeping-bags and went on a recce as far down the river as he could to get the best view of the hut.

While gathering driftwood I looked at the river through the eyes of someone who had spent every day of every school holiday fishing alone on the banks of the Thames. I remembered the search for eddies where fish might lie during winter floods; remembered swimming the Thames in flood, in dinner jacket, shirt and trousers, to impress a girl on a late January night in Maidenhead; remembered my night swim of the Wye at Hereford on the SAS selection course. I had rowed the Atlantic, sailed it alone, sailed round the world a couple of times, run my own School of Adventure for seventeen years. I had seen a good deal of rivers and oceans. Could this river be swum?

An hour passed. We signalled to three men moving about in a small field of what looked like oranges and bananas, well below the house, but there was no response. Midday came and went, and I saw frustration taking the place of joy in the faces of those around me.

'John, I reckon I could swim it,' said Justin at my elbow.

I looked him in the eye. 'Do you?'

I looked away, remembering exactly the same dilemma in 1970. We had waited all day, and the *balsero* hadn't answered our fires. Mac, the medic, had offered to swim across and find him. Mac had been in the Army swimming team when we'd been in the 3 Para together. But I had thought of his wife back in Putney and forbidden him to try.

'I was quite a good swimmer at school,' Justin pleaded. I knew this was important to him. I looked at him again, that familiar sinking feeling returning to the pit of my stomach. 'At least he's not married,' I thought.

'It's not worth the risk, Justin, old top,' I replied. 'I've been on two Boards of Inquiry into river drownings, one in Wales and one in Malaysia. It's such dangerous stuff, water.'

But he persisted, and I knew I was going to let him try. To a young blood like him, this was a great challenge, just as rowing the Atlantic had been for me.

After some further prevarication, I said, 'OK, but listen. I've had a real look at the river. The eddy on this bank will wash you right upstream and into the middle of the rapids—that 'Lion's Mouth', just past the centre of the river. Swim lazy breast-stroke to that point. Then let the rush from the rapids carry you for the thirty yards down to the tail of the big rock. Then you must put in a twenty-five yard sprint to the bank there, and you're out.

'If you miss that chance, you've got fifty yards to the next rapids. You might be washed back on to this bank, before you get there. Otherwise, just bowl through the rapids and take your chance . . .' I heard my voice trail away: there wasn't much point in going on.

Ten minutes later Justin was ready, wearing jungle trousers and white t-shirt. Round his waist he'd tied his training shoes to the continuous length of plaited nylon line which we'd used on the cliff descent the previous afternoon. Sealed in a plastic bag in his pocket he carried Bec's phrase book and a little money.

He grinned self-consciously and waded cautiously into the eddy. At once the water seized him. His breast-stroke looked hurried and off-balance. The back eddy washed him swiftly upstream and across the river, directly below the rapids. I sensed it was all happening too quickly for him.

At the 'Lion's Mouth' the boiling surge bashed him about, impeding his breathing, as he came bobbing down towards us. Too soon he was at the tail of the big rock, hurtling downstream all the while. He made a brave effort with his racing crawl, but he was no more than a twig in the flood. Then he was past us, heading for the rapids. He made a despairing effort to reach our bank, rolling his head and wallowing with fear. Then he was gone: into the rapids and under the surface.

Ed dashed down the bank with Becca, shouting incoherently. I sat on the rock, certain that I had sent Justin to his death. What could I say to his mother? How much more callous I had become. Fifteen years before, I wouldn't have—hadn't—allowed such a risk. Why had I done it now? Wasn't even life sacred?

'He's up! Oh, look! He's up!' M.C. was tugging at my arm. I stared. There was his head. I never moved. How long had he been under? Had he hit a rock? Was he hurt?

The head was a tiny black dot on the brown flood, way down the river. Now and then Justin lifted leaden arms until, by a miraculous fluke, he was washed helplessly into the one place where he could get out, a sandy bay on the far side of the river, near the outer edge of the bend. Downstream of him lay the sheer rock walls of the bend. For a long time he lay on the sand like a corpse. Then he crawled out of sight, up into the jungle above the beach. The four of us huddled together on our bank, shaking with the release of tension and watching for him to come into sight on the bottom edge of the field where the men were working.

'I'll get some soup on,' said Marie Christine, while the rest of us swatted away at the black-flies.

An hour after he waded into the river, Justin re-appeared on a strip of brown path leading to the raft. He hadn't gone up to the *balsero*'s hut. Maybe he was just too exhausted; maybe he felt a need to get in touch with us again. He disappeared behind the rocks to look at the raft, emerging a few moments later on the rocks directly opposite us. Cupping his hands round his mouth, he motioned he wanted to say something. We stood in silence.

'The raft . . . it's dismantled . . . no sign of a cable,' he called, and I gave him a thumbs-up to signal we understood.

I made a slow sweep with my arm, pointing first at the bedraggled figure on the other bank and then up a thousand feet or more towards the *balsero*'s hut. Justin waved wearily and turned to make his way up the path.

We took the opportunity to bathe. The jagged shore was full of little bays where we could submerge almost every part of our bodies to escape the pitiless biting of the black-fly. The yellow-brown waters rose and fell rhythmically against the rocks, as if we were in the clutches of some living, breathing, liquid monster, panting with rage after losing a victim.

'He's reached the field, Dad,' Becca called, nearly an hour later.

Twenty minutes later we spotted him in a clearing, almost down to the river again. He was trailing behind three Indians, who were bouncing down the hill with excitement. Even at that distance we could see that Justin had managed to impress the locals.

Back on the bandstand, he signalled he was going to shout, and we leaned out over the water to catch every word.

'The *balsa* and the cable have been dismantled by the military . . . Nobody's allowed to cross the river . . . Elvin is dead. He was killed three years ago . . . There've been massacres at Lucmahuayco and Osambre . . .'

He was pausing between each message.

'They say the river's too high . . . but it'll go down in the night . . . Then they'll try and get a rope across for you . . . tomorrow at eight in the morning.'

We waved acknowledgement, and sat down to absorb the information.

'Elvin's dead,' I said, half to myself. Feeling sick and dazed, I looked across the river and up into the thickly-forested mountainsides, blueing into the distance. To me, at that moment, this was the whole world. The rest of my life seemed to dissolve into nothing. For fifteen years I had been meaning to return to Osambre. Now it seemed only yesterday that Elvin and I had parted at the Benedictine Mission. My mind could not accept that he would not be at the farm to greet us. I clung to straws.

Quite likely Justin had misunderstood, and it was one of the other brothers who the Indians told him had been killed.

I jerked myself out of the reverie and got down to the business of trying to put a line across the river. Ed, who had been good at throwing the cricket ball, began to throw a line-carrying stone across the torrent, and almost succeeded, but his best effort fell short, and the approach of darkness found us still *in situ*. With the coming of night the air cooled and the black-fly stopped plaguing us. There was a little thunder and lightning, but not much rain. M.C. cooked up a good, hot soup with what little food we had left, and then we got into our bivvy bags under the stars.

I spent a good deal of the night going over and over a plan to get a line across the river. I felt sure that our 7.7lb nylon line was the key to success. If I could stretch it off the spool, to prevent it kinking, and then flake it out in layers across an area of smooth rock, it should fly up behind Ed's stone with hardly any resistance. It should be carefully knotted on to a cricket ball-sized pebble, and masked with a layer of two-inch plastic insulating tape, smooth in the palm. Compared with the roaring power of the river, 7.7lb is a tiny breaking strain. Once we had the line stretched across the water, we would be able to feed the white 4mm plaited line across from high up on either bank. If the fine line once touched the water, surface drag would snap the monofilament instantly. And, even if we got the line across, could I risk M.C. and Bec on it? It was only a series of six-foot lengths held together by reef knots; at the very least we should secure each side of every knot with a half hitch . . . There was so much to go wrong.

Over in his rocky hollow Ed was fretting about his throwing arm, twitching his shoulders with imaginary throws. M.C. and Bec also lay awake, trying to imagine hauling themselves across the river along a tight line. What if the current dragged them under?

At the first sign of dawn Marie Christine was up making tea and porridge and Ed had built a small pyramid of suitable stones before it was even properly light. I was snapping at everyone to keep clear of the invisible monofilament which I had got zig-zagged out across the polished rocks.

'The river hasn't fallen, Dad. It's come up about three inches. I put a stick in here last night.' Bec was cleaning our fire-blackened saucepan with gravel at the water's edge.

Eleven Indians came down through the jungle with Justin, and I was relieved to see them carrying the huge balsa-wood paddles which I remembered from the last time I'd been this way. One sturdy-looking fellow had a thick black rope coiled round his shoulders, but it looked a good deal too short to cross the river. They were an hour earlier than planned, but we'd been ready for some time. Our kit was sealed inside the red plastic survival bags we had brought so far for just this moment, the plastic protected in turn by our Army lightweight ponchos. At a pinch we could float the rucksacks, using the bubble trapped between poncho and pack.

The Indians were chattering with excitement, and Justin shouted over to tell us they'd come from miles around. Apparently they were all very nervous; savage military reprisals in the recent past had made it all too clear that no strangers were to be granted hospitality in any village. Messengers had already gone out asking the military what to do with the five *gringos* who were trying to cross the Apurimac.

Ed's first throw was a mighty effort. Arcing high over the river, the stone clanked down right on the rock where the Indians stood. Somehow they failed to understand its importance, and the current caught the monofilament, dragging the black pebble in short bounces back towards the water's edge. Justin seized it in the nick of time.

I took the spool of 4mm line and clambered up the bank as high as I could get, right into the edge of the jungle. M.C. and Bec paid it out down by the water, and inch by inch Justin took in the monofilament on his side. The white line passed up and over my hands and slowly began to reach across the flood. Would the length of white line suspended in mid-air weigh more than

Justin just afloat, and out of control, by the
Big Rock in the Apurimac

John on the raft, about to hit the Big Rock

Above: Crossing a *torrentina* on the way up to Pacaypata from the rafting

Left: The Apurimac valley

7.7lbs before Justin could grasp its leading end? Luckily for us, there wasn't a breath of wind. The line sagged within inches of the turbulent brown waters, and the weight on my hands seemed a deal more than 7.7lbs, but at last Justin managed to catch hold of the white line, and we'd done it. Tremendous cheers rang out.

One of the Indians tied himself first to the end of our line, and then to the end of Justin's line. Lowering himself into the water, he began swimming out into the current. All four of us took in from our end, while Justin and two others paid out their end. We had the Indian controlled from both sides. The current engulfed him; he disappeared from view, and we really heaved to hold him. He was washed well downstream and got tangled in the outgoing line from the far side. By the time Ed helped him ashore he was pretty far gone, and bleeding from his left leg.

'*Impossible para señoritas,*' he gasped, flashing his white teeth and pumping my extended hand with excitement. After taking a minute or two to gather himself, he told us his name was Saul, and that he'd travelled overnight from the village of San Fernando to come and see us. Once he had recovered, his excitement and chatter increased tenfold. '*No hay documento—no hay balsa!*' he declared, and I quickly produced the book and letters.

'*Ah, Elvin—es muy buen amigo. Está muerto, muerto!*' he cried, shaking his head. His sadness created an instant bond between us.

I felt very low, and weighed down by doubt. If Elvin really was dead, were we wise to risk crossing the river? But there was no stopping Saul: he was already waving and shouting instructions, and a great volume of noise came up from behind the rocks as the *balsa* was rebuilt for launching. A tremendous *joie de vivre* seized everyone: the river was a great challenge. In the innocent fun of it all, the Indians soon seemed to forget they were risking death from the military for helping us.

The raft was ready in half an hour and soon three men were wielding the huge paddles on their way over. We hauled in the line to a rhythmic chanting from the other side. Several times the raft was awash, and I shouted to M.C. and Bec that when they crossed they must sit further towards the back, to help keep the front above the waves. Minutes later, I was watching them being pulled across by Justin and his team, and checking the reef knots as they slipped through my hands.

By ten in the morning we were all across, amid great rejoicing and munching of fresh bananas. It seemed a miracle.

'*Los militares tienen muchos problemas de seguridad!*' laughed the man we christened Blue Cap, peering at the documents and running a finger across his throat.

The Indians were much interested in the story of our time lost on the ridge. '*Cómo han sufrid!*' they cried, not allowing us to carry any of our gear on the way up the mountain to the ferryman's hut.

Chapter Seventeen

Even without kit I found the thousand foot climb heavy going, and I was quietly relieved when we entered small fields of dark green coca bushes when still only halfway up. I could see a little hut over to the left, and knew we would find some pretext for a short rest there.

Walls of slightly spaced vertical bamboo poles made the most of the faint cooling breeze, and we could still hear the roar of the river, now some 500 feet below us. We sank down on rough coir mats which were carefully laid on the beaten earth floor, their real use being for pounding the leaves of the lethal crop. Although we had seen Indians chewing coca leaves ever since arriving in Cuzco, this was our first glimpse of the raw product. The *balsero*—a very old-looking man of forty-nine with a narrow, emaciated face and wispy grey beard that gave him a Confucian look—told us he was paid two dollars a kilo for his share in supplying the vast expansion of demand for Peru's abundant coca leaves, which now feed an illegal cocaine trade estimated to be worth 800 million dollars a year.

I was feeling all-in. Heat, lack of food and continuous nausea combined to give me a jaundiced view of life. Vivid television films in Britain had shown me the devastating effects of cocaine —and here was the plant being grown within the law. I hadn't the energy to launch into the familiar argument about whether it would be easier to remove the demand for the substance in the Western world or to destroy the supply in places like the jungles of Peru. Feebly, I just thought how glad I was that it wasn't my job to destroy this field and go searching for other, similar clearings in the dreadful forest. I was not at my best.

Eventually, just before noon, we arrived at the *balsero*'s two-storey mud hut which had been the object of so much interest to us in the past few days. From a table outside the building wife and daughter doled out bowls of steaming soup and chunks of sticky white yucca root—woolly and tasteless—to our party of eleven Indians and five *gringos*. We rested on benches in the shade of the building and began rebuilding our strength for the long climb to the village of Pacaypata.

As we gulped down the soup, Justin described his epic swim across the Apurimac. He had found the river overwhelmingly powerful from the very start. Immediately he had allowed the eddy to carry him up towards the rapids above the rafting point, the undertow had tried to drag him down; he just couldn't keep his feet up, let alone make headway against the current. When he'd disappeared under the water in the second rapids, he had struck a rock with his backside, and decided he was going to drown. Coming out of those rapids, he had seen the beach on the outside of the approaching bend, and realised it might be his last chance. Now, looking back down at the river, we could see —and hear—three more sets of thundering rapids just round the end of the ridge. Justin had been amazingly fortunate and we had all shared in his good luck.

The Indians were a varied lot, from an almost urbane young official from some distant village, who had come to check us out and carried a small sample of gold sifted from the sandbars of the Apurimac, to toothless old men with eyes permanently glazed from years of chewing coca. But most of them were superbly fit-looking young fellows in their mid-twenties, who had come from far and wide to investigate our mysterious back door arrival in their world. Confident now that we would be taken to the military for questioning, they enjoyed discussing the excitement of the rafting. When they had finished their food they dispersed, returning to their villages with their news of us.

It was still only 12.30 when we began the walk up to Pacaypata.

In spite of a good rest at the hut, we were always glad of the breaks, but the Indians didn't like stopping and seemed to bounce along on legs like rubber springs. Their daily life led them up and down this mountain, and that was only on the way to and from slogging days in the fields.

Soon, we came to a roaring torrent of ice-cold glacier water, where delicate rainbows hovered in the shifting curtains of spray, and butterflies settled on our boots. The water we splashed over us here helped us up another section of hillside to the homes of Benito and Ricardo, two of the fittest of the rafting party. Their wives gave us a whole juicy papaya each and a delicious drink of lemon-flavoured water.

I don't think we would have made it in one hop to Pacaypata on our own: probably we would have stopped along the way for the night. But the presence of the Indians, who had done so much to help us already, kept us going. There was one longish halt when we reached a coca-field where the crop had been burnt to the ground. This was uncontrolled brush clearance by a neighbour, and a large-scale meeting was convened on the spot. When we started upwards again, one of the men gave us each a piece of sugar cane which he'd cut during the coca discussion.

We came into Pacaypata past the football field. From the moment we arrived it was perfectly clear that we were in a different land from that out on the other side of the river. The teacher was a twenty-one-year-old called George, a smart-looking boy from Abancay who had a young wife called Julia and a baby. He briefed us on the situation as he led us to the clean and tidy school. By his estimation only sixty of the usual 200 inhabitants of the village remained, the rest having elected to leave, preferring to become refugees rather than endure the menace of the terrorists.

To leave one's village is a desperately serious step. Since the agrarian reforms, the rule has been that if a family deserts the community in time of emergency, that family forfeits its share in the land, the most precious of possessions. There is no coming back.

Little transistor radios are common in the villages, and they give Indians access to the same programmes heard by their sophisticated countrymen in the distant cities. Most Indians have relatives or friends in the cities—in fact a third of the population of Peru lives in Lima alone. There is little chance that departing families go to the appalling city slums without a fair knowledge of what they are giving up and what they are letting themselves in for.

George had no problem in letting us sleep in one of the three schoolrooms: there were only twenty school-age children left in the village, and there had been 100.

All the villagers gathered outside the school to decide what should be done with us, their faces anxious. *Seguridad* was the word they used most. We produced our documents and the book for the fourth time in the day. Benito, from down the hill, turned out to be the *gobernador*. A barrel-chested, dynamic fellow of no more than twenty-five, he would be a good man to have on your side in a fight; his youth and vigour contrasted strongly with the quiet old men who held power in many of the villages we had visited on the Altiplano.

The fact that the meeting went well was entirely due to Benito and the others who had been on the rafting with us. Justin's feat in swimming the river was already a legend, and we could feel goodwill slowly growing among the rest of the villagers. Sixty is a small remainder from two hundred. *Guerrillas, los terroristas, subversores*—these were the terms used for the *Sendero Luminoso*, whose presence was felt in the very trees around the village. Indeed, it was generally believed that most villages contained *Sendero* sympathisers. But most people appeared content with the proposition that we should be allowed to stay in the school, pending the return of the messenger who had already left to inform *El Comandante*, the military leader in Amaybamba, a village some two days distant.

Benito carried his responsibilities well, usually managing to smile cheerfully whenever he spoke to us. He told us he was returning down the mountain to his home for the night. 'Simeon is at your service in my absence,' he grinned, nodding at an unusually large young Indian, and I rather felt that Simeon might be more of a guard than a friend.

It was soup and yucca and early to bed for us. I was worried about the effect which the black-fly bites were having on us: Justin was covered with ugly weals, the result of his lack of clothing after he had swum the river, and Becca's hands were badly swollen.

Lying in the dark in my bag on the school floor, I pondered the latest information from Benito. He confirmed that Elvin had been dead for three years. It was impossible to visit the villages of Hatumpampa, Lucmahuayco, or Osambre, for nobody lived there any more. The *Sendero Luminoso* had attacked them the previous year, and after a while the military had counter-attacked and recovered them. The military took the view that anyone choosing to live in a village held by terrorists should be treated as a terrorist. It was a story as old as time: either way, the villagers were losers. No wonder so many people had fled the district.

One final piece of information was especially disturbing. During the past week thirty-six houses had been burned to the ground in a raid by 500 terrorists on the village of Amaybamba, which was most likely to be our next destination, in the Red Zone of the Emergency Area. Almost certainly it was there that we would meet *El Comandante*.

Simeon proved friendly, even if he did arrive very early next morning. He climbed trees and brought us fruit, and for the first time we had the long, leathery beans, whose juicy, white fluff was so refreshing. But he never let us out of sight.

When a troop-carrying helicopter lumbered across the sky, George checked his watch and told us what it was doing before disappearing into the classroom to teach the seventeen children who'd come for school. His nerves were a little frayed too. He taught by rote, the children chanting back his instruction regardless of meaning. A couple of times the chanting stopped and we heard the swish and slap of the leather belt, followed by wails of pain.

We visited houses around the village and bought potatoes, tomatoes, cabbage, carrots and bananas. Even at Simeon's father's house we noticed the coca-chewing old men were suspicious of the way we had come in through the back door across the river, and I felt it would take little to persuade them we were terrorists.

We seemed to be living on borrowed time, in a sort of limbo. The villagers spoke to us as if we were moving through, rather than staying in their *pueblo*. After lunching on a can of sardines with raw cabbage and carrots, M.C., Bec and I decided to go for a bathe in the nearby *torrentina*.

We stretched the ten minute walk into thirty: there was much asking how the others felt, and several breaks beside graveyards and gateways. We three luxuriated in being alone together, like prisoners exercising outside their cells. The butterflies looked brighter than usual, the waterfall unreally white and cascading. Even the black-fly were defeated as we sat on polished boulders with our feet and ankles in the icy water and every other inch of skin carefully covered: the thunder of the falls and the moisture-laden air seemed just too much for the little biters. Water-cooled, we managed to achieve a perfect body temperature, while sucking fresh limes dipped in sugar and searching for nuggets of gold among the sand and gravel between the stones. Enwrapped in a bower of tall, slim jungle trees, this racing stream seemed far from the strife-torn Apurimac valley. As a family, we felt especially close.

We took even longer on the walk back, and it was already late afternoon by the time we returned under the arch into the school compound. Benito, the *Gobernador,* was waiting for us, loudly blowing his whistle to summon a full village meeting as we came into view. Indians crowded round the schoolroom windows. A young messenger stood by, looking exhausted, important and agitated all at the same time.

'We must go to San Fernando tonight,' said Benito, holding

out a piece of graph paper covered with writing in spidery red biro. Two blue rubber stamps made it look official. '*El Comandante* has called for you to be brought to him immediately. You should cook a meal, and be ready to start as soon as it gets dark. My men will carry the packs for you.'

Marie Christine and Becca prepared a hot vegetable soup, and the villagers stared as we packed. I felt we were now prisoners in all but name, and when the time came to depart, George shook our hands as if we were heading for some sort of interrogation, while others looked on with undisguised hostility. Benito chose nine men, including himself, to accompany us, and I was disturbed to see one of the escort nearly in tears when he was pressed into service.

Darkness lent an air of excitement as we hurried along the narrow jungle path. Fireflies swam in the inky blackness among the trees. When I nudged Benito to point out some bats which were flapping about as we forded a stream, he grinned and hissed, '*Vampiros*'.

We climbed above the trees and followed the main north wall of the Apurimac valley as it tended north-west towards the village of Piquipata, or San Fernando, as it had been renamed after some revolution or other. We had to cross one major re-entrant, and Benito halted the march as soon as this came into view. Deliberate, long, yellow dashes of torchlight from the far side of the valley answered Benito's urgent signals. I knew the *pueblos* had formed their own vigilante groups, and anyone travelling after dark could expect to be fired on. It was good to know we were expected.

We hurried on. A sliver of pale moon came up, lighting the path for us, and we rehearsed ambush procedures. Numbered from first to last, we decided that odd numbers should dash right and evens left of the path, and rendezvous were agreed at various points as we moved along. I saw three more tarantulas on the moonlit path, and wondered how many others I had missed. Our team went really well. Bec and M.C. kept pace perfectly, and Ed and Justin were full of cheer, always ready to give a friendly hand or word. Marie Christine and I, discussing why the team was working so well, had decided that danger and uncertainty were bringing us closer together than on easier expeditions.

All the same, we were pleased enough to reach the village of San Fernando. It was bigger than Pacaypata, and the crowds seemed rather more hostile as we came in out of the dark. Benito showed us into a big, tile-roofed barn, where much of the floor space was taken up with builders' equipment, a mud kiln and a pile of brick-clay. The place was dusty and strewn with waste hay; by lantern light it looked just the place for fleas. A small hatch in the wall opened into another room, where the villagers were busy signing a register, watched over by an Indian with a hideous cleft palate. The scene was like rent day in a Dickensian nightmare. Justin made a cup of tea, and we went straight to bed, nursing our itchy bites.

We slept in until 6.30 next morning. Emilio, the agitated *gobernador*, appeared as soon as we showed signs of waking. Taking me into the registry room next door, he recorded our time of arrival and passport numbers. He was older and more serious than Benito, and showed me a note from *El Comandante* demanding the five *gringos* be brought forward to him personally —*rápido*.

'I will be killed if this is not done immediately,' he said. 'Every *pueblo* is prohibited from having visitors. The raft is *prohibido* as well—they should never have brought you across.'

Justin and I went off to the stream for a wash and shave. Our minder was a friendly fellow, and on the way back he told us a new version of the sacking of Osambre. The farm had been attacked by thirty terrorists a year ago, he said. Elvin had been killed in the battle, but his brother Olaf had shot two terrorists with his pistol and escaped. Again I grabbed at straws, hoping that with the stories conflicting so much, Elvin might still be alive.

We left for Amaybamba under heavy guard at 10am. Our leader was Mismeo, thin-faced and with all his front teeth missing. He had been the second Indian to reach our bank during the rafting, and had become a firm friend. He claimed to have known Elvin personally, and to have travelled with him often.

We had an immense, five-hour climb to a tiny *pueblo* named Corca. Marie Christine was suffering severe stomach pains, but kept gamely on. In any other circumstances, taken steadily, the walk would have been splendid, but now it was mostly just a slog. For lunch we could only produce potatoes, bananas and unripe mangoes, but the Indians shared with us their rice, yucca and a very good, brick-hard white cheese.

The white horse carrying our rucksacks broke down in mid-afternoon, and I would have been quite happy to stop for the night, but Mismeo insisted we press on. We paused for a while in Corca, where a friendly Indian woman gave us fresh milk and fresh cheese. Unfortunately, the smoked, uncooked meat we accepted was not as fresh, and perhaps was the cause of future troubles.

Progress deteriorated as the afternoon drew to a close. We had climbed all the way back up on to a ridge at over 11,000 feet, and found ourselves in thick mist, plodding through dank woodland: it was remarkably like hunting for golfballs on a wet autumn Sunday afternoon in Surrey. Harsh words were needed to keep us all together. Justin, Ed, and I were already carrying our rucksacks, and it struck me that if we went much further we should become dangerously exhausted as we approached the *zona terrorista*.

Darkness was drawing on as we straggled down a neat irrigation channel into the village of Incahuasi. Sadly the delights of its Inca layout were lost on us in a combination of failing light and poor humour. The Indians were openly hostile, and we ended up spending a cold night under a rough porch outside a hut. I barely remember loud voices and people treading over me in the dark.

We awoke to a wet, misty morning and the sound of Mismeo's voice imploring us to be on our way. M.C. treated an old lady for recurrent diarrhoea with a course of Immodium and in return received a welcome gift of four eggs and some potatoes.

We were a pretty miserable, unwashed team, with upset stomachs; but spirits rose with the clearing mist as Choquesapra outlined its 16,700 foot white summit against the deep blue of the heavens some seven miles to the north. A good wash and shave got me on an even keel, and we set off without regret. The villagers of Incahuasi were clearly worried about our presence among them, and we resented their hostility.

Although we were still moving forward, we had lost our momentum. I doubted if we could progress beyond our meeting with *El Comandante*. Had I been in his position, I would hardly have welcomed five snooping foreigners. It looked as if the whole expedition was about to end; after today, it might simply be a matter of making our way home to Scotland. With this gloomy thought I led the way slowly down the ridge towards the village of San Martine. Amaybamba lay just out of sight 3,000 feet below.

Entering San Martine, I had that same clearing of vision which I had experienced at the site of the raft. 'I know this place,' I said. 'I've been here before—we came in from the other end in 1970.'

But our direction of entry was not the only change in San Martine; I remembered it as a bustling row of stores and bars, but now it was deserted. The few remaining people looked dejected and lifeless. Over a can of lukewarm beer in an otherwise deserted bar we learned how the terrorists had come and, with a bit of calculated murder and menace, had virtually emptied the village.

From a grassy bank beside the path we could see down into the bottom of the Mapito valley, 2,000 feet below us. David, the schoolteacher of San Martine, pointed out the big school and houses in Amaybamba, which had been burned by terrorists on 10 November. He said there were 200 terrorists in the attack, not 500 as had been claimed by Benito. With his bushy, black beard and powerful physique, he looked afraid of nothing but even his conversation turned mostly to describing our best route back to Cuzco.

Now we were looking at what was really the front line. The

two distinct paths cut into the far side of the valley, leading on towards Hatumpampa, Lucmahuayco and Osambre, were virtually controlled by the terrorists. Osambre, our goal for so long, was no more than a couple of days' walk from where we lay. But David told us what we had heard so many times before: we should not go on past Amaybamba on any account.

We heard the slow beat of a military helicopter whacking up the valley from the direction of the military base at Andahuaylas. It was a big, camouflaged troop-carrier, which did not land at once but made several turns round a playing field in front of a large square building with a red tile roof. It looked to me as if the pilot was uncertain of security.

'*La reunión!*' David pointed at a crowd of people rushing from the building towards the playing field. 'About 400 senior people of the district are meeting to discuss the *ronda*—the security patrols of the villages.'

The helicopter landed, and kept its rotors turning. It was engulfed by the crowd so that we couldn't see who got in or out. Within five minutes it was on its way back down the valley.

Mismeo was anxious to get moving, increasingly worried by what might happen if our meeting with *El Comandante* was delayed much longer. In Indian terms, our movement thus far could hardly be termed *rápido*. But it was hot, and we were worn out, and rather dreading the meeting, so we dragged our feet a bit on the descent. We stopped for a sparse lunch beside a rapidly-expanding graveyard on the hillside, and while we were there, at 2pm, the helicopter returned. Again it landed only for five minutes, but this time there was a lot of ragged rifle and machine gun fire. I had serious doubts about going any further, but Mismeo and his friends assured me that the noise was simply the soldiers discharging their weapons for show, and we kept on down towards the sound of the firing.

As we entered the jungly trees just above the valley floor, I thought how feeble I had been, how weak and easily led. If anything happened now, I had no excuse whatsoever for walking straight into trouble. Again we stopped, this time on the pretext of accepting a refreshing drink of orange juice from a friendly young local whose wife and children had long since left the area.

The path was nearly vertical, and the Indians were now arranged in front and behind us. Both Justin and Ed had been encouraged to carry their packs and I wondered if this was a ploy to prevent them escaping. When we reached the magnificent Mapito river, a strip of white thundering through the green of the jungle, we simply lay on the bank and submerged our heads in the glacier melt-water. Once more the black-fly took advantage of our weakness, but at least we felt a bit cooler for the stiff, half-hour climb.

The ascent was a major test for Justin and Ed, with their heavy packs. By now we were surrounded by a crowd of Indians, and the two boys wanted to arrive in Amaybamba with colours flying. They were to regret using up so much energy.

Chapter Eighteen

We were led straight into a square building with a red-tiled roof, a sort of district headquarters but quite unfinished. The windows were rectangular holes in the mud-block walls; there were no doors, and the floor was red earth turned to fine dust.

Four hundred people make a fair-sized crowd, and they thronged round the entrance to the building as we were led in like prize prisoners and sat down at tables in an open-fronted alcove. Having heard a single shot as we came up the cliff from the river, we felt a little nervous.

The crowd was made up mostly of visiting leaders from other villages. I looked around for those who might actually be doing the work and identified an elderly clerk whose hat and demeanour gave him a striking resemblance to the founder of the Boy Scouts, Lord Baden-Powell. We got on well together from the start. He seemed impressed with my book and the Norwegian newspaper cutting about our search for Elvin, and said he knew the Berg family personally.

'How is it this letter from the *prefecto* of the Department of Cuzco is dated 14 October, and you are here on 24 November?' he asked, raising an eyebrow.

'We did some training up on the Altiplano,' I replied, pointing at the pictures in the book. 'We've been retracing the steps of our 1970 expedition.'

Evidently this did not sound entirely plausible. 'Perhaps you wouldn't mind if we searched you, then?' he suggested.

'Not at all.' I thought it was time to grasp the initiative. 'If we line up on this side of the tables, with all our gear, and you select five men to conduct the search, we can go ahead directly.'

My suggestion was greeted with hoots of laughter from the crowd, but Baden-Powell was clearly surprised by my frankness. He had expected a private search in one of the rooms, but I thought that to make a funny spectacle in public might help reassure the locals.

As usual in impromptu searches, some of us were thoroughly dealt with, every last sheet of loo paper being checked, while others underwent only a token examination. The operation provoked great hilarity and good humour towards us among the crowd, who craned their necks to get a view of what the *gringos* really did have in their big packs. At the end of fifteen minutes or so, with all our kit on the far side of the tables from us, and the body-searches complete, even the most zealous of the examiners was satisfied. Baden-Powell stood up, and called for silence. He made a little speech, thanking us for our frankness and professing astonishment that we carried no weapons at all.

While everyone's attention was on him I took the opportunity of scanning the faces in the crowd, noticing one or two more sophisticated Spanish-looking people, obviously not Quechuan Indians. I was surprised there were no teachers present: I wasn't sure if this was because it was Saturday, or if the teachers had left the district after their burning of the *colegio*. Most important of all was the complete absence of the military! Where was *El Comandante*?

A ripple of applause greeted the end of Baden-Powell's address. I asked the others to watch the kit closely and develop our good relationship with the crowd while I concentrated on the content of a document being hammered out by two fingers on the community typewriter. Baden-Powell worked on composition and a bright-looking young fellow called Fabian supplied the two fingers.

La reunion was evidently over, and there was to be a communal supper outside the square building that evening. Out at the back a cow was being cooked over open fires by half a dozen women.

When the document was finalised I was given the blue carbon

John and Ed resting on Boot Hill, on the way
down to Amaybamba

The square building in Amaybamba

Dusty alcove in the square building

'Baden-Powell' stirs the EEC butter-oil outside
the square building

Above left: Gobernador of
Amaybamba (right),
with visiting officials at
'La Reunion'

Above right: Military
helicopter coming into
Amaybamba

Right: The burnt-out
school at Amaybamba

Crossing the bridge over the Mapito River, on the way from Amaybamba to Accobamba, after terrorists destroyed seven of ten logs

Accobamba village. Looking up the path towards Choquetira. The two school buildings are a few yards down the hill to the left.

copy. As well as detailing our names and passport numbers, it outlined our search for the Berg family as the reason for our visit to the area. The paper bore many official stamps and signatures, and was a grand passport for *la zona roja*—the Red Zone of the Emergency Area.

With the formalities over, Baden-Powell briefed me on the situation. *El Comandante* and a detachment of soldiers had been billeted here, in the square building, ever since the terrorist attack on the night of 10 November. They had only just left: the helicopter we'd seen had been taking them away earlier in the afternoon, and the firing had been the soldiers discharging their weapons before being lifted out.

'We are alone now,' said Baden Powell. 'The terrorists are watching us from the forest.' He spoke very correctly and waved his hand at the other side of the valley. 'They have seen the military leave. This is a dangerous place.'

The officials who had signed our document told us we must wait in the village until *El Comandante* returned in a few days' time. They gave us two eight-foot-wide dusty rooms on the ground floor of the square building for bedrooms, and told us most vehemently that there was no way forward from here. If we so much as set off along the path towards Hatumpampa, the *Senderos* would at the very least rob us of our clothes and equipment. In any case, nobody lived at Hatumpampa, Lucmahuayco, or Osambre any more. Osambre was burned to the ground. Elvin had been tortured and was definitely dead. The rest of his family had fled the district.

With everything so bleakly definite, there seemed nothing for it but to retreat. That evening we watched the *ronda* prepare for the night ahead. The patrol consisted of eight men. Armed with pointed sticks, two ancient hunting rifles and a bugle to sound the alarm, they looked anything but fearsome. Proudly they showed me their weapons, which I dated at roughly 1890 and 1930. I was horrified to see the riflemen squatting on the ground scraping the brass cartridge cases of the bullets with knives to make them fit the breech.

Manifestacion de los Turistas de la nacionalidad , Británicos.
son las siguientes personas.

01	John Manfield Ridgway	47 años	Pasap.	G 882681
02	Marie Chistine Ridgway	40 años	,,	G 063218
03	Rbecca L. Ridgway	18 años	,,	H 190258
04	Justin Matterson	22 años	,,	H 361164
05	Edward J. Ley Wilson	21 años	,,	H 178124

Quienes se manifestaron en la forma siguiente : Poniendo a la
vista un documento de fecha 15 de Octubre del presente año es-
tificado expedido del Prefecto Departamento del cusco DR, Julio
Jara Ladron de Guevara, fundamentando su manifestacion de acuer-
de así documete, de su pais de Inglaterra, ha llegado al perú
hace 2 meses a la fecha, con el fin de vecitar a un pariente lla-
mado familia Verge, que radicaba en el lugar denominado Usambre
de quienes no ha recebido nengunacommunicación hace tiempo, por
que los manifestantes ha vecitado a la familia indicada hace 15
años antes a la fecha, y no sabia que esta sona estaba Infiltrado por los terrorristas, por lo que recien al pasar Rio Apú-
rimac, con tanta deficultad se ha enterado que esta sona estaba
Infiltrado por los terrorristas, por tal razon los manifestantes decidieron descansar en este lugar Huarancalqui, con conocimiento de las autoridades de la comunidad, para luego reter-
nar de este lugar al departamento del cusco. Por haber sido
declarado en sona roja , tambien manifestan a ha solicitud del
Ejercito se ha constituido a este lugar. Al mismo tiempo se les
hizo comprender que sus vultos se les heciera la revición de cada
uno captando los mencionados, esto para seguridad legal de la
comunidad y no encontrando nada el revision de sus vultos, so-
lamente sus pertenencias personales, como equipes de viage y
sus vestimentas. con la presente manifestación se dió su libre
tránsito para su retorno. leyda ha6 sus manifestaciones y no tiene nada que agregar ni quitar. Con lo que terminó el acto fir-
mando junto con los autoridades los manifestantes.

Huarncalqui, 23 de Noviembre de 1,985.

The Amaybamba document

The party was not much of a jamboree. We felt guilty about eating the villagers' precious chunks of meat, and worse about drinking hot, sweet cocoa which was made with EEC Dairy Crest dried milk from Surrey and never intended for the likes of us. We began to realise that the population of Amaybamba was largely made up of refugees from the ruins of Hatumpampa and Lucmahuayco. There was little food, and practically nothing was being planted for the future, as many people who owned small plots of land had fled.

Zipped in our bivvy bags, fully clothed, with knife and torch to hand, we felt lumps of mud plaster raining down on us from the ceiling above as the occupants of the upper storey moved about on their unfinished floor. After a while the last curious locals left the window spaces and went off to bed. There seemed nothing for it now but to wait for *El Comandante* to tell us to get walking out of the *zona roja*. I felt a great sense of anti-climax after all we'd been through. Why had we come at all?

Next morning was Sunday. There had been no alarm in the night, and we awoke to the sound of murmurings at the windows as the crowd gathered to watch. Becca did not enjoy dressing under such intense scrutiny and the fine dust from the floor was getting into everything.

Breakfast was only yucca and cocoa, but at least we were allowed to pay for it. Bright sunshine and blue skies began to dissolve the atmosphere of menace but when I lent my Zeiss monocular to Fabian, the alert two-fingered typist of the previous day, he soon had a flag hoisted and a bugle sounding to signal the alarm. He had spotted terrorists in the trees on the outskirts of the village. He gathered a few men and was on his way within minutes, armed with the two old rifles and a few wooden spears. His departure left the rest of the villagers feeling vulnerable, out of sight or call of the military for the first day since the attack of 10 November.

Bec, M.C. and I walked a couple of hundred yards through waist-high scrub to see the burnt shell of the *colegio*. Charred desks on a carpet of black ash still faced their concrete blackboards on walls now open to the sky. That was all that remained of the village's proud, self-built, six-classroom hope for the future.

According to the *Senderos'* Maoist dogma, modern Western-oriented education is the very foundation of everything which has to be destroyed. Names of school teachers, Guarda Civil, village officials, the *ronda*, are marked on death lists pinned to villagers' doors at night. The idea is that after the cessation of the *ronda* patrols, the terrorists will come into the *pueblo* and live happily side by side with the villagers, building a new Maoist society, freed from the tyranny of democracy.

As we were looking at the ruins of some of the other thirty or so incinerated houses nearby, we met a frantic old woman refugee, who had been burned out of her home in Hatumpampa, just a couple of hours' walk up the path, and she told us the place was now *ardiendo* [on fire]. Somehow she looked to us three for some kind of help, and we felt oddly guilty.

After a while we gathered ourselves, and returned to the square building for the worst lunch any of us had ever eaten. Passing through a queue of mothers who were drawing cans of melted butter-oil donated by Southern Ireland through the EEC, we were issued with a mess tin full of parts of the cow not eaten the previous evening. In full view of the throng, we set about choking down the rubbery, almost raw sections of chopped intestines. We smothered it in curry powder and salt, but the taste of dung still came through. To his eternal credit, Ed managed to eat his portion and Marie Christine's; we used him as our demonstrator, while the rest of us took turns at hiding our mess tins in the bedrooms, planning to dispose of the contents after dark. Again we felt guilty at wasting valuable food, and sank down on to our bivvy bags in the heat of the afternoon.

We could find no food for sale in the village. Either people were unused to money, preferring barter, or they simply had nothing to spare. A large proportion of the population were refugees, without land of their own; food was not being produced, and livestock was being sold off to raise funds in case the remaining villagers had to flee. In the late afternoon we set off to visit another village, Pacaybamba, where we'd heard there was *bastante* [plenty] of fruit ripe on the trees. But it was still too early in the season, and all we got were some unripe oranges and tomatoes, hard avocado pears, a few onions and a cabbage. It wasn't much for five people, but a giant step forward from the 'tubes' at lunchtime.

On the way back we had just paused to eat some of the green fruit, sharing a rough seat at the top of a cliff, when a young fellow appeared at the top of the steep path leading up from the river. He turned out to be a refugee from Hatumpampa, and had known the Berg family all his life. He confirmed Elvin's death, in May 1984, saying that everyone knew about it, because it was the attack on Osambre which had signalled the real beginning of the terrorists' infiltration of the district. Apparently Elvin's brother Olaf and his unmarried sister Bertha were now living in Huanta, near Ayacucho. Another brother, Virgilio, had escaped, but his whereabouts were unknown. Stories of women's bodies floating down the river and children burned alive did nothing to cheer us.

This gloomy news—this final blow to our hopes—delayed our start down the cliff towards Amaybamba, and we found ourselves scurrying along in the dark after curfew, with the added worry that we might be fired on by the *ronda*. Eventually we stumbled into the square building, hot and breathless, to learn from Justin that Fabian had returned with the patrol. Apparently my Zeiss *large vista* had enabled him to see and capture two terrorists, whom he'd marched to the military post in Hatumpampa. I almost gave him the monocular as a present, but then I thought we might need it ourselves before we were through.

We were pretty low as we settled down for the night in our dusty room. The near-certainty of Elvin's death and the increasing unlikelihood of our being able to get any nearer to Osambre had produced an inevitable mood of anti-climax. The windows were crowded with chattering, laughing Indians and their constant presence was proving really hard on the nerves for Justin, Bec and Ed. Strangely enough, it didn't seem to bother

M.C. or me very much; for some reason, our tolerance of such intrusion seemed to have improved with age, even though nothing much else had. Becca and I had a row about her spreading the *polvo*, or fine dust, on my kit as she stepped across me, and this ended with her in a storm of tears, about which I felt awful.

Dogs barked interminably, and we all spent a disturbed, anxious night. 'Bad night, blur of heat, dust, unease,' M.C. wrote in her diary. 'Effort to keep going.'

'If you listen to the sounds, and look at the blank walls, you could be in Ardmore on a summer's morning,' Becca said wistfully, as we lay in our bivvy bags just after first light. No one wanted to move, and for a moment everything was all right. Then reality came slowly into focus. Dust, dust, dust—we were lying in a pit of the dreadful *polvo*. I found it difficult to hide my depression; it seemed all the anxiety and effort of the past weeks had been for nothing.

Somehow we ground through another day. When the helicopter returned I saw that the people were delighted: there was no question but that the villagers were on the side of the military. They brightened up still more when an Army patrol came in.

The first soldier in was the scout, a crew-cut, tough twenty-year-old. He came running up to the square house, sweating like a racehorse, a good quarter of an hour before the officer and ten other men. Considering the heat, I was surprised at their dress: cap comforter, polo neck sweater and gloves were all made of thick black wool, which they said was for the cold on the mountains at night. Although they had good jungle boots and light-weight jungle-green trousers, their webbing was old-fashioned and worn out, and the white blanco hadn't been touched for some time. But the rifles were relatively modern, high velocity 7.62mm Belgian FNs, very businesslike.

'Old heads on young bodies,' commented Ed, looking at the tired young faces. M.C. gave some hot sweet tea to the scout, who flopped down in our quarters, hoping the gesture might lessen the chances of him shooting us.

The young officer was limping badly, having been kicked in the right thigh by a mule as he came running down the path only half an hour previously. But when Marie Christine and Bec produced the medical kit, the best medicine turned out to be a good slug of our Johnny Walker whisky.

'My Colonel drinks this,' he laughed wryly. 'Nobody below that rank can afford it!'

I never asked the officer's name, and this is an indication of just how delicate I thought our own situation: I didn't wish to give the slightest impression of spying on his patrol. I explained what we were doing and produced my documents as usual. Quite properly, he told me as little as he could, simply mentioning that he had been patrolling the area for a week; a tiny squad searching for an invisible enemy in a huge jungle. I noticed that all the soldiers, and the officer, were strangers to the district: on purpose or by coincidence the patrol was made up of men from the Pacific side of the Andes. On the other hand, the *Senderos* were mainly locals. This practice of having only an occasional military presence, made up of strangers, opposing an indigenous army, was a powerful element in favour of the terrorists in their struggle for the hearts and minds of the villagers.

The patrol took over the square building; young and vigorous, they were a great support to community morale. The villagers cooked food for them and generally made them feel welcome. We moved all our gear into our two tiny rooms, and the soldiers reassured us with flashing smiles that now they were here we could sleep safely at night.

One of the officer's problems was being out of contact with his base, far away over the mountains in Andahuaylas. His soldiers cranked away tirelessly at the hand-powered generator on their American radio, but to no effect.

That night—25 November—brought yet another worry in the form of a story from a villager who had been kidnapped in the attack on Amaybamba on 10 November. The man had escaped after a few days, but not before he had overheard the *Senderos* claim that they would control the whole Mapito river valley by 1 December. If this were true, the sooner we five unarmed *gringos* were out of the valley, the better.

At midnight four rifle shots rang out. We knew that they were pre-arranged, to scare off the terrorists. But they sounded surprisingly close, a crashing volley in the blackness. We all stared at the window holes in the walls, as if expecting *Sendero* heads to appear over the mud sills at any moment. It was time to go.

Chapter Nineteen

'Papa Cuatro! Papa Cuatro! Papa Cuatro!' called the radio operator, and his assistant sweated at the hand generator. At 7am he finally got through, and could just make out a voice crackling through the static from Andahuaylas. It said a helicopter would be coming to lift out the patrol at 9am. The soldiers greeted this news with a cheer, but the villagers looked grim, and I wondered if the politicians in faraway Lima understood how their voters felt when they were abandoned in this way.

We were washed, shaved and all packed up for an early start. The left side of my face was badly swollen from black-fly bites, and the itching was driving me crazy. In spite of obvious enthusiasm to be on our way to a higher, cooler place, we felt sad at leaving the good friends we had made at the square building and in the village. Shaking hands with them all, I felt I must try to bring some attention to their plight: but how? Why didn't the Army protect them? Surely the outgoing patrol should be replaced by another?

As ever, we were happiest walking on our own, under clear blue skies. It was a beautiful day, and we made our way up the leafy valley in the cool of early morning, along the narrow, tree-lined path through Pacaybamba, where we had bought the unripe fruit a couple of days before. The jungle was a splash of vivid greens in the Mapito valley floor to our right, and the brilliant glacier melt white of the tumbling river matched the glittering peak of Choquesapra, five miles north and on our left.

After nearly two hours the sun was blasting down on us again as we came to a scattering of huts called Chirimayo and called in at a well-to-do looking place on our right-hand side, just below the path. We must have looked as hot and bothered as we felt, and the old woman of the house responded kindly to our request for something to eat and drink.

While we filled our water bottles from the stream, she spread sheepskins in the shade of her open bamboo bedroom. Over sweet black home-grown coffee and cold yucca we learned that she was Baden-Powell's sister; indeed, he had lived here ever since her husband's death. It was a beautiful place, high above the river, and surrounded by its own coffee, bananas, limes and avocados. Cobs of maize were stored neatly in the roof to dry, and the hut was filled with good quality old saddles and harness for horses and mules, much of it in hand-tooled leather. As she saw us looking at the piles of rawhide cargo nets, saddle-bags, and bridles, the old woman's face turned sad: she told us how the terrorists had come a few nights ago and stolen all ten of her horses and mules, depriving the family of their living as muleteers in the valley.

She said the terrorists were nothing but robbers, and they had taken the animals for food. It seemed Amaybamba was effectively surrounded. Without military support, the *Sendero* forecast for 1 December might well come true and then the valley would suffer the same fate as Hatumpampa, Lucmahuayco and Osambre. The old lady told gruesome tales of women and children fleeing with no more than the clothes they stood up in. Again we felt guilty to be leaving.

The sweet coffee gave me some zip at a time when I was feeling low. Soon we found ourselves walking along a level path, something unusual in Peru, and I asked myself, Do I want to be miserable today, or shall I be happy? I realised I was exquisitely happy, moving well in a beautiful place with my family beside me. Soon Becca would be starting a new life in London, as far from Ardmore as the Pyrenees or Munich. I'd better make the most of the day. Bec was brighter in herself, and although she was suffering from bites like the rest of us, she was no longer as apprehensive as she had been.

The path crossed the river half an hour up the valley. Terrorists had all but managed to destroy the single-span bridge of tree trunks which passed some twenty feet over the rushing Mapito river. The Indians had succeeded in keeping the crossing open, with just three of the ten logs in position, one of them badly split in the middle. It made for a tricky passage, difficult for humans, impossible for animals.

We rested on the far bank, cooling ourselves with Ed's trick of plunging our heads under the icy water. We took turns with the Zeiss monocular to scan the forest on either side of the valley for signs of movement. We were in no doubt that terrorists were watching the path. They were there, stuck out in the jungle, with no support, desperately short of medical supplies, armed with little more than their own savagery and the few weapons which they had managed to steal in raids. Above all they needed food.

Because of our heavy loads, we'd been advised to take three days over the journey to the nearest trucks in Huancacalle. The first day should take us as far as the little village of Accobamba, at 9,000 feet, and we were hoping for cool English summer weather, without the black-fly.

We had already done a fair bit of climbing by the time we stopped for lunch in the village of Tranco, at the home of a woman we met on the path. She had been taking food to her husband in the fields, and the young child and a dog she had with her had slowed her to our pace. She had no food for us, but the yucca which the lieutenant had given us now tasted a lot better. Ed cut up a section of sugar cane he'd been carrying for days, and among our kit we found a nearly-ripe mango. Somehow we managed to spin this far from heavy meal into about an hour's break. The woman told us that most of the villagers had abandoned their houses and left for Quillabamba. Across the river we could see overgrown fields, and she said the villagers had been warned by the terrorists not to cross the stream.

The track wound only uphill now, and we saw several mule trains, invariably heavy laden going out, the animals usually carrying nothing on the return journey from the outside world. It was a one-way trade, for the terrorists were emptying the district. Several of the muleteers carried rifles slung across their backs, and one went so far as to warn us of the chance of terrorists robbing us on the track.

Although Justin and Ed never complained, M.C., Bec and I found the climb getting harder as each hour passed. We stopped for five minutes every fifteen now, grabbing every opportunity to dip our heads in cold water and drinking heavily from the crystal streams that rushed down out of the forest above. Butterflies fluttered round us in dazzling shades of orange, yellow, white and blue; they settled on the toecaps of our boots, and we found all manner of reasons for not disturbing the gorgeous creatures.

My good humour departed. I felt exhausted. Why had we gone through so much bother to struggle through Huanipaca to the salt mine? Our night on the dry ridge and the dangerous descent the following day were all to no purpose. I had wantonly risked Justin's life; I'd known how dangerous the river was, even if he and the others had not. Elvin was dead. Now, in a rush of self-pity, I remembered his high spirits when we were shooting the rapids in 1970. 'The days of man are but as grass: for he flourisheth as a flower in the field,' I thought. 'For as soon as the wind goeth over it, it is gone: and the place thereof shall know it no more.' I had reached the stage in life at which funerals become more common than weddings—a gloomy thought.

My 203-day, non-stop sailing voyage round the planet, from and to the mooring under the wood at the foot of the croft at Ardmore, over the previous couple of years, had left me with a strong feeling of the finite nature of our existence. In the Southern Ocean the great whales and albatrosses seem everlasting to the sailor who ventures to pass through their domain; every time he comes, they are there, apparently unchanging. But in fact they are living out their lives like all other creatures; they have their time, and only the ocean itself, and the mighty weather systems, endure.

During a break by the stream I glanced across at Justin and Ed, twenty years my junior. I remembered how it felt to be lean and taut and filled with boundless energy. They were definitely thin, rather than lean, now, and they weren't talking much either. Sagging on a boulder, halfway up an endless path to God knows where, I felt like a Michelin man with a slow puncture. Altogether, our progress was in danger of becoming five minutes of walking with fifteen minutes of rest. We were all running on our reserves: the shortage of food for so long had burned up a lot of fat.

My dark cloud of anti-climax was lightened only by a loose aim somehow to find the surviving Bergs, Olaf, Virgilio and Bertha, so that we could at least give the relatives in Europe a clear account of what had happened at Osambre.

At four in the afternoon, as the sun fell behind the mountains, we finally straggled into Accobamba. Set on a natural step in the mountainside, the village reminded me of a hill station in India, and I almost expected to see steep fields of tea. Dense forest clung to the mountains on both sides of the path, which ran above and parallel to the thundering headwaters of the Rio Mapito, below us to the left.

The disappearance of the sun emphasised the blessed cool of altitude, and shadow darkened the moist green forest which entirely surrounded the village. There were only a few huts, some padlocked and forlorn, scattered among tall blue eucalyptus. Cows and donkeys grazed among chickens and ducks on a gentle slope clothed with patches of bald green grass. The surprising central feature of the place was the pair of long, low, tin-roofed huts, lying end to end.

'*Señor!*' A short, crafty-looking storekeeper called to us, walking over from a cat's cradle of freshly cut rawhide cargo netting which he was pegging out on the ground to dry.

'I am the *Gobernador*. Show me your passports!' he said gruffly, and I wondered if he wasn't just a little frightened.

The letters and book calmed him, and our obvious delight in finding basic commodities such as rice, sugar and pasta in his dark and dusty shop, among boxes of Camay soap and crates of long-empty beer bottles, seemed to reassure him that we weren't the gun-runners that passing muleteers had warned him of.

At the school the Director, a charming man in his mid-thirties called Abelio, showed us to an empty classroom, explaining that only forty-three children remained out of the original 120, and many of these were so nervous that they couldn't concentrate on their lessons. The terrorist threat was so serious that all schools in the district were closing fourteen days early, on Friday, 6 December, for the Christmas holiday, which lasted until March.

Apparently Accobamba, astride the main path to the outside world, was the administrative centre for education in a large district, and as such it presented a real target for the terrorists. The teachers slept poorly in their straw-thatched hut at nights, fully clothed and ready for flight. Their colleagues in Hatumpampa had had the thatch burned over their heads, and the school in Choquetira, the next village up the path, had been burned to the ground a few months earlier. Abelio had buried the school records in the garden, just in case.

The villagers were suspicious of us, and we were able to buy only a few potatoes. We were told they were frankly frightened of strangers, unwilling even to supply the teachers, whom they identified as a threat to their own safety. *Sendero* notices, pinned up by night, warned the community to isolate themselves from the teachers, who were trying to brainwash their children into the evil ways of a capitalist society.

As far as the teachers could tell, the community was staunchly against the *Senderos*. Distrustful of political dogma, they simply wanted to be left in peace. They too had formed their own *vigilantes* or *ronda*, and warned anyone thinking of leaving home that this was the time for the community to be united and drive off the terrorists. To leave Accobamba now would mean to leave for ever.

Eventually we were able to buy a kilo of fresh red steak which, fried up with the potatoes by M.C., put new heart into us. It tasted a little odd, and enquiries revealed the accidental death of a mule the previous day. The unfortunate beast had slipped and fallen from the mountainside a few hundred feet above the village. Now I remember the new, rawhide cargo nets the storekeeper had been pegging out when we'd arrived—but it tasted very good, whatever.

A young teacher called Cesar, who spoke American-accented English, told us that the Indians had little time for the Peruvian Government, *campesinos* had never really been recognised as citizens of their own country, though they made up half the population. Other than education, they believed, the Government gave them nothing. And this outlook exactly suited the main plank of *Sendero* philosophy: since democracy had never benefited the *campesinos*, and never would, the only path forward lay in a completely new Maoist system, in which the *campesinos* would be equal partners. Not for nothing had the *Sendero Luminoso* movement begun in Ayacucho, a city in the centre of a huge concentration of impoverished *campesinos*.

The *Senderos*, Cesar said, were like the Khmer Rouge in Kampuchea: they refused any link with the national Communist Party because it favoured a dialogue with the democratically elected government. If the *Senderos* came to power, they would make a completely fresh start, with history beginning again at Year One.

Here in Accobamba, the terrorists might launch an attack at any time from the thick, steep jungle across the Mapito river, which was only twenty feet wide. From the villagers' point of view, the Government was represented by the military, but they were only in Accobamba very rarely. On the other hand, the terrorists, with their political views, were ever-present: they had already stolen all the community cattle on the far side of the river and forbidden the villagers to cross.

Topographically, I felt that the narrow defile at Accobamba was an excellent place for terrorists to cut the path and seal off the valley, all the way back to the Apurimac.

In spite of all these anxieties, we were so exhausted that we slept soundly though the night on the concrete classroom floor, with our emergency kit to hand. Next morning it rained, and I woke up with the beginnings of a cold. We needed little persuading to spend the day resting in the village. Justin and I joined a game of volleyball with the school during the mid-morning break, and Cesar, with his unusual height, was the star of the show. Ed went up the mountainside to a little plateau by a spectacular waterfall, to find some Inca ruins. Apparently the Incas fled to this inaccessible place after their defeat at Machu Picchu.

By lunch time my nose was running like a tap. I lay on the floor in one of the administrative offices, feeling seedy. M.C. and Bec set off in the rain to see if they could buy bread from a wily old woman whose husband had been baking rolls in a beehive-shaped mud kiln for forty years or more. After much bargaining and laughter, they had thirty of the little beauties in the bag.

Unable to resist eating a few on the way, they meandered back along the leafy path, lined with blue flowers and running with water. Smoke, rising from the sodden thatch of the huts, mingled with the mist hanging low over the village and seemed to enclose Accobamba in a lost world of its own, surrounded by a dark green wall of forest.

After yet another look round the almost-bare shop, they stopped at a little bamboo house with a thatched roof and, seeing a couple of bottles of *chicha* maize beer on a bench outside, M.C. asked the woman of the house if they could buy them. The beer was light and fizzy: Bec found the refreshing, sweetish taste similar to that of elderflower champagne.

Refugees came trailing up the path all day, large families and small, even pathetic teenage couples with no more than a baby and a mule, heading for the city slums. Shortly after dark two men called Elliot and Jude appeared, driving twenty cows and bulls brought from the despairing villagers of Amaybamba. They also brought worrying news. Yesterday, a concentration of terrorists had been observed crossing to our side of the Apurimac, near the mouth of the Mapito river. The military had responded to the alarm and sent in a helicopter force which had destroyed the *Senderos'* boats with hand grenades, but not before the terrorists were safely away into the jungle. The military were then air-lifted back to Andahuaylas. There had been rumours of terrorists seen crossing fields and heading up the valley. There were three days left before 1 December.

M.C. fried up the rest of the mule for supper, and I slept badly, with a roaring cold. During the night I thought about Becca's *otitis media* on the Altiplano, and decided not to chance making for the 15,000 foot pass which we had heard was metres deep in snow.

Dawn came late, with rain drumming on the corrugated iron roof. Poor Becca found that her neatly folded clothes had been piled right under the only hole in the roof. It was miserable weather for walking anyway, and there was no argument against staying another day in Accobamba. Six small, brightly-speckled brown trout given to Ed made a delicious breakfast; then we cleared our gear out of the classroom for the day's school.

It was no day for a streaming cold. Heavy rain had set in, and we needed a fire to sit by. M.C. and Bec took me to the little bamboo hut by the path where they'd bought the *chicha* beer the previous afternoon. Stationed opposite the shop, on a bend, it made an ideal place for travellers to stop for a cup of coffee and a gossip. Marie Christine knocked on the door, rattling the light bamboo poles. There was no reply, and I was just thinking about going back and getting into my sleeping-bag when the door opened a bit and a face looked up at us from about knee height. I expected to see a child, but I was looking at the face of a grown young woman.

'Come in!' She smiled sweetly. 'My mother is out, but soon she will return.' She pulled the door wide open and suddenly I could see she was crippled, only able to drag herself around with her arms. My first reaction was to think how difficult it would be for her to escape if the terrorists came.

The woman had a strong, intelligent face; I got the impression of a powerful person trapped on the floor. We sat down by the door in a tiny dark room, hanging with soot and overrun by about twenty cooing guinea pigs. The girl told us her name was Virginie, and hauled herself into the left-hand corner, where she tipped a handful of homegrown coffee beans into a black pot on a small fire of twigs. 'Whoosh! Midgi!' she hissed at a skeletal black cat, covered in fine grey ash, which prowled dangerously close to the flames. Ducks and chickens tried to join us out of the rain, but we beat them back, and they fluttered their wings with displeasure.

Becca picked up a squeaking black piglet, about nine inches long and attached to a bit of string. The coffee beans began to crackle, and thin, aromatic smoke curled out of the pot. Then Virginie put them through a cast-iron grinder and poured boiling water over the coarse powder. When the coffee was infused, she drained it through a long sock-like tube and poured it into three bright-white enamel mugs. All we had to do was stir in rough sugar and drink the delicious stuff. Becca was just too quick for the piglet, which began piddling on its way down to the ground.

Virginie give us a plate of toasted maize to nibble while we drank the coffee, and began working at her crochet. I noticed blackened pigs' bladders, bottles and gourds up in the ceiling.

It was all I could do to join in the conversation, I felt so rough; but inevitably we turned to the reason for our visit to Peru. I suppose I should have realised Virginie would know the Bergs. They must have called in many times on their way to Quill-abamba with coffee—I remembered old Abel telling me it was Quillabamba they went to.

Now Virginie confirmed that Abel and his wife had died ten years ago.

'Abel was a very good man,' she said, looking up from her crochet. 'Always friendly and laughing.'

'Yes. He loved Osambre.' I felt devastated by the thought of how it had all turned out. But then the bombshell burst.

'You know Elvin's daughter is living here in Accobamba,' said the cripple.

Silence fell. I don't think any of us could believe we'd heard right.

'Did you say *Elvin*'s daughter?' I thought maybe she'd said Abel's daughter. I remembered an unhappy eighteen-year-old, fifteen years back. Bertha would be thirty-three now; it was possible that she might be up here somewhere. But Virginie said:

'Yes, Elvin's daughter. Her name is Lizbet. She has lovely curly hair—not straight, like us Peruvians.' Ruefully she stroked her own black hair, which was straight and lustrous.

'Where does she live?' M.C. burst out. 'How old is she?'

'Oh—she's six or seven, and she lives just along the path. It's only a few hundred metres, to the left of the track by the cemetery.'

Chapter Twenty

The news of Lizbet's presence in Accobamba completely changed our outlook: we had found a Berg. Had we subconsciously been expecting something to happen, after all the trials of the past weeks? Doesn't something always come up if you hold on long enough? Or was it simply an extraordinary coincidence? The odds against us finding a child of Elvin's must have been astronomical. We had stopped only because we didn't get the mules in Amaybamba. We had stayed only because I had a cold; and we were two or three days' journey from where the child's father had lived.

Virginie's mother came in with her sister Simeona—two strikingly handsome women in their late forties. Simeona was instantly excited by our eagerness to meet Elvin's daughter, and we took an immediate liking to her. Within minutes we were on our way, through the dripping trees to where the girl was living.

'Go quietly,' Simeona whispered. 'This family has suffered terribly. They are very nervous.' We clambered over a broken-down wall covered by clinging, sodden undergrowth and found ourselves in a small, ill-kept meadow, looking downhill at the back of a single hut some thirty yards away.

'Lizbet's mother, Leocadia, is away working in Huancacalle,' Simeona went on, as we followed her across the field in the rain. 'The girl will be with her grandmother, Josephina. We must not frighten them.'

Coming round the hut, we stopped in front of the central section, which was open to the air, with a fire burning in a back corner. Two women and three young children were sitting in the dark and smoky recess. Immediately I focused on one small girl.

'That's Elvin!' I said instinctively. 'I can see him in her face.' A second later, without thinking, I added, 'How will she look at Ardmore?'

It was done on impulse. In that moment of setting eyes on the child, I knew I must see Elvin right and do what I could for his daughter.

The small figure was sitting cross-legged on a sheepskin, slightly apart from the others, drinking soup from an enamel bowl. Her skin was unusually pale and her hair a deep, wavy brown, not black, under a grimy, crocheted yellow and white hat. Her pink knitted dress looked as if it had seen many owners. She stared at us unblinking, with a solemn, rather sad look.

There were four others in the alcove: Granny Josephina, her daughter Marcilina, and her two little children. Josephina looked about sixty. She sat by the fire, very much the matriarch: as Simeona spoke to her in Quechuan, her careworn face took on a hunted look and anxiety caused her chest to rise and fall sharply with hyperventilation. There were no smiles, only nervous looks —but also some dignity in the distress.

While Simeona began to explain who we were, I took *Amazon Journey* from the flap of the top of my pack and turned the pages until I found the photo of Elvin in 1970. Both Josephina and her daughter recognised him immediately, pointed excitedly at the picture. At once the atmosphere improved a lot, and the women began smiling towards us while they chattered in Quechuan. Did they think I was a relative of Elvin? Did Lizbet even think I could be her father? We were offered sheepskins to sit on, against the left-hand side wall of the alcove. Simeona stayed on her feet and began to interpret the family's story for us.

Josephina and her husband Juan Huaman Chavez, who was away working in the fields, came originally from Lucmahuayco. Juan Huaman had been the *Teniente* [Lieutenant Governor] in that village for fifteen years, and when the *Sendero Luminoso* attacked in May 1984, after destroying Osambre, he had fled into the mountains. The terrorists first murdered his old mother in revenge for his having escaped, and then brutally dismembered his only son, throwing his bloodied trousers at Josephina's feet as a warning.

These terrible events had unhinged Leocadia's mind, and she had developed periods of madness. The other daughter, Marcilina, had been in Lucmahuayco as well, with her husband and two children, Freddie and Johannie; rather than die, the husband had joined the terrorists—the only alternative. Recaptured, he was now in prison in Quillabamba.

With the village virtually destroyed, and their home burned, Josephina and her family had become refugees. They set off on foot, looking for somewhere else to live. Two months later they arrived in Accobamba, where Juan Huaman's brother was *Gobernador*. At first they had stayed in a borrowed house, but when, after three months alone in the forest, sixty-three-year-old Juan Huaman staggered down from the mountains, they bought the house we were now in. The sale had been an act of compassion, by a man with two houses: the hut was bare, save for rags and a few black cooking pots. It was not what you would call a home.

'*Lizbet está triste. No tiene mama, no tiene papa. Pobre niña.*' Simeona looked sadly across at us.

'Does Elvin have any other children?' I asked.

There was a pause while Simeona put the question to Granny Josephina, and we knew by the shake of her head that she meant Lizbet was an only child.

Marie Christine and Becca were both gazing hard at her. All our minds were racing ahead, but it was a time of intense emotion rather than of reason.

'We must give her something,' I mumbled, 'to mark our visit here.'

'I'll give her my Irish Granny's ring,' said M.C. '*Her* name was Elizabeth.' With hands trembling she slipped the silver ring off her thin brown finger.

'My confirmation chain!' Instantly Becca began to take off her most precious possession. 'She can hang the ring on it.'

As Marie Christine knelt down to put the chain and ring round Lizbet's neck, I could see Becca fighting back her tears.

We asked if Becca could take photographs for the relatives in Norway; even if Elvin was dead, they would surely be delighted to have a picture of his child. Granny agreed, and clearly she had a sense of occasion, for she rummaged in an old sack of clothes and brought out a bright green dress which she slid over the top of the pink one. Marcilina began washing Lizbet's face and wetting her hair, while the girl sat on the floor, uncomplaining, but with her lively eyes fixed on us.

The atmosphere had become so highly charged that we felt we must leave, at any rate for the time being, to let everyone calm down. Granny took Marie Christine's hands and embraced her. As we walked down the steps, Lizbet came out into the light, as if she didn't want us to go, and called to me, 'Ciao, Pappi.' The little salutation took my breath away. Not knowing that *Ciao, Pappi* was a standard form of Quechuan greeting to any man, I thought the girl had said, 'Goodbye Daddy.'

By the time we got round the side of the house, we were all speechless. Becca went ahead, to avoid having a talk, but Simeona stopped and looked me straight in the eye. The child was pining, she said: with a dead father and no mother to look after her, she had no future. Then came the words I'd been hoping for: 'The grandmother has asked, will you take Lizbet home with you?'

As we walked the few paces up to the broken wall at the top of the field, Simeona suggested in so many words that we adopt Lizbet. I thought of my 203 days' sailing non-stop round the world and how, during that period, I'd made one or two decisions about the rest of my life. I made another now. If Marie Christine and Becca both agreed, we would adopt Elvin's daughter.

We stepped across the cemetery and started down the path towards the village. Becca walked ahead, still wanting to be on her own.

'What do you think, Flower?' I said quietly.

'I don't know, Johnny,' Marie Christine was crying. 'I'll have to think about it.'

I could see that she wanted to do it, but was astonished that I did: it was completely unlike me. For the moment I left it at that, embarrassed by the presence of our guide.

We turned off the path and began going down through the scattered huts, towards the two school buildings. Curtains of pale grey rain swept up the valley, obscuring the forest on the far side. I caught up with my daughter, and put my arm round her shoulders.

'What do you think, Bec? Should we take her home with us?'

'It's all so unfair, living here,' she sobbed.

'But would you want her in the family?'

'It's you and Mum who'll have to look after her. It's up to you.'

'That's not what I mean. *Do you want Lizbet for a sister?*' I felt I must find this out before we reached the school and had to share any news with Justin and Ed.

'Of course I do!'

Simeona left us at the archway into the school compound. The empty classroom echoed with the noise of the opening door as we stumped in, dripping water on the dusty concrete floor.

'It's all changed,' I blurted out. 'We've found Elvin's seven-year-old daughter. They've asked us to adopt her and take her back to Ardmore.'

The others were stunned. Normally so quick to comment, they could not find anything to say.

'Have you thought out the consequences?' asked Ed incredulously.

'No—we just feel this is something we must do.'

We had the whole afternoon to kill, as we planned to go back and discuss the adoption with Juan Huaman Chavez, Lizbet's grandfather and the head of the family, when he came back from the fields at five o'clock; but first we had to decide whether or not we really wanted to have the girl.

'La Ronda' Accobamba. Accounts for the month of November 1985

Elizabeth and Grandfather Juan Huaman

From bottom: Virginie, Theresa.
Top from left: MC, Simeona, John

From the left: Freddie, Elizabeth with Becca's confirmation chain and
Marie Christine's ring round her neck, Elizabeth's Granny Josephina,
Marcilina, Johannie

It would mean a huge change for both of us. We had been married over 20 years. Marie Christine was one of four children from a good, secure home, and she would have liked a large family. My own views were different. An adopted child, I have always felt insecure. One of my beliefs, perhaps simplistic, has been that a way of reducing the world's problems would be to halve the population. I have not seen much in my travels to shake this view.

But my non-stop voyage round the world had changed my perspectives. Now, I thought, here was something positive I could do in the years remaining to me. Lizbet was already alive, and in adopting her we would not be adding to the population. Besides, the timing was an extraordinary coincidence, miraculous almost. The three of us had met in a hut in deepest Peru. Lizbet had become known to us just as Becca was about to leave home and step off into the outside world. Maybe it was meant to happen.

'Mum keen, and Dad, although I never thought he would be,' Rebecca wrote in her diary, a little ambiguously.

Our visit to the grandfather would be a serious matter, so I asked Cesar, who spoke English and Quechuan, to come with us. I wanted to avoid any possibility of our misunderstanding Simeona's Spanish, especially as I was feeling so ill.

Cesar was visibly moved by the idea of the opportunity which adoption would offer Lizbet. He had already told me of his own difficult upbringing. His father was a well-to-do civil engineer in Cuzco, but his mother had been just a servant in the house. His father had dismissed the girl straight after the birth, so that Cesar had never met his mother. This situation had led to much trouble between father and son, and they were no longer communicating. Thus Cesar immediately sympathised with Lizbet.

At last it was 5.30. Cesar and Simeona came with us to see Juan Huaman. Lizbet was still sitting on the sheepskin, chain and ring round her neck, half-smiling at us.

Juan Huaman sat on a box on the opposite side of the alcove

from us, occasionally burying his face in his hands with anxiety. A gaunt old man of sixty-four, with a fine brown poncho and a bright woollen hat, he was still proud enough to manage a smile now and then. He told us he was now old and in poor health, and not able to maintain Josephina and Lizbet, and Marcilina and her two children as well. He was sure the terrorists would come any day; they were in the forest overlooking the village, he said, pointing out at the trees across the valley. Leocadia—his daughter, and Lizbet's mother—was *media tonta*, driven half-mad by what had happened. She had been so upset by the dreadful events that she was no longer able to look after her little girl. She had been sent away to work for her keep as a domestic help in the house of a cousin, Guillermo, in Huancacalle (the village in which we hoped to get a lift on a truck for Quillabamba.)

Juan Huaman quite clearly saw this extraordinary visit by five *gringos*, with their picture in a book of Lizbet's dead father, as her chance for a decent existence. He was adamant, frequently using the word *oportunidad*, that he wanted us to take her to Europe, to give her an education and a chance in life. He said he would gladly sign the papers for her adoption, but that there was a problem: all documentary record of her existence had been burned in the fire at Lucmahuayco. Yet, as she had been baptised here in Accobamba in September 1984, shortly after her arrival, Cesar thought there must be a record of the baptism in the village.

Juan Huaman said that, since terrorist attack was imminent, he was going to take the girl to Huancacalle. However, he could not leave for another three days, until Monday, 2 December, because he must attend an assembly of the Community Council at which he hoped to be granted a piece of land to work for himself. If we travelled with him, he said, we could arrange the adoption in Huancacalle and finalise it in Quillabamba. Then we could take Lizbet back to Britain with us on the plane on 18 December.

The old man's confidence was touching, but I thought we'd need several more coincidences to make all that happen. Looking out, we realised darkness had fallen, and the grandfather urged us not to linger. 'The *ronda*', he kept saying, 'the *ronda*.'

We trooped out into the night, across the field, over the wall, past the cemetery and down the wet lane to the school, feeling a little dazed and worried lest we got shot by a trigger-happy patrol. I asked Cesar if he thought a life in the materialistic West was really preferable to one in Peru? I guess there were very few suicides in Accobamba, but he was in no doubt that Ardmore was the place for Lizbet.

Simeona and Cesar stayed for supper in the classroom, to share a very tough and expensive chicken which Ed had bought the previous morning. Justin had it stewed up and ready for us when we got in, but M.C. was too overcome by events to be able to eat anything. During the candlelit meal a couple of bats flew out of the rafters, causing the English ladies to put their hats on in double quick time. Once in their sleeping-bags, both of them lay awake, wondering what life would be like with little Lizbet at Ardmore.

During the night we heard a shot. We lay tense and frightened in our sleeping bags, but when nothing more happened we slowly drifted off again.

Next morning the place was alive with the news that the *ronda* had seen lights on the other side of the river, near the ford where the terrorists were expected to cross.

We were now faced with another three days in Accobamba. I was quite happy to stay put and get over my cold, and there was plenty to think about. As M.C. wrote, 'We are, the three of us, almost numbed by the possible enormous change in our lives. It's as though we all feel it was inevitable, and we accept it unquestioningly. Bec and I wander round in a daze, overcome by events which seem outside our control. She would love Lizbet as a sister. And I have much room in my heart for her.'

Becca's entry for the day was simpler: 'Thoughts about Lizbet running through my mind—I'd love to have a little sister (aged seven).'

Juan Huaman brought his brother Alexandro, *Gobernador* of

Accobamba, to see us in the classroom. Alexandro told us there was no certificate of baptism for Lizbet in Accobamba. The brothers agreed that Leocadia was *media tonta* and therefore Juan Huaman as grandfather would need to be accepted by the authorities as next in line of responsibility for Lizbet. For the adoption, both mother and daughter, as well as Juan Huaman, would have to appear in Quillabamba. I tried to imagine what Quillabamba would be like: an overcrowded, steaming jungle town, with us trying to find the right church, the right priest and the right record book.

Cesar turned up a rather startling piece of information. Apparently Elvin had never been married, but he had two young sons, both now living with his brother Olaf in Huanta. Cesar said that although this might seem unusual for Europeans, in Peru it was quite normal. Marie Christine, Becca and I all agreed this was not relevant to our adopting Lizbet: nor were we deterred by the possibility that her mother's insanity might have been inherited.

Again a single rifle shot woke us. Lamplight still shone through the gap under the corrugated iron roof from the meeting of the *ronda* which was still in progress next door. It was midnight by my watch. We sat up on the concrete floor, holding our emergency kit in our hands, reluctant to make a dash for the door unless there was further evidence of terrorist activity. The lamp in the meeting room was put out, and the members began to disperse quietly. After a while all fell silent again, and we slowly sank back to sleep. But Cesar's warning from Amaybamba that fifteen terrorists had been seen crossing a field, heading up towards Accobamba, was never far from our minds.

Next morning, Saturday, 30 November, we lay in bed. We weren't moving towards Huancacalle until Monday morning. My cold felt better, and the sun lifted our spirits. For the first time in Accobamba we could see over the valley to the wondrous snowy peak of Choquesapra.

I joined Marie Christine, Bec and Justin at the nearby water hole, where they were busy washing clothes, and squatted down by the water to shave and brush my teeth. I suppose the luxury of borrowing Justin's badger shaving brush, and the warm sun, extended the business to five minutes or so, and when I'd finished I stood up, mopping my face with a lightweight towel made from a baby's nappy. Then life took a sudden change.

'John! Are you all right?'

I could make out a face swimming towards me across the water, but I could recognise neither face nor voice.

'Must have fallen asleep,' I thought. The water looked silvery and very close, enclosed within a circle of mist.

'Are you OK?' said the voice again, and I recognised it as Justin's. The mists began to dissolve, and I found I was lying on my right side by the irrigation channel. My right eye was no more than three or four inches from the edge of the water, giving an unusual perspective of the silvery reflective surface of a stream no more than a couple of feet wide and an inch or so deep.

'I must have fainted!' I said, astonished, pushing myself up into a sitting position. My right shoulder hurt, and there was a sizeable dent where it had dug into the mudbank of the channel. I'm about six feet tall and weigh thirteen and a half stone, and I must have gone over like a falling tree. I thought it must be very easy to die.

I soon recovered, but feeling a little unsteady, I slept for the rest of the morning. This was an extreme example of the dizziness we had all felt over the past few weeks whenever we stood up too quickly from a kneeling or sitting position. It was an interesting sensation—one which it was always tempting to increase, to see how much dizzier it was possible to get without actually collapsing. Now I knew.

I think the act of standing up causes a change in pressure, which restricts the flow of blood to the brain. I'm told giraffes require a special physique for pumping blood up to their brain, but I can only think that in our case we were somehow affected by altitude and poor diet. Nevertheless, this experience was a shock to me. I had never fainted before, and never been knocked out at boxing, and psychologically this wasn't the best time to start. Perhaps my heavy cold had just tipped the balance.

We visited Lizbet twice in the afternoon, and M.C. wrote, 'Go up to Lizbet and find out if mules are OK for Monday. No grandfather, who speaks Spanish (*poco*), so we can't say much. Lizbet looks at us fixedly, Granny takes my hand in both of hers and shakes it warmly as we leave.'

Of our second visit she recorded: 'Back to Lizbet's—soup and potatoes. Kind, they haven't much, we don't want to take what they need, but it would offend them if we refused. Sit waiting for the return of grandfather, looking out on papaya tree and jungle greenness. River below and steep, tree-covered hill ahead. Darkening with dusk—thunder and bright flashes of lightning. Grandfather returns from work in fields. He has mules organised for Monday. He urges us to go before dark because of *ronda*. We hurry back.'

Our minds were very much occupied with thoughts of taking Lizbet home with us, but still we could not miss the underlying feeling of menace which pervaded everything in Accobamba. Families were being broken and loyalties tested. We were deep in a jungle-clad valley, cut off from the sight of any other habitation, and our knowledge that terrorists were somewhere in the trees gave the place a claustrophobic atmosphere. 'Menace' is the best word I can find to describe it, particularly during the eleven hours of darkness each night.

Cesar described the attack on Amaybamba, giving details he'd heard from a teacher. The raid took place at eleven o'clock at night and lasted until five the following morning. The *ronda* raised the alarm, and the villagers fled up the hillside into the trees. Nearly 180 terrorists were counted against the light of the burning houses, many of them children about twelve years old, carrying spears. Only two shotguns and three rifles were actually seen in the hands of the *Senderos*, and one of the *ronda*, who was apparently drunk, turned and attacked them: he was shot dead.

The thirty-six houses burned were selected by the leader of the gang, who was recognised as a lazy malcontent from Lucmahuayco, well known locally as a man who would not work his own land.

The people of Amaybamba claimed that a military patrol of fifteen and an officer had been close to the position of the *Sendero* leader's group during the attack. But the patrol did not attack, because they were frightened; the soldiers weren't used to the jungle, but they knew very well the terrorists were literally at home in it.

With sparing use of ammunition, a patrol armed with sixteen automatic rifles should have routed 180 practically unarmed marauders. There was a strong feeling, locally, that the terrorists were winning simply because the military would not commit themselves on the Cuzco side of the Apurimac. The Department of Cuzco would not pay for a military presence.

We slept lightly, knowing tomorrow was 1 December. When a shot was fired at 8.30 in the evening, we slipped out of our sleeping-bags in the dark, fast and silent, and stood outside the door wearing belt-order and each carrying an emergency bag. As Marie Christine put it: 'Nerve-racking. Dark, torches, fireflies, dogs barking.'

The enemy would almost certainly be coming up a path from the river. If they appeared, we planned to run left, along the face of the long, low, school building and attack using the bags and knives, rather than simply chance running before faster opponents. It was an uncertain strategy, but we didn't have a very high regard for the enemy, feeling they might be routed by a sufficient show of aggression reinforced by surprise.

We had plenty of thoughts, standing there in the dark, while torches flickered and shouting gathered in intensity and then slowly subsided. After ten minutes or more we crept back to bed, hoping to be quicker next time. Becca was a bit groggy; she'd taken some Piriton tablets before turning in, hoping the anti-hystamine would stop her from scratching the hundreds of bites in her sleep.

Next morning was bright and sunny, but when I visited Cesar's hut, I found him very nervous. Today was Sunday, 1 December, and he was convinced the terrorists would attack. He said the shot last night had been accidental; apparently it had blown the barrel off a rifle, and everyone was asked to look for the barrel if they were down by the river.

We spent much of the day drinking coffee in Theresa's house, up by the path. We were anxious not to pressure Juan Huaman and Josephina by visiting Lizbet too often, but we bought some fresh rolls from the bread lady and took them the extra few yards to Lizbet's home. Everything seemed in order for our departure next day, and Juan Huaman came to the school to see what sort of a load the rucksacks would make for the mules.

It was awful saying goodbye to all the friends we had made in the village; the common fear of terrorist attack produced a rare warmth in even the most casual acquaintanceship. Just as I had often wondered how the Bergs were getting on at Osambre, now I will think about people like Simeona and Virginie in years to come.

We packed our gear and went to bed early, thinking this was the last night: if there was no attack, we'd be away first thing next morning.

Chapter Twenty-one

The rain was back, drumming on the roof, when M.C. got up at 4.30am to make tea and fry five little trout for breakfast. An hour later we were all psyched up and almost ready to go.

Then Juan Huaman arrived, water dripping from the torn sheet of blue plastic which he wore over his fine brown poncho. In such bad weather, he said, he didn't want to go. If it was raining in Accobamba, it would be snowing higher up.

I had already delayed our departure by four days to suit him, and now I was in no mood to stay any longer. The chances of the terrorists attacking were every bit as good as the odds on the weather improving. I was for going, whatever.

By six we were at Lizbet's home. It was in disorder. Josephina looked anxious and kept saying that her husband was a sick man; there was something wrong with his stomach, and he shouldn't be going on such a long journey at his age and in his condition. I'd heard it all before. There were tears and much wringing of hands from Josephina.

Cesar made an excellent interpreter. Juan Huaman confirmed that he was sick, but said that since he'd agreed to go, go he would. Then Marcilina made a move. She loaded one of the three mules with all her gear, stuffed a couple of chickens in a cloth poncho and wrapped it round little Freddie's shoulders. She picked up Johannie, gave the mule a whack, and set off in the misty rain for the path to Huancacalle.

This was the first we'd heard about her coming with us. Cesar said she was taking her children to Quillabamba, to await the release of her husband from prison.

Quite clearly, the two remaining mules were insufficient to carry all our kit. We had arranged to have three. Then we noticed Lizbet was not ready to go. Excuses were made: she had not eaten, she had no waterproofs, she had no shoes for walking, there was no saddle for her to ride. Marie Christine bustled about, finding her shoes and putting two woollen dresses on her. Ed, resourceful as ever, said he would carry the girl up to Choquetira if necessary. When it appeared that none of her excuses was working, Josephina said the little girl was sick. Who, she asked, would be responsible if Lizbet died in the snows on the pass?

By now it was 8.30, and Cesar was due to begin school. He was as upset as anyone. Bitterly denouncing the grandparents for their shortsightedness, he began a see-saw battle of words with Juan Huaman: '*Sí o No? Sí o No?*' he kept asking the old man, who looked fixedly at the ground, trying to avoid the issue. At last he looked up and said quietly: 'No.'

Cesar was almost in tears. Josephina began to lift the necklace and ring over Lizbet's head, to give it back. '*No! No! Regalo, regalo!*' [a gift, a gift] we cried, and the old woman let the necklace fall back round the little girl's throat.

Bec was sobbing quietly as we followed the mules up across the field towards the path. Once on the track, Cesar turned right, and we went left: I could see he was still hoping for some kind of miracle. Before parting, we shook hands and agreed to meet in Cuzco eight days later, after the school term had ended.

We walked in silence for some time, each locked in personal thought. It was a mournful, wet morning. Tendrils of mist hung about the mossy trees and creeping plants, dank and gloomy. Why had the whole plan crashed about our ears? Was it because old Josephina couldn't bear the thought of being left alone, with the terrorists so close? But why, if she had never intended us to take the little girl, had she asked in the first place?

I caught up with Marie Christine and we walked hand in hand. 'We'll see Leocadia in Huancacalle, the day after tomorrow,' I said. 'Then we'll get hold of Olaf Berg in Huanta—he'll make it work.' She just nodded miserably, and we walked on in the rain.

The team was not in good shape. Justin was carrying the lightest of the packs, and the remaining four were in coffee bag nets on the mules. Ed was suffering from sunburn. Becca had about twenty bites on the inside of her left ankle and they had turned into one solid lump which was itching desperately as it rubbed against her boot. I feared it would rub raw and go septic.

The path wound steadily uphill and the trees began to thin out. For a while the weather cleared, and after a couple of hours we reached a little place called Lusana and took a fifteen-minute break. I was finding it all I could do just to keep going, with no load at all. The mule trains we passed were all empty, and many of the huts were padlocked and deserted.

The long, zig-zag climb to Choquetira had really taken it out of me, and I was pleased when Juan Huaman said we should stop in the village for the night, even though it was only 2pm. We'd caught up with Marcilina and the two children, but they looked tireless—an example of what the human frame can achieve even on the poorest of food.

Choquetira lies at close on 13,000 feet. The community is a long straggle of well separated huts, leading up a bleak Altiplano-style valley. But all we could see was mist and thatched huts with round stone fanks for the sheep, as if we had been at home in the Highlands. The terrorists had burned the school six months earlier, and the group of four men and two women whom we found doing accounts in a big ledger were a miserable, suspicious-looking lot. They weren't prepared to let us stay in the evangelical hut which now served as a school; instead, we found ourselves squeezing out of the rain on to the lean-to, open verandah of a deserted hut, whose padlocked doors showed the owners had fled.

We'd just settled in when Juan Huaman appeared with a couple of narrow-faced fellows, well muffled in long ponchos. 'I cannot go on, Señor Juan,' he said, 'my stomach is bad. I must rest here and go home to Accobamba tomorrow.'

Marie Christine looked desolated: our last link with Lizbet was about to be cut, and without the help of Juan Huaman we would never find her mother.

'What about the mules?' asked Justin.

'This man will supply them, and a guide to get you to Huaca-calle.' The sad old fellow pointed at the elder of his two companions. I could see the doleful undertaker-types calculating what to sting us for. Sure enough, they wanted double the price for half the distance. Protracted negotiations led to a compromise. For the first time I had the whole deal written out in long-hand and signed by both parties.

I was feeling cold and sick, and it was a raw night, but I managed to sleep the best part of fourteen hours. In the morning the mules weren't due until 8.30, but we were ready to go an hour earlier. Ed was practising with his catapult, out on the grass, and for the first time the mist was clearing.

'Hey! Look!' he cried. 'It's Juan Huaman and Marcilina. They're not going back to Accobamba after all! They're heading our way.' He bellowed with outrage and before we could calm him made a rude Anglo-Saxon gesture which I felt sure Juan Huaman must have seen.

We all began arguing about what his real motives were, and what he was doing. Adulado, son of the undertaker-type with whom we'd made the deal, had brought two good mules. No more than eighteen, he didn't say much, but he loaded the animals in a sound, professional manner. Unfortunately, he seemed upset by something.

I felt much fitter and was keen to get on with the walking, hoping it would help me think out what to do about Lizbet. Just as we got underway, however, a bugle sounded the alarm. We were heading up a gentle incline of short-cropped grass towards the path. Bugle calls and urgent whistles summoned the community to a low mound with a rough wooden cross on top, fifty yards to our right.

Adulado looked even more miserable. He told us a messenger had brought bad news. The terrorists had captured the village of

Tortora, six miles to the north and at about the same altitude, on top of the cordillera. Coming as it did right on the heels of their triumph in forcing the schools to close early, this was a major coup for the *Senderos*. They'd crossed the Apurimac, and now they'd secured a base on top of the cordillera. In Tortora they were no more than a day's march from cutting the arterial path at either Accobamba or Choquetira, and/or striking an equal distance to the north-east and attacking Vilcabamba, a major settlement on the northern slopes of the mountain chain.

Our thoughts were with Lizbet, Simeona, Virginie and our other friends in Accobamba. Adulado was worrying about his own family here in Choquetira. In spite of every warning, we still felt, 'Surely it can't happen to *us*.'

According to the map we were well over 15,000 feet, though it didn't feel that high. The mountains had shed all vegetation now. The rocks and gravels had those raw bright new shades of red, yellow, green and black which always make me feel in a foreign land, where the minerals are new and constantly in motion.

We were well acclimatised, and I felt much better after a good night's sleep. We had been moving up towards the pass, with good rhythm, for an hour or more, when we saw a horseman coming after us. He galloped up and, without dismounting, handed Adulado a folded message, written on the familiar, squared graph paper. Looking grim, he told us it was for the *gobernador* of the village on the other side of the pass, then pulled at the bridle and galloped back down the mountainside towards Choquetira.

Near the pass the glaciers looked to be on our level or below us, and almost close enough to touch. Above us, on the watershed of the Cordillera, condors played the wind.

'*El paso!*' grunted Adulado, at his most communicative. Surprisingly there was no snow on the path, though the red-brown gravel had that mushy texture which follows a thaw. We were at 16,000 feet, the highest on the whole trip. The pass was a narrow path, perhaps half a mile long, cutting round a right-handed curve on the steep and exposed mountainside. A large memorial wooden cross stood ominously at either end. In snow, it would be difficult to keep upright: one slip would be goodbye. But under present conditions, with Lizbet probably free of problems with the altitude, we would have managed to take her through all right.

Adulado was a good man: he didn't bully the mules, and after the pass we were well able to keep up with his swift descent.

We pushed on at good speed all afternoon, dropping down into a deep, narrow valley, well grown with beautiful flowering trees and bushes. Peaceful water-meadows fed both cattle and sheep. A man and a boy were fishing their way from pool to pool, the boy lugging a cluster of fine trout on a forked stick. This was perhaps the most beautiful valley I'd seen in Peru, but spots of blood on the path reminded me that we might yet be cut off from the trucks, if Adulado's news of the Tortora attack proved true. Certainly he showed every sign of wanting to get his guiding job done so that he could go home.

After crossing the stream by a rickety wooden bridge, and hauling the mules through a ford, he arranged for us to stay the night in a leaky cattle shed, near one of the only houses we saw in the valley. Next morning he set off at a cracking speed, but luckily the mules soon tired and the pace slackened a bit. Then, way above us, we saw three tiny figures and two mules. They were moving more slowly than us, and soon we identified them: Juan Huaman, Marcilina with Johannie on her back, and little Freddie. Closing on them, we found that both the adults had big lumps of coca in their cheeks, and as they seemed pleased to see us, we slowed down to walk with them. Freddie was walking very well for a six-year-old. With cap set at a jaunty angle, and ancient check jacket with sleeves much too long, he was now carrying two hens, each with its head poking out of the cloth poncho on his back in a most comical fashion. Marcilina looked very pregnant, and with Johannie on her back as well, it was remarkable that she managed to walk at all.

At the summit we stopped for a while and dished out some

Dextrosol glucose tablets and salt for the children, and M.C. produced one of her emergency packets of dried figs. Walking down the steep path with Juan Huaman, I was reassured by his friendliness and warmth, and impressed by the courage of this sad, battered old man with his ulcerated stomach. In thinking he had double-crossed us, we had misjudged him. He was still keen for us to take Lizbet back to Britain, and we agreed to meet at Guillermo's house in Huancacalle.

Then two horsemen came hurrying up the mountain on their way back to Incahuasi. Their horses looked as if they'd been ridden hard, and the men told us breathlessly that seventeen terrorists from Tortora had raided the village of Vilcabamba on the previous day, burning several houses, and apparently cutting the truck route out to Quillabamba. If this was true, it meant there would be no vehicles leaving Huancacalle. But I couldn't believe we were trapped: there just weren't enough terrorists to prevent us from making a detour around any blockage in the valley. Even so, Adulado became even more anxious to press on, and we had to leave the little family party behind so that he could get us to Huancacalle, and set off for home again as soon as possible.

At last, just after noon, hot and weary, we emerged from the undergrowth at the point where dusty red path meets rough mining road on the outskirts of Huancacalle. Of terrorists, there was no sign. Justin, Ed and Adulado took the mules on into town so that Adulado could unload and get going on his homeward journey.

Marie Christine, Becca and I sat at the edge of the track and waited for Juan Huaman and his family party. We were much lower now, around 9,000 feet, and it was desperately hot. Trees drooped under the midday sun. Elder bushes looked out of place among the bamboo, but the place seemed reassuringly civilised, with an occasional new house set beside the road, bright with red or blue wash. Surely these were the homes of successful tradesmen, not of people who would wish to wreck the system?

The enforced wait turned our minds towards Lizbet. It would

be all too easy, now, just to get on a truck and disappear back to our active and entirely diverting lives in Scotland. But we waited, and after half an hour the little team of refugees trooped into sight. They looked tired and Juan Huaman suggested we follow them down to Guillermo's house.

Eventually we came to a neat-looking, mud-walled house with a shiny roof of corrugated aluminium, shaded by trees and just back from the road. Juan Huaman hitched the mules to a tree and led his party over a low stone wall into the house. We three waited in the shade on the other side of the road, unwilling to push straight in on a family reunion.

When Juan Huaman came out again to unload his animals, with his patient, worried look, I suggested we leave the family to discuss the idea of the adoption. We agreed to go up into the village and return in half an hour.

The hands of my watch slowly turned towards two o'clock. We were dreading the possibility that Leocadia might have reacted badly to our proposal, and our feet dragged as we made our way those few hundred yards back down the road. But we felt Lizbet's future was out of our hands: the whole thing was being decided by fate. Each time we'd lost hope of ever getting her to Britain, something had always started the process up again.

Guillermo was just in from working in the field of maize at the back of the house. A tallish, balding figure in his mid-thirties, he was intelligent and 'less shell-shocked' as M.C. put it. We made sure he understood our plan: the family were to complete the documentation on their side, and get Lizbet to Lima. We would arrange adoption from our side, and fly the child to Britain.

Marie Christine wrote: 'Leocadia comes out. She is pretty—wide, innocent happy face—like a simple child, and perhaps she is *media tonta*. Does she know we might take her Lizbet to Britain?'

When I showed her the picture of Elvin in *Amazon Journey* Leocadia laughed excitedly; but I felt maybe she'd have been

Crossing Chucuito Pass

The trout stream near Abra

Relaxation at Machu Picchu. From left: Justin, Bec, John, Ed

John showing Leocadia (second from left) Elvin's photograph
in *Amazon Journey*. Cousin Guillermo on the right

excited at being shown any photograph. Although Guillermo pointed at the picture and said 'Elvin' several times, I couldn't really tell if she recognised him.

Just then Justin came running down the road, shouting to us there was a truck leaving for Quillabamba in fifteen minutes. 'We'll be there,' I called back, anxious not to prolong the agony.

Guillermo, his wife and Juan Huaman were all clearly thrilled at what they kept calling *oportunidad para Lizbet*. Becca took some photographs of the family, and I noticed that Guillermo guided Leocadia into position, holding her shoulders as if she were a child, while she continued to smile vacantly.

There was no time for emotional farewells. We left the family and ran up the hill to catch the truck. The jovial driver and his enormous wife evidently ran a successful franchise for a large beer company. They wasted no time in loading the lorry with crates of empties. There was a whirl of paying for our drinks and buying bread for the journey, and then we were away.

Just as the truck lurched forward, I recognised Guillermo's balding head coming up the street after us. He was at least fifty yards back, and running as fast as he could, waving frantically; but the driver hadn't made his money by hanging about, and he wasn't stopping for anything. Poor Guillermo slowly dropped back, waved his hands in frustration, and turned into a side street.

I could only think he wanted our address in Scotland, so I jotted it down and gave it to a young lad who was coming as far as the next village. Showing off his English, the boy was singing us a song. The tune was familiar, but for a moment we were puzzled because we'd never heard the words in English before. Then we realised: it was *Frère Jacques*.

Chapter Twenty-two

We thought Huancacalle was civilisation, and that Quillabamba was only forty or fifty miles down the road, but our imagination had been playing tricks. Even in a newish light truck the journey took nine hours. And we were lucky: toothless Carlos, the wiry Indian who rode shotgun, protecting the cargo on the back, told us the road was closed by the rains for months each spring, when access was possible only on foot.

The first twenty minutes of bumping brought us down to Pucyura, at just over 9,000 feet.

'Guarda Civil, John,' warned Justin as we entered the *pueblo*. The vehicle stopped right in front of the police post. One of the pistol-packing cops, in snappy uniform and dark glasses, strutted purposefully across the rutted track to the tailgate, demanding to see our papers. Passports and the *Prefecto*'s letter saw us through. We were only leaving the area: coming in might have been quite different.

The track wound down the valley beside the Vilcabamba river, with jungle-clad mountains rising steeply into the clouds on either side. There was ample cover for the terrorists to come right down and cut the road without being seen on their approach. We hung grimly to the sides of the truck, trying to shake off the feeling of menace which had become part of our lives.

We had lengthy stops for broken springs and punctures, and we got stuck in fords, where everyone had to get off and push the vehicle up on to the opposite bank. Trees scraped their boughs across the cab, and twice Bec pulled green mangoes from passing branches. When we realised the road was no more than a tiny shelf scratched across a near-vertical cliff, the sweet scent of blossom helped calm our nerves. Thunderstorms drenched the vehicle, but our tent-like ponchos kept us dry, and we were only averagely 'tired and weary', by the time we rattled into the tawdry street-lighting of Quillabamba just before midnight.

We had asked to be put off at the cheapest *hostal* in town, and the Hostal Commercial certainly fitted that bill. Much rattling of the steel gate and ringing of bells eventually produced a janitor of great age and frailty. We took a couple of rooms and collapsed into a wonderful deep sleep. It had been some time since we'd slept in a bed, and the *Sendero Luminoso* seemed far away.

When I woke up it was already broad daylight, but M.C. and Bec were still sound asleep, and there was no movement from Ed and Justin next door. The room fronted on to a central courtyard full of tall green tropical plants. The high yellow ceiling and faded blue walls were darkened by the wire mesh of mosquito netting on the windows, and a chipped enamel jug, basin and chamber pot sat on a small dark table under a window. The lavatory was just one door to our left: the usual appalling stench of the *baño* was made even worse by a water shortage in the town. Even so, and all in all, I thought it was no bad place, at 45p a night per head. At least we could rest easy, safe in the knowledge that we wouldn't be attacked.

Lying deep in the Urubamba valley, Quillabamba is only 2,500 feet above sea level. Our main reason for coming to the town was the *bastante frutas* which everyone we met on the Cordillera had told us we'd find there, and even the steaming heat didn't stop our trip to the fruit market that morning. We found the colour and the variety all we had dreamed of during the endless meals of gnawing sticky yucca. By eleven in the morning we were struggling back to the shade of our rooms laden with avocados, melons, mangoes, bananas and oranges, and talking of taking the train on to Cuzco in the morning.

The sun drummed on that South American market town. Tawdry low multi-coloured buildings edged the broad concrete main street which was thronged with wheezing, rickety vehicles and people going about their business. It seemed a long way back to Hostal Commercial.

The lanky old Brit stood out from the crowd. He looked too old to be riding a motorbike, but he saw us as he came wobbling along the other side of the street and, hauling the battered Honda through the traffic in a risky U-bend, he pulled up beside us, perching one foot on the kerb.

'You from England?' he asked, his voice gruff from too many cigarettes. Perished red elastic secured his glasses high on the edge of his receding grey hair. He looked like an old-time aviator, reminding me of Francis Chichester.

'Yes—are you?'

'Oh no, I'm from much further north—Aberdeen.'

And so we got to know Len Young, then sixty-five and the only Briton living in Quillabamba. Again, it was a momentous meeting, apparently arranged by fate.

Although an engineer by training, Len was addressed as 'Doctor' by the customers who came to his pharmacy. Visiting him there, I listened to stories of school at Fort Augustus on Loch Ness, then Burma with the Chindits, diamond-dredging off East Africa, and later pearl-fishing and gold-prospecting spread over thirty-five years in Peru. At first he seemed only half-interested in our story, and quoted an old saying, 'Don't breed ravens, they'll peck out your eyes.'

Our shrunken stomachs prevented us from eating much, but our minds thought of little else besides food. The fruit turned out to be a disappointment. I'd been looking forward to avocado pears for weeks, but our room was dark, even at noon, and I failed to notice that the ones we had bought were full of maggots, until I had eaten a good portion of them. I fell asleep in a poor frame of mind: sodden with sweat and somehow comparing the rotten fruit with the chances of bringing Lizbet to Ardmore.

Knocking on the door woke me. M.C. and Bec were out. It was already dark, and my humour hadn't improved. The aged proprietor handed me a message. Scrawled in soft pencil on a scrap of paper was: 'Have news of Bergs. Must speak with you. Len.'

He joined us for a meal at an almost empty cafe by the Plaza de Armas. He told us he'd had a chat with an old friend, Padre Santiago Echeverria, a Dominican priest who, as head of the vast parish of Quillabamba, regularly visited remote villages in the course of his pastoral work. Although Osambre was just outside his parish, Padre Santiago knew of the Bergs, and Len had arranged for us to meet him. Even Len was now warming to the idea of the adoption, and he left us with his favourite dictum, 'When in doubt—strike out!'

Next morning he took M.C., Becca and me to a nondescript modern church by the square. Padre Santiago was slight and pale, obviously Spanish, with close-set blue eyes. Dressed in grey slacks, with a pale blue, short sleeved shirt, he looked every inch a European foreigner, and could have been mistaken for a lawyer. I feared he might be worried by the fact that we belonged to the Church of England, but this didn't deter him one bit. He had seen just about every human injustice during his decade in Quillabamba; he was short of funds, and virtually under siege. This was not a man to stand on ceremony.

Without knowing it, we had been in his parish since crossing the Apurimac on the raft. He listened patiently to our story, then silently crossed the bar room and picked up an enormous baptismal register.

Thumbing the pages, he stopped at No. 1894 in Folio 475 of the twenty-second Book of Baptism. Here was the only documentary evidence that remained of the existence of a small human being called Elizabeth Huaman Berg, born in Lucmahuayco on 8 June 1979 and baptised in Accobamba on 22 September 1984 by one Padre Santiago Echeverria.

He smiled quietly at us. I swallowed hard and felt tears pricking my eyes. Everything in Lucmahuayco had been destroyed, and yet . . . here was another miracle. With this document, adoption was a possibility. Padre Santiago knew Leocadia, Simeona, and

PARROQUIA de Quillabamba
La Convención - Cuzco
VILCABAMBA

PARTIDA BAUTISMAL DE ELIZABETH BERG HUAMAN

El suscrito CERTIFICA que en el Libro de Bautismos Nº 22 Folio 475 con el No. 1894 se halla una partida cuyo fiel extracto es el siguiente:

NOMBRE ELIZABETH BERG HUAMAN

BAUTIZADO (A) EL 22 de setiembre de 1984

LUGAR DEL BAUTISMO Accobamba

NACIDO (A) EL 8 de junio de 1979

LUGAR DE NACIMIENTO Lucmahuayco

PADRES Elvin Berg y Leocadia Huamán

PADRINOS Policarpo Altamirano y Ricardina Huamanguillas

SACERDOTE BAUTIZANTE P. Santiago Echeverría o.p.

NOTAS MARGINALES

Quillabamba, 6 de diciembre de 1985

C E R T I F I C O la autenticidad de la firma d
Fr Santiago Echeverría o.p.
por ser la misma que usa en todos sus actos
Quillabamba, 6 de diciembre de 1985

P. Francisco Panera o.

The baptismal certificate

Virginie, and he confirmed the suffering and probable illness of Juan Huaman.

He assured us he would confer with the family, and act in Lizbet's best interest, when he next visited Accobamba, probably within the next couple of months. He felt that as she was still only six— not seven as we had thought—Lizbet should still be young enough to cope with the tremendous changes involved in living at Ardmore instead of Accobamba. The alternative prospects for her were not bright. If Juan Huaman and Josephina died, she would be very vulnerable; the usual course for Indian girls was an illegitimate baby at thirteen or fourteen and a life of drudgery.

We walked out on to the Plaza de Armas feeling strangely calm. The chain of coincidence seemed to stretch on and on. Padre Santiago was a good man. If Lizbet Berg was destined to become Lizbet Berg Ridgway, she would. All we had to do was keep pushing.

Boys with nets on long poles were dragging mangoes from the boughs of huge trees in the centre of the square. Purple bougainvillea and scarlet flame trees shaded those taking it easy in the noonday heat. We joined them, and made plans to leave for Cuzco next day. Len had to leave us for a business trip out of town. We thanked him for having become another link in the chain binding us to Lizbet, and watched him clamber on to his faithful Honda. 'Look out for the *ladrones* on the train,' he laughed. 'They'll try to slit your rucksacks!'

Walking down to the station, in steamy heat and pitch darkness at 4.30 next morning, we kept in a close group. It was a bad time for muggers, particularly in the secluded area by the bridge across the Urubamba, and we had to warn off a couple of youngsters who got a little too interested in us.

The railway winding beside the Urubamba for the forty-odd miles up to Machu Picchu has been operating only for a dozen years. The grade is steep and the mountains on either side precipitous. There is little space for the track, so in some villages the railway has taken the place of the main street.

The train was packed solid, but we had a seat in the first class carriage, and the three and a half hour journey was a lot better than walking. Even so we were relieved when we pulled into Machu Picchu station and got off to visit the astonishing Inca ruins, high on the ridge above. In spite of the culture shock brought on by finding ourselves among other *gringos* again, the ruins made a dazzling memory.

We were lucky to get on the 5pm local train to Cuzco, which was so full we had to hang on the outside for a while. We stacked our packs together at the end of a second class carriage and took turns at guarding them. As there wasn't even standing room in the adjoining first class compartment, I left the others by the luggage, and made my way down the second class carriages, which are normally never used by foreigners for fear of robbery.

Carriage No. 1861 had bare wooden seats. The overhead racks were filled with baskets and the white cloth bundles favoured by those large Indian ladies with hard faces who travel up and down Peruvian trains selling refreshments. I was surprised by the friendliness shown me. The raffish, wiry young men with darting black eyes ignored me, but the women smiled and encouraged me to sit well up in the middle of the carriage, though there were other empty seats along the aisle. From the start I had the impression I was somehow in a special seat, and this made me feel alone and alert. Len's warnings of robbery were ringing in my ears.

M.C. and Bec had places at the entrance to the carriage, and I could see Justin and Ed guarding the rucksacks, some forty feet away. They began having trouble with a middle-aged American who resembled a thin version of Orson Welles, beard and all, and was brashly hanging on the outside of the train, close to our luggage. He was being unduly friendly with the Indians, in a rather patronising way.

I couldn't quite put my finger on it, but something was wrong. I had the feeling that too many people knew each other. Girls kept running up and down the aisle in some kind of conspiracy, and they were controlled by the fat lady in a white blouse and stained grey skirt sitting across the aisle from me, who had put me in my seat in the first place.

When we stopped in a small village, some of the girls leaned out of the windows, chattering excitedly in the darkness, and took heavy parcels from men on the tracks below. I recognized the parcels as drums of compressed coca-leaves, and accepted them as part of the Peruvian way of life. It was none of my business.

Just then there was a lot of shouting up by our packs, and word came down that the noisy American had been robbed. His passport, money and air ticket home—all were gone. He was creating quite a fuss, and held an Indian by the throat against the side of the carriage. Ed tried not to become involved, as he did not want to leave our pile of gear.

The ticket collector looked disinterested and moved on down the train. But other officials quickly gathered round the unfortunate American. First a young plain clothes policeman, sporting a .38 revolver under his fawn windcheater, took charge of the investigation. Then a uniformed Guarda Civil and a blue-bereted member of the PIP secret police appeared from nowhere; and they were joined by a burly, overalled figure in an official Peru Railways hat. Ed quietly watched the four men interview the American, who was foolishly abusive about Peruvians in general.

It was soon established that the poor man pinned by the throat either was not the thief or had already managed to dispose of the goods. Either way, he was released and duly disappeared. The American kept bellowing that he wasn't concerned about the money: all he wanted was his passport and air ticket, 'so I can get out of your crummy country.'

The four policemen came down the carriage together, and the man in the fawn wind-cheater smiled at me as he passed. I wondered how difficult it would be to lift the .38 from the back of his belt. They disappeared into the lavatory at the other end of the carriage for a brief conference. Then they returned to the American, and Ed—as he told me afterwards—watched the railway official hand back the passport, air ticket and money, less fifty dollars—whereupon the American gave him ten dollars, but nothing to the others; and this was not well received.

I did not then know that the passport had been recovered, and so I was hardly surprised when the Guarda Civil and secret policeman began a search, coming up either side from the back of the carriage.

Watching them check the passengers and overhead racks, and move slowly up the carriage towards me, I suddenly realised they were looking for the drums of compacted coca-leaves, not the passport at all. I was sitting right in the middle of a team of coca-smugglers. The ring-leader was the fat lady in white blouse and dirty grey skirt, who now looked cruel and bitter. It dawned on me that she'd put me here on purpose: I might be a useful diversion for her team.

One of her girls sat next to me, and opposite us were a couple of doubtful-looking young Quechuans. All three had been moving about the train continuously, but now they sat still, tensely awaiting the search. The girl had a sack of six coca drums at her feet, and another, wrapped in white cloth, she had stuffed down between me and the back of my seat, protesting that she didn't have enough room for all her luggage.

Perhaps I should have stood up and walked away to rejoin the others near the luggage. But nobody was moving now. I thought my flight would be construed as guilt or, since I had nothing incriminating on my person, at least as evidence of my implication with the smugglers. The coca would be found on my seat.

So I sat where I was. The Guarda Civil and the secret police moved in parallel down the carriage, and as they came level with us, the fat lady set up a diversion. Making an obvious attempt to hide the basket on her lap, she created such a fuss that the Guarda Civil had to wrestle with her. Distracted by the struggle, the secret policeman, on our side of the aisle, turned to watch; instantly the girl beside me seized her chance to kick her sack of six drums under the seat opposite to an accomplice who'd just been searched. The fat lady began whining and pleading to be allowed to keep the coca, and she hung so grimly to the Guarda

Civil's hand that the secret policeman had to help him drag the drum from her.

I shut my eyes; the coca felt like a burning hole in my back. The secret policeman turned and looked at me, then he moved on up the aisle to search the next seat. I struggled to stop myself from shaking.

The fat lady was philosophical about the loss of her one drum. She wasn't even reprimanded for possession, and by the end of the search only a single drum had been found. To my certain knowledge there were ten others that the police failed to find in that one carriage, on that one train. I wondered if the police were really trying to find the stuff; but I had to admit, I had been lucky if they were. The raw coca was flooding into Cuzco for refining into cocaine. As soon as the carriage was clear of police, people began moving freely about again, and I moved swiftly to rejoin the others.

The journey to Cuzco took five hours. We spent long periods stopped without lighting, so we just sat in the dark holding on to the gear and hoping robbers wouldn't take their opportunity. The darkness worried the American, who tried to calm himself by chewing coca. What made the Indians giggle was the way he would insist on swallowing the leaves and starting on a fresh lot when the flavour went.

The city of Cuzco lies in a valley, and the Incas called it 'the navel of the Earth'. To reach it, the train zig-zags down from the heights above, halting and reversing at every zig and zag. By quarter to ten in the evening we'd reached the first of the zigs and were feeling pretty tired. The train was running hours late, and the passengers were restless, milling up and down the carriages as they prepared to get off at the end of the line, now no more than ten minutes away.

A scuffle broke out by our packs, and a hard-looking little Indian began screaming abuse at Justin, waving a piece of cardboard in his face and ranting that he had no right to block off a carriage doorway with the rucksacks. I moved up to support Justin. Three more Indians loomed up in the poor light at the junction between the carriages, supporters of the man waving the cardboard. Justin was flustered, penned back against the packs. The abuse increased and one of the supporters tried shoving me away, while the other two squeezed in between Justin and the rucksacks. Ed came up beside me, and I feared a full-scale fight might start. The Indians were so small that I worried in case one of them might be accidentally killed, plunging us into a very difficult legal situation.

'Watch they aren't slitting the packs!' I shouted above the commotion, as the train stopped on a zag. And suddenly all four robbers were gone, dropping into the night between the carriages.

'Phew!' I was trembling with excitement. 'That was lucky. The packs haven't been cut at all.'

'No, but they've bloody well got my camera,' snarled Justin. 'I had it on top of the pile.'

We weren't quite ready for civilisation.

Chapter Twenty-three

Safely back in Cuzco, we quickened the pace of our efforts to bring Lizbet to Ardmore. We had only ten days before our flight home, and after that it would be almost impossible to make anything happen. Feverishly we searched through telephone directories, which seemed our only hope. We found only two names listed under Berg, and these were both in Lima, so we had to go there straight away.

In my search for the Berg family, two factors were uppermost in my mind. First, in Quillabamba, Padre Santiago had warned us that for financial reasons the family might deny Lizbet's connection with them. And second, the family had already suffered so much at the hands of the *Sendero Luminoso* that I was very much aware they might not wish to be found at all. Clearly, the first telephone call that got through to them would be critical, and I thought a sympathetic, Spanish-speaking female voice would be the least alarming.

While M.C. and Bec and I flew on to Lima, the two boys stayed in Cuzco for a few days, waiting for Cesar to arrive home from the Accobamba school. We wanted to give our friend some of our useful gear, which was otherwise unobtainable in Peru.

Our glorious jet flight across the Andes brought us right back into the twentieth century. But the crooked taxi drivers at Lima airport only served to develop our growing concern that nobody in the capital would show the slightest interest in our quest. And by the time we struggled off the bus with our rucksacks, in the centre of town, we were feeling distinctly jaded. Nick Asheshov, co-owner of the *Lima Times*, was our main hope; and even he was away on business. Somewhat dispiritedly, we decided to contact the paper's Assistant Editor.

The *Lima Times* offices are a few storeys up in one of those massive stone relics of the South American rubber boom. At least it was cool as we walked in from the sweltering street. Our clumsy walking boots clattered across the marble floor and we squeezed our rucksacks into an ancient lift which took us clanking up into the dusty past. Heavy, dark wooden furniture and solid, reassuring silence lent an atmosphere of integrity and honest dealing to Peru's newspaper for the English-speaking community.

Once more fate took us in hand. Ellie Griffiths, the Assistant Editor, listened with interest to our story. Sitting in her busy office, she told us of new rules for the speeding-up of adoptions in Peru, which had been in operation for less than a month. In an effort to help the thousands of children orphaned or abandoned by the war, the President's wife had created the Foundation for the Children of Peru. Simplified paperwork was intended to finalise adoption within fifteen days of application.

'Go and see Captain Hogg at your Embassy,' Ellie suggested. 'He's very good at adoptions.'

The British Embassy, which we had visited in such a hurry on the day we arrived in South America, is high in a modern green skyscraper. Good fortune was surely with us, for here I discovered that in the early 1950s I had been at the Nautical College, Pangbourne, with Captain George Hogg, RN, the British Defence Attaché for Peru and Bolivia.

The notion of 'being very good at adoptions' brought a warm smile to his urbane nautical features, but for us it was an extraordinarily fortunate coincidence. George was familiar with the new rules for adoption, and he quickly came up with the excellent suggestion that Margaret, his fluent Spanish-speaking secretary, might be the best person to make the critical first telephone contact with the Berg family.

Margaret's telephone manner was all we could have wished.

Kindly and skilfully she arranged a meeting with one Victoria Berg for the next morning, and offered to come with us to help with any language difficulties.

The Defence Attaché's car and driver created a favourable impression as we swept to a dignified halt outside a modern detached home in a smart residential quarter of the city. The sitting-room was bare, save for a small sofa and a television set. My halting Spanish wasn't getting us very far until the old lady asked politely, 'Do you speak English?' and we all burst out laughing.

Victoria Berg had spent thirty-five years nursing in America, and she was in Lima only to sell her house before moving back to retirement in California. Straight away I knew we had come to the right place: her features strongly resembled those of Abel. Could she be his sister, and therefore aunt of Elvin and great-aunt of our Lizbet?

Looking into her strangely familiar face, I heard again the first words spoken to me fifteen years ago by the head of the clan to which I now found my own family so inextricably linked.

'Welcome to Osambre,' Abel had said. 'I am Señor Berg, and this is my son, Elvin.'

Now, sitting in another empty room we listened intently to Victoria's story. In her soft, broken American voice she told us she was indeed Abel's only sister, and Elvin's aunt, but that she had never been to Osambre.

In the early years of the century she herself had been sent away to school, and when their father died, money had come from Norwegian relations to enable her to continue her education. Abel had also had his naval college education paid for by these same relatives so far away; but, unlike Victoria, who had studied hard and taken up nursing, her brother had a wild streak. He had left college and headed for the jungle, where he had built Osambre. The next part of the story I knew, but when Victoria spoke of Elvin—her favourite nephew, her hope for the family's future—her voice began to falter. She still had not come to terms with his death.

But she knew nothing of Lizbet, and our story came as a total surprise to her. She looked long and hard at Rebecca, Marie Christine and me, lean and weathered from our journey. And, like us when we heard of Lizbet's existence in Accobamba, her spirit lifted again at the revelation of life continuing, her blood, a child bearing the name Berg. She clasped my hands in hers, and I knew she would do all she could to help her small great-niece find a new life with us in Europe. When we left, she immediately wrote to Elvin's brother Olaf, urging him to go to Accobamba and bring Lizbet to her in Lima.

At the British Embassy I found a note asking me to telephone Father Michael Smith at the Benedictine Mission in the outskirts of Lima. I remembered Father Michael from the Mission at Granja Sivia on the Apurimac in 1970, where we'd said goodbye to Elvin. I was pretty sure he'd told me Osambre was the extreme limit of his parish, and that meant it must have shared a boundary with Padre Santiago. I hoped he would be able to tell me something of the Bergs.

Arranging to meet was difficult, as he was so busy. In the end he agreed to fit us in after Mass at nine in the evening. There were plenty of taxis on the street, but the drivers of the first eight vehicles simply shook their heads and wound up their windows when we gave our destination. Suddenly we realised we were going to be late for our appointment.

Grudgingly, I agreed to the ninth taxi driver's demand for five times the normal fare, and we set off at good speed. The driver was a cocky young buck, given to one-handed steering. He boasted that the Mission was close to Lurigancho prison, where the terrorists were held, and that other drivers wouldn't go there for fear of break-outs and hi-jackings.

Lurigancho district was not attractive in the darkness. But we soon met Father Michael, an agile, inspiring seventy-year-old with thinning white hair and that rare, enviable calm found in those with an absolute certainty of purpose. I was glad to see he still possessed the charming uncertainty of detail which I'd so much admired fifteen years before. Something of a legend in

Peru, the slim, ultra-English Oxbridge graduate had spent many of his years with the Mission at Granja Sivia, travelling the jungle alone and totally absorbed in pastoral work.

Just before the *Sendero Luminoso* had forced him to leave his life's work and return to Lima, Father Michael had visited Osambre. It was the year after Abel and Esther had died, and he remembered seeing their grave. Elvin, Olaf and Virgilio were running the farm, and Bertha was talking of moving to Huanta to study languages. Their mother had instructed the Campa Indian farmworkers in Roman Catholicism, and Father Michael had been impressed by how much a part of the family they were. In fact they had cried when he had had to leave the farm to continue his journey round the parish.

A few days later Justin and Ed arrived in Lima. They had seen Cesar in Cuzco, and he had brought them a cutting from the day's edition of the local paper, which gave a typically vague account of bloody battles between terrorists and *campesinos*. Details were hard to fit together, but the article worried us, because it was clear that Lizbet's home village had been attacked.

Cesar's account of his own experience was far more vivid. After crossing the Apurimac, the terrorists had been sighted in strength near Amaybamba, on their way up the Mapito valley. They had attacked Tortora on the day we left Accobamba, and moved on to attack Vilcabamba and Accobamba simultaneously on the following night. They had missed us—or we them—by less than twenty-four hours.

Lizbet and her granny were lying defenceless and alone in their hut on the outskirts of the village as a squadron of twenty terrorists crossed the river under cover of darkness and began moving silently up the path towards the school. (This was the very path we had planned to run down as we stood outside the school, during the alarm, three nights earlier.)

The *ronda* lay in wait for them and sprang an ambush at midnight as the terrorists were bunched together, labouring slowly up the steep hill. In the volley of fire two terrorists fell mortally wounded. The remainder fled back down the hill, across the river and on up the path through the jungle towards the snowy fastness of Choquesapra.

Lizbet, along with all the villagers, including Cesar, the teachers and the crippled Virginie, spent the whole night cowering in the jungle. Next morning everyone returned to their homes, and Cesar saw the two bodies, with a deadly automatic rifle lying beside one of them. Fearing another attack, he joined the villagers in hiding out among the trees for the next two nights. When the school term ended the following day, he set out immediately on foot along the route we ourselves had taken, to rejoin his young wife and baby in Cuzco. As far as he knew, Lizbet was safe.

Passing through Choquetira, Cesar heard of another action which had taken place on the day we left that village with Adulado, just as the *ronda* was assembling on the mound with the wooden cross. A strong patrol set off towards Tortora and discovered a large group of terrorists in a jungle clearing. Ravenously hungry, the *Senderos* were totally preoccupied with eating a cow and had failed to post sentries. With the benefit of complete surprise the *campesinos* achieved a stunning victory: thirty-three terrorists were killed and twenty captured. The *campesinos* lost four dead and three missing.

In our few remaining days in Lima three people helped us form a plan for bringing Lizbet to the capital and adopting her in Peru. By lucky coincidence, international direct dialling between the United Kingdom and Lima had just come into operation, and Nick Asheshov, with his sympathetic approach and the practical benefit of many years in Peru, set up an invaluable chain of communications for us. We felt sure that if anyone could push things along, he could.

Victoria Berg filled in many gaps in our knowledge of her family in Peru, so we felt we would be able to tell Lizbet something of her father in later years.

More important, the great-aunt offered to care for Lizbet when she arrived in Lima until we could fly over to take her to Scotland. Finally, George Hogg, Margaret, and all those we met at the

Embassy went to endless trouble to reassure us and help with the bureaucratic procedures necessary to protect the child's welfare. The big city had turned out to be much more sympathetic than we had feared.

On the morning of our flight back to Britain, we were up early. Victoria telephoned to say she must see us before we left, and within minutes she had arrived at the apartment. She produced from her bag three small packets: for Rebecca and Marie Christine, simple silver bracelets; and for me, a silver sugar spoon. The bracelets seemed to us further links in the chain of coincidences, so like the silver chain we had hung around Lizbet's neck, about which Victoria knew nothing. Partly because of their symbolism, we were deeply touched by these little presents.

Then it was time to go. Soon we were standing in the busy concourse of what could have been almost any international airport in the world. As we took off, I looked out of the window. The wing of the big jet pointed down towards the distant foothills of the Andes, and my mind turned yet again to Osambre. In 1970, I had written, 'My own feeling is that at the end of my life there will still be Bergs at Osambre—just as there will be Ridgways at Ardmore.'

My prophecy had not been fulfilled in the way I had hoped it would be. But perhaps after all we would be able to bring a small Berg to live with us at Ardmore, and I like to think old Abel and Elvin would approve of that.

Epilogue

At midnight on Saturday 10 May, five months after our return from Peru, the phone rang:

'Will you accept a transfer call from Cuzco?'

This was the moment I had been waiting for. I held my breath, suddenly wide awake.

'We've got Lizbet with us, John, she's absolutely fine.'

Once again my old pal Nick Asheshov had come up trumps. With Igor, his 23-year-old-son, Nick had gone into the Apurimac valley and miraculously brought out Lizbet, with her family's blessing.

Hungry for news of the child, I strained to hear how they had carried her out on horseback over the two mountain passes—how she had stoically withstood the journey with the two strangers, only whimpering a little as she got tired. How excited she had become when they reached the bright lights of the jungle town of Quillabamba; she had never seen electricity before. How she ducked on the train for fear of the passing branches hitting her; she had never seen glass before, or been in anything that moved so fast.

A whole new world lay before this small one-eighth Norwegian Quechuan six-year-old. And I knew that it was now up to us to give her the home, the love and security that she had never had.

Nick took Lizbet on to Lima where she is now with his wife Consuela, and together with Captain George Hogg, the Defence Attaché at the British Embassy, they are all trying to speed up the bureaucratic processes so that Lizbet can soon come to Ardmore.

Funny how things turn out. I was an adopted orphan, given a chance. Lizbet's prospects were nil, but through this chain of co-incidences she will be coming to us—I mustn't fail her.

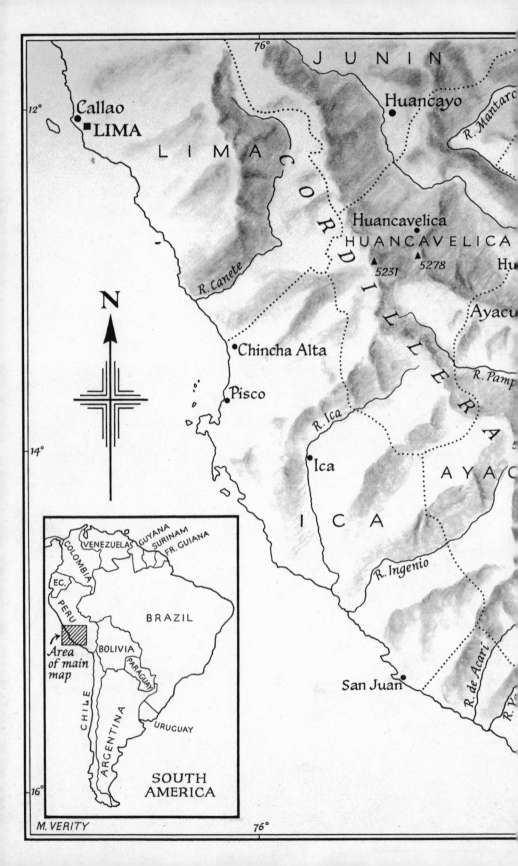